Alaska Wilderness

ALASKA
WILDERNESS

Exploring the Central Brooks Range

BY ROBERT MARSHALL

Edited, with Introductions by George Marshall

Foreword by A. Starker Leopold

Second Edition

UNIVERSITY OF CALIFORNIA PRESS

BERKELEY, LOS ANGELES, LONDON

University of California Press, Berkeley and Los Angeles, California
University of California Press, Ltd., London, England
Library of Congress Catalog Card Number: 73-116025

SECOND EDITION

Originally published as Arctic Wilderness
Printed in the United States of America
Designed by Marion Jackson

ISBN 0-520-01710-2 (cloth)
0-520-01711-0 (paper)

3 4 5 6 7 8 9 0

Foreword

THE VANGUARD OF AMERICAN FRONTIERSMEN WAS COMPOSED largely of unlettered trappers, traders, and prospectors who pushed their way into the virgin continent and left a scant record, or none at all, of the wonders they saw. There were exceptions, to whom society is deeply indebted—men like Pattie, Work, Smith, Lewis and Clark, and Escalante—who kept the journals now pored over by historians. Most of the chroniclers, however, came in subsequent eras, when the wilderness was being "reduced to possession."

In interior Alaska there were some literate pioneers too, such as Pike, Schwatka, Stefansson, and Schrader. But most of the territory was first explored by nameless sourdoughs whose thoughts and adventures died with them. Parts of this inhospitable land were not penetrated at all until long after the gold rush had subsided. Robert Marshall was one of the fortunate latecomers who found a great reach of Arctic wilderness to explore and whose literary talents leave us an exceptional chronicle of the event.

The stark and awesome wonder of the Brooks Range is not easily recreated in writing. Canyons are deep, torrents are dangerous, ridges are knife sharp, and the peaks ordinarily are shrouded in a leaden sky. Vegetation is scarce, mosquitoes are abundant. There is nothing to create even a flickering illusion that this is a land of milk and honey. But in a receptive mind like Bob Marshall's, the very unfriendliness and threatening facade of the landscape aroused a tingling sense of high adventure, such as climbers must feel on the bleak spurs of great unconquered peaks. A glow of irrepressible excitement is evident on every page of the Marshall text. The accomplishments of the author not only make good reading but represented in their time a substantial contribution to the then existing knowledge of northern Alaska.

Marshall could scarcely have anticipated the manner in which the airplane, that he himself used to reach his jump-off point, would facilitate later arctic exploration and permit exploitation of such resources as exist in the north. In the span of three decades much of the tundra zone has been intimately examined from the air. An oil field already is developed on the plain north of Anaktuvuk, with labor and machines flown over the Brooks Range. Remote outposts have grown into substantial villages. Defense units are scattered along the coast of the Arctic Ocean, maintained from the air with a shuttle service nearly as dependable as many suburban railroads. Hunters, fishermen, and prospectors (including the new subspecies equipped with Geiger counters) are reaching the most remote fastnesses. The arctic wilderness is fast shrinking.

The concept that some wilderness should be preserved, even in heavily populated regions, was championed by Marshall throughout his life. The principles that he fought for in the Adirondacks and the western United States can now well be considered in planning an orderly course of growth for Alaska.

It is characteristic of frontier societies, and Alaska still is such, to become so engrossed in the process of development as to fail to look ahead to the point of diminishing returns beyond which more development becomes a social liability rather than an asset. The idea of wilderness preservation finds little favor in Alaska today, because the more obvious and immediate problem is wilderness subjugation. But although growth and economic expansion are indeed important to Alaska's economy, it does not necessarily follow that complete disruption of wild-land values is in the best interests of that economy. On the contrary, the tourist industry and recreational values that attract visitors are important potential sources of wealth. Among the assets that should be staked out and jealously guarded are some representative blocks of completely undisturbed wilderness, of the sort Marshall describes. For as more and more North Americans cluster in cities to earn their daily bread, the recreational value of wild country increases in social value almost exponentially. And the airplane that is carrying civilization to northern Alaska can carry a vacationing urbanite there as well.

In addition to recreational value, samples of original North America have tremendous scientific interest. Our efforts to manage the land and its life often falter for lack of clear understanding of how the soil and its plant and animal dependents maintained their balance in the first place. Specifically, in northern Alaska the complex interrelations between the grazing animals (caribou, Dall sheep, moose, and muskox) and the range on the one hand and predatory wolves on the other is only incompletely understood. Long-term studies of such natural interdependencies would prevent many a blunder in land management. Carefully preserved wilderness check areas are prerequisite to conduct these investigations.

Dissemination of the Marshall account is timely for its documentary value and for bringing into focus the majestic charm of the arctic mountains, now threatened with accelerated disruption by virtue of a new oil strike at Prudhoe Bay. The fragile veneer of vegetation that holds the surface soil to the permafrost is being carelessly disrupted in some areas by roads and tracked vehicles, preparing to lay an oil pipeline over the Brooks Range. The integrity of the arctic is more endangered than ever before.

It is appropriate indeed that the words of Robert Marshall, champion of wilderness, can be published to contribute to the appreciation and possibly to the preservation of some of the northland.

A. STARKER LEOPOLD

Introduction to the Second Edition

In our militant enthusiasm to throw back the wilderness and open up this continent for man, we have been so far successful that we are about to destroy a part of us that is as indispensable as it is irreplaceable.—Ian McTaggert Cowan, "Science and the Wilderness" in *The Meaning of Wilderness to Science.*

But most men, it seems to me, do not care for Nature and would sell their share in all her beauty, as long as they may live, for a stated sum. . . . It is for the very reason that some do not care for those things that we need to continue to protect all from the vandalism of a few—Henry David Thoreau, *Journal*, Jan. 3, 1861.[1]

THE GREATEST REMAINING WILDERNESS IN NORTH AMERICA, AND perhaps in the world, is the Brooks Range which stretches some six hundred miles across arctic Alaska. When Robert Marshall made his journeys of exploration and enthusiastic enjoyment in the Upper Koyukuk Drainage and across the Arctic Divide in the Central Brooks Range (the Endicott Mountains) during the decade of 1929-1939, there were virtually no signs of man north of the small gold mining communities of Wiseman and Nolan, and some outlying one- or two-man mines on the neighboring Middle Fork of the Koyukuk, and at Big Lake to the east and Wild Lake to the west. The only exceptions were a few tree stumps in remote spots along migration routes cut by Eskimos in years gone by with stone age axes.

The great expanse of mountain country with peaks sculptured by wind and water and ice, high cirques and hanging glaciers, waterfalls and precipices, steep-sided glacial valleys with untamed rivers, northland wildlife, and plants ranging from lichens to sedges to spruce, all added to a wild magnificence and untrammelled beauty not altered by man since the dawn of time.

There were signs of change even as the first edition of this book was published in 1956, but until the winter of 1968-69 the Central Brooks Range—in fact the greater part of the entire Brooks Range—remained wilderness.

The first violent change, the first major intrusion of the modern in-

[1]From *The Heart of Thoreau's Journals*, edited by Odell Shepard (2d ed.; New York: Dover, 1960), p. 334.

dustrial world, occurred in the early part of 1969. News filtered south that a winter road had reached the Yukon, that it had crossed the river on an ice-bridge, that it had reached Bettles on the Koyukuk, that it was moving up the wild John River, that it had crossed the Arctic Divide at Anaktuvuk Pass, that it had gone down the North Slope to the Sagavanirktok River, that trucks were crossing the Divide, that the great Range had been split and its unity with past ages destroyed— destroyed without a public decision, destroyed without the knowledge of most Americans.

The purpose of this road was to bring equipment to the site of the great oil strike made in the summer of 1968 near Prudhoe Bay on the Arctic Ocean. This road, and proposals for a four-foot oil pipeline with accompanying year-round road across the Divide and down the Die- trich River—the easternmost tributary of the Upper Koyukuk—and a further proposal for a railway up the North Fork of the Koyukuk, if carried through, will destroy the greater part of the unique wilder- ness Bob Marshall explored and which he described vividly in this book.

II

Before giving more detailed consideration to the present situation, it would be well to summarize the history of the past fourteen years or more relating to wildlife, people, wilderness atmosphere, knowledge of the region, and efforts to give it long-range protection.

Estimates differ on what has been happening to wildlife, but it ap- pears that, except for natural cycles, there has been relatively little change except in some localities and for certain species. One wildlife expert writes:

"Wolves were hunted ruthlessly in the 'fifties and 'sixties by a few bounty hunters using aircraft. They often took 150 or more per year apiece. Wolves became very scarce in the Arctic, which I presume means the Upper Koyukuk, although by the early 'sixties populations in forested areas were greater than in the tundra. Restrictions on aerial permits and on hunting by non-residents seem to have been effective because wolves became more common by 1966-67. More recently they have been hit hard, again by only a handful of people, and populations seem low."[2]

There was a shift in the population of the Upper Koyukuk between 1939 and 1956, and again between the latter year and the present. In

[2] Letter dated November 19, 1969, from an Alaskan scientist.

1948 or 1949, thirteen Eskimo families moved to Anaktuvuk Pass on the Arctic Divide at the head of the John and Anaktuvuk Rivers where they have lived by hunting and trapping. Almost from the start a post office was established and planes landed near the village. The airstrip has been enlarged over the years and in the present village, nearby, the traditional Eskimo houses have in large measure been replaced by structures more typical of the "Outside."

With the diminution of gold mining, only about six or seven people were living around Wiseman throughout the year in 1956, and the number remained about the same in 1969. There also have been a few summer visitors and some non-resident prospectors who have come to do assessment work on their claims.

The main change in the Upper Koyukuk, other than at Anaktuvuk Pass, has been the appearance of some six couples living at different isolated places. Two do a little mining; four from the Outside apparently just like the life of the wilderness. During the summer months, there have been increasing numbers of people coming into the region for recreation or hunting.

The detailed knowledge of the region has been increased by the United States Geological Survey's mapping in the middle nineteen-fifties with "topography by photogrammetric methods from aerial photographs taken in 1955, field annotated 1956." The maps were "not field checked."[3] The area in the Upper Koyukuk Drainage and the places across the Arctic Divide explored and mapped by Robert Marshall are included in the following U.S. Geological Survey quadrangles, all dated 1956: Survey Pass, Wiseman, Chandalar, Chandler Lake, and a corner of Philip Smith Mountains. Although there are some differences between the U.S.G.S. maps of the Upper Koyukuk region made by sophisticated methods and Bob Marshall's made with relatively crude methods and instruments, his maps on the whole are remarkably accurate.

The five quadrangles covering the Upper Koyukuk region include 29 new place names which were proposed by Robert Marshall in his 1938 and 1939 journals and on the maps which accompanied them. The U.S.G.S. maps include three more of his names, but with different spellings. These 32 new names are in addition to the 132 he proposed following his 1929-1931 journeys and which were approved in 1932.[4]

The major factor, until 1969, in changing the environment of the

[3] Information contained on U. S. Geological Survey Alaska Quadrangles, 1956 series, named below. The Wiseman quadrangle was not printed or released until 1959 according to a letter from the Topographic Division of the U. S. Geological Survey. Denver, January 8, 1970.

[4] See p. xxix, below.

Brooks Range Wilderness has been aircraft. In the postscript to the 1956 edition of this book I wrote: "More planes penetrate the north country, and DC-3's land in Bettles on scheduled flights." Now larger planes land there, although Bettles Field remains a frontier landing strip. Commercial and military planes fly over the mountains, and, within the past year, a great many planes have carried passengers and many tons of freight to the Prudhoe Bay oil developments. Even more significant for the fate of this wilderness—other than what the air transportation to Prudhoe Bay portends—has been the increasing number of hunters and fishermen, prospectors, and, yes, recreationists who land within the wilderness.

There is a great difference between flying to the last community at the edge of the wilderness, as Bob Marshall did, and landing within wilderness. When Bob and his companion walked with heavy packs to Grizzly Creek near the Arctic Divide, where they camped one hundred and one miles from the nearest other human being, they would have been outraged and their splendid wilderness solitude shattered had a plane landed with a prospector, a hunter, an administrator, or a hardware-laden mountaineer. The environment of their wild camp would have been disturbed further, although not to the same degree, had there been sound pollution from a plane overhead. Eventually, if there is to be any full wilderness left, it will be necessary to zone areas where aircraft may and where they may not land.

There have been two major efforts, since 1956, to preserve large areas of Brooks Range wilderness. Secretary of the Interior Fred A. Seaton, following several years of field studies and educational efforts by Alaskans, scientists, and conservation organizations, such as The Wilderness Society and the Sierra Club, established the nine-million-acre Arctic Wildlife Range in the northeastern corner of Alaska. It extends from the Canning River on the west to the Canadian boundary on the east, and from the Arctic Ocean some 140 miles south across the Brooks Range. It is especially noted for its wildlife, its high peaks, and the extent and variety of its wilderness.

The second effort grew out of studies made by the National Park Service of areas of national park quality. It also grew out of an increasing concern among a number of Alaskans and conservationists throughout the Nation, that reasonably large parts of Alaska be retained in their natural condition because here was where most of the big wilderness of America remained. In December, 1968, Secretary of the Interior Stewart L. Udall proposed the establishment of The Gates of the Arctic National Monument. It was to have two units. The smaller eastern one was to be about half a million acres. It was to include Mount Doonerak and its neighboring dramatic mountain and deep valley country, extend across the Arctic Divide to about Cocked-hat Mountain, and include the upper North Fork of the Koyukuk and its tributaries, the upper Hammond River, and the Gates of the Arctic.

The larger western unit was to be about three and a half million acres. It was to include the upper drainages of the Alatna, Noatak, and Kobuk Rivers, Mount Igikpak in the Schwatka Mountains and the Arrigetch Peaks, and Walker Lake. It was to extend in part from a little north of the Arctic Divide to the Arctic Circle. The John River Drainage and the western part of the North Fork Drainage were omitted. Despite its weakness, especially making the eastern Mount Doonerak unit much smaller than desirable and splitting the area in two, had the Gates of the Arctic National Monument been established at that time, it would have been most welcome. Although a proclamation to establish it awaited President Johnson's signature, he failed to sign it before leaving office.

Later in 1969, Representative John Saylor, House Interior Committee minority leader and staunch conservationist, introduced a Gates of the Arctic National Park bill with boundaries identical to the Udall proposal. Since then a far superior plan has been advocated. It would extend the national park as a single unit from the Bornite area on the west to the Dietrich-Hammond Divide on the east, and considerably farther north. This plan is closer to what is required.

III

The speed and scale with which the oil companies have proceeded with developments and plans to change the face of Arctic Alaska, following the discovery in the summer of 1968 of a major oil field near Prudhoe Bay, have been unique in American industrial history. Within a month of the discovery, the companies had crews seeking a route for an oil pipeline.[5] They also wished to have a road for ground transport. In the autumn, under the leadership of Walter J. Hickel, Governor of Alaska and later Secretary of the Interior, the State of Alaska Department of Highways started to bulldoze a winter road across the Brooks Range by way of the John River, Anaktuvuk Pass, Anaktuvuk River, and down the North Slope toward the Prudhoe Bay development. Trucks were taking equipment over the mountains by mid-February.

The decision to bisect the Brooks Range wilderness was made with-

[5] U. S. Senate, Committee on Interior and Insular Affairs, 91st Congress, 1st sess., *Hearings on the Status of the Proposed Trans-Alaska Pipeline*, October 16, 1969, Part 2, p. 102.

out public hearings or consideration of basic public policy. The road goes over Federal lands administered by the Bureau of Land Management which, under existing weak laws, apparently had little choice in the matter. However, after hearings, the Bureau established a transportation corridor along the route of the winter road which protects land from "strip settlement, illegal mining claims, and other unauthorized land uses."[6] Locally the road has been called the "Hickel Highway," and when warm weather came and water filled the road's ruts for many miles, some changed it to "Hickel Canal."

At the same time that the wilderness of the Central Brooks Range was being bisected by the winter road and threatened by additional injury by other transmountain transportation proposals, the Arctic Slope—the great Arctic plain north of the mountains with its remarkable tundra country and wildlife—was being damaged beyond repair in large areas. Tundra is fragile country. Caterpillar and jeep tracks remain for years. When the thin plant cover is removed, the permafrost beneath is exposed, melting occurs, and what was ground becomes water.

Serious damage to the North Slope has been going on since World War II. Military activity then and in postwar years was destructive. Now, with the oil development, injury to the tundra is proceeding at a rapid rate. Large sections have been lined by seismographic tracks. Much of the plain is sprinkled with oil drums, old and new. A growing number of oil rigs and structures, airstrips, and ground vehicle tracks mar the landscape. To keep structures and roads from sinking into the tundra, gravel has been taken in large quantities from rivers or river benches.

The threat to wildlife is increasing and will continue unless there is far greater protection than now of both mammals and birds and their habitats. Caribou numbers, for example, will almost surely decline if their calving grounds are not made safe from developments and predatory men, and if historic migration routes are blocked or diverted.

Unfortunately, there seems to be a similar attitude toward tundra as there has been toward deserts in the other states. Both are fragile and damage is not easily healed or it may be incurable and both have been regarded by most people as inhospitable waste land where anything goes. There has been a growing appreciation of the desert as it has become scarcer; but tundra is being lost at a rapid rate without

---

[6] Letters from the Bureau of Land Management, Alaska Office, January 31 and March 18, 1969. These hearings were on a proposed transportation corridor classification, not on whether or not a trans-Brooks Range road should be built.

benefit of adequate interpretation or understanding or protection.

The Prudhoe Bay oil lands were selected by the State of Alaska from the Federal Government through its rights under the Alaska Statehood Act of 1958 which permits it to select 103,550,000 acres of vacant, unappropriated, and unreserved Federal public lands. The State leased these oil lands to several companies following competitive bidding. There was an understandable desire of the companies to cover their investments and make profits, of the State of Alaska to obtain rich oil revenues to solve its financial problems, and of many Alaskans to believe oil development would be the bonanza they had sought since World War II. All, therefore, wish to bring large quantities of North Slope oil to market as rapidly as possible.

The main method proposed by the oil companies to accomplish this is the construction of a four-foot pipeline extending 800 miles from the Arctic Ocean to Valdez, an ice-free port on the Gulf of Alaska. The route selected goes from Prudhoe Bay up the Sagavanirktok and Atigun Rivers, across the Arctic Divide at about 5,000 feet, skirts headwaters of the North Fork of the Chandalar River, descends the Dietrich River (the most easterly branch of the upper Koyukuk) and the Middle Fork of the Koyukuk to Wiseman. From here it goes south, crossing the Yukon River and passing near Fairbanks, to Valdez. It would thus cut through many miles of wilderness on the North Slope and in the Central Brooks Range.

The plans include building "approximately 390 miles of roadways to furnish access to the pipeline during construction" between Livengood south of the Yukon to Prudhoe Bay. The road was to be as near to the pipeline as possible. It was estimated it would carry some 240,000 tons of freight during construction and it was "considered to be at least a semi-permanent, all-weather road."[7] Among other features, twelve pumping stations were planned between the pipeline termini.[8]

In order to implement its plans, the oil companies organized the Trans-Alaska Pipeline System (TAPS). On June 6, 1969, it submitted a formal application for the construction of the pipeline to the Bureau of Land Management and requested a right-of-way permit within one month.[9] This the Bureau would not do without more time for study and for preparation of stipulations. After a summer of conferences between the Department of the Interior and TAPS, and preliminary hearings in Fairbanks in August, the Senate Committee on Interior and Insular Affairs held hearings on "The Status of the Proposed Trans-Alaska Pipeline" on October 16, 1969.

[7] U. S. Senate, *Hearings . . . Proposed Trans-Alaska Pipeline*, p. 102.
[8] *Ibid.*, p. 96.   [9] *Ibid.*, p. 82.

These hearings were held because when Mr. Hickel appeared before a Senate Committee earlier in the year for confirmation as Secretary of the Interior, he agreed that he would make no change in the existing "freeze" on the classification and withdrawal of public lands in Alaska pending the settlement of Alaska Native Claims without bringing any proposed change before the Senate Interior Committee. At these hearings, Secretary Hickel requested that the "freeze" be lifted in order to permit construction of the oil pipeline as soon as he believed essential technical problems were solved and the Department of the Interior's stipulations would be met. He believed these stipulations were strong and would be effective. The Department was represented at the hearings primarily by Under Secretary Russell E. Train.

Based on testimony presented to the Committee, it appears that many essential technical and environmental problems have not been solved for bringing a 48-inch pipeline carrying oil at temperatures to 170 degrees across 800 miles, most of which are over permafrost and many over tundra. The unsolved problems in general and for particular areas are too numerous to cover here. However, they include: danger of a buried pipe melting its support; the danger that the portions above ground, which would in effect be five-foot fences, would seriously affect wildlife movements even if each section is only a few miles long; the danger of pipe on unstable hillsides slipping and breaking; the danger of breaks in several earthquake zones; the danger of serious erosion from the removal of plant cover over pipeline trenches, roads and access roads, borrow pits and graded areas; the effect of bringing in large numbers of people during construction and later as tourists into sensitive areas; the net effect of all the manipulation involved in the project on the environment; and, above all, the danger of oil spills.

Although TAPS introduced testimony on its automatic and manual leak detection and control system, it was not convincing that they would be able to prevent spills under all conditions. That pipeline oil spills are a dangerous reality was brought out in an article placed in the record from *Science,* October, 1969, by Luther J. Carter. He warned:

"During 1968 nearly 500 oil pipeline leaks, each involving a loss of 50 barrels or more, occurred in the United States, and about a fifth of those were spills between 1,000 and 12,000 barrels. The pipes involved in these spills were mostly in the 8 to 12-inch range, and none was larger than 20 inches. The 48-inch trans-Alaska pipeline will be the largest ever built, and, at capacity, will carry 500,000 gallons of oil per mile."[10]

[10] *Ibid.,* pp. 212-213.

Commenting on testimony presented at the hearing and elsewhere, Robert B. Weeden, representing the Alaska Conservation Society, stated:

"I am dismayed by the lack of solid facts and pertinent experience that should firmly undergird a project of this magnitude. I would maintain that some of the information we do not have is so important to the safety of the pipe, itself, or relates to such significant aspects of the environment that I cannot conceive of starting construction at this time."[11]

The reasonableness of this statement is fortified by Under Secretary Train's statement:

"In a project of this magnitude involving the first hot pipeline to be partially constructed within the North American arctic, there are inevitably some unknowns that cannot be resolved fully in advance, and uncertainties that cannot be eliminated."[12]

Before the end of 1969, both Houses of Congress in effect lifted the Native Claims land freeze on the pipeline route and turned over to the Secretary of the Interior authority to decide whether or not to grant the right-of-way, to work out to his satisfaction construction details and stipulations for the oil companies to follow, to approve or not approve their plans for each mile of the route, to change stipulations if he feels it desirable and to enforce stipulations.

What the outcome will be is not too difficult to guess. Unless a much larger segment of the public becomes aware and aroused by what is happening, and unless some very fine legislators and public servants, and some wise oil executives reconsider what is being done and about to be done before it is too late, the pipeline and transmountain road will be built and serious long-range environmental damage will follow.

There are two additional aspects of the pipeline and road preliminaries which it would be well to consider not only in connection with plans to invade the wilderness of the Central Brooks Range, but also in connection with policy making for many types of publicly owned lands.

First, apparently the oil companies were so sure they could get what they wanted once oil was discovered, that they went full steam ahead with their program and schedule without waiting for authorization of some of their acts. For example, the 48-inch steel pipe was ordered in Japan and some of it was landed at Valdez prior to the October Senate hearings and prior to authorization of the pipeline. In places along the proposed route, serious scars and unauthorized grading oc-

[11] *Ibid.*, p. 174.   [12] *Ibid.*, p. 107.

curred before authorization for the line was given. This was protested by two leading Congressmen who observed it. On October 1, 1969—also before the pipeline was authorized—the U.S. Forest Service issued a permit to TAPS for a tank farm to be constructed on the Chugach National Forest near Valdez and authorized the first stage of the permit to commence. The company then proceeded with "clearing and surveys necessary for the first part of their construction."[13] The Forest Service found the tank farm "consistent with the multiple use plans for the area."[14]

Second, the major questions concerning the pipeline and road project were not seriously raised, if at all, during the discussions by government agencies. Among these questions are the following.

1. What will be the influence of the oil pipeline and road via the Dietrich River on the over-all environment of the North Slope, the Brooks Range, and the regions south to Valdez?

2. Can ecological studies be made with a reasonable degree of reliability in a few months or even a year in relation to the proposed pipeline?

3. What will be the effect of the pipeline and road and activities related to them on the wilderness through which they pass?

4. What will be their effect on the rare, vast, and magnificent wilderness to the west of the Dietrich Valley in the Gates of the Arctic areas, and on the wilderness to the east?

5. What will be their effect on local and migrating wildlife?

6. Will any rare species of plants be eliminated?

7. If the pipeline and road are built via the Dietrich River route, will proposals for other trans-Brooks Range transportation routes, including the reopening of the Anaktuvuk Pass route and constructing a railroad or road along the North Fork of the Koyukuk, be abandoned?

8. If the pipeline and road are built via the Dietrich, will an over-all plan be put into effect for the entire Brooks Range designating the greater part of it, and, in particular, the greater part of the Central Brooks Range, as wilderness?

9. Why is there so great a rush to bring oil from the North Slope before many essential questions can be answered in regard to environmental effects and public policy?

10. Why are oil companies accelerating their production programs both on the North Slope and at Santa Barbara, elsewhere on the West Coast, along the Canadian Coast, in Cook Inlet, as soon as possible at Bristol Bay, and at various mainland fields?

[13] *Ibid.*, pp. 143-145.   [14] *Ibid.*, pp. 143-145.

11. Why have the dangers of oil spills from the trans-Brooks Range pipeline been played down by companies and officials in view of the *Torrey Canyon* and Santa Barbara disasters?

12. Why has very little attention been given to the fact that oil spills from the pipeline in the Brooks Range would pollute upper watersheds of from one to three major river systems and could spread many miles downstream?

13. Why is there a rush to pump oil in vast quantities from the North Slope and elsewhere at a time when petroleum products may become obsolete for transportation and industrial power because of the necessity to stop air pollution from making our cities from New York, to Los Angeles, to Fairbanks uninhabitable?

14. Should the oil industry receive the kind consideration of the United States and Alaskan governments in view of its major responsibility, along with the automobile industry, in befouling the atmosphere over much of the Nation?

15. If the pollution of the biosphere, unless stopped or reduced severely, may shorten the time mankind can continue to live on the Earth, as a growing number of scientists warn, would not the acceleration of oil production and the opening of new fields in the Arctic and elsewhere best be reconsidered?

These questions may go beyond the Central Brooks Range and Bob Marshall's explorations. However, the future of Brooks Range wilderness, in fact of all wilderness, is related to these problems. If one agrees that the continuation of large and magnificent wilderness is a necessity for humanity, one can hardly consider the future of wilderness in isolation.

IV

We have discussed in detail threats to the Central Brooks Range from the John River and Dietrich River developments. Unfortunately there are additional threats. The most ominous is the proposal for a railroad along the North Fork of the Koyukuk, the heart of the finest part of the entire region. In 1967, the Governor of Alaska urged extension of the Alaska Railroad from Nanana, about fifty miles west of Fairbanks, to the Arctic and funds were appropriated by the State Legislature to plan and survey this route.[15] One hopes that this proposal has been dropped, but that it may not be dead is indicated by the map tipped into the U.S. Senate Interior Committee's Trans-Alaska Pipeline Hear-

---

[15] Robert Weeden, "Alaska's Oil Boom," *Alaska Conservation Review* (December, 1968), p. 3.

ings, October 16, 1969, Part 2, opposite Page 108, which shows two "Proposed Railroad Extensions." The one appears to follow the John River Transportation Corridor across the Brooks Range. The alternate seems to go up the North Fork of the Koyukuk along its outstandingly beautiful and wild length and cross the Divide to the Itkillik and Sagavanirktok on the North Slope. Anyone reading this book, I am sure, will fully understand what will be lost should this or similar proposals be carried out.

There are two more threats to the Brooks Range which should be mentioned. One is the growing danger that the Arctic Wildlife Range will be opened to prospecting and oil leasing, and that permits may be given to bring an oil pipeline across the northern part of the Wildlife Range from Prudhoe Bay to Canada.

The other is a million-acre BLM classification (withdrawal) made early in 1969 at Bornite in the Kobuk Valley not far from the western section of the proposed Gates of the Arctic National Park. This is a potential copper mining area and if developed probably would be reached by a new railroad extension from Fairbanks that would cross the southern part of the proposed National Park.

Events move rapidly in Alaska even as this book goes to press. The future of America's greatest wilderness in the Brooks Range is uncertain unless there is a change from the present policy which makes a grab bag out of Federal and State lands. Unless there is a clearer realization among Alaskans and all Americans that this particular wilderness is a unique, irreplaceable, and essential asset to both State and Nation, little of it will remain.

Its future will also depend on strengthening the frustratingly weak Federal and State land laws in all respects, and on the creation of a broad regional plan that will preserve the greater part of the Brooks Range as wilderness and which will designate those areas where there may be certain types of development.

If the great wildernesses of the Brooks Range and of the Upper Koyukuk in particular are to be saved, many more individuals and organizations in and out of government must speak up now, and many have done so. One of them is Samuel A. Wright, biologist and former professor of social ecology at a graduate theological seminary. He and his wife are spending a second winter in an isolated cabin at Big Lake in the eastern Koyukuk Drainage. In his testimony on the proposed trans-Brooks Range pipeline and road at the Interior Department hearings at Fairbanks, August 26, 1969, he warned of the fate of the Brooks Range wilderness unless people speak out. He said:

"We have chosen to live in this last great wilderness, disturbing it as little as possible and becoming a part of its ecology. One reason for this choice was the recognition that at this moment in history this great wilderness is doomed unless voices speak out in its behalf. And, certainly, a voice should come from the wilderness itself."

Forty-one years ago, Robert Marshall gave his now famous call to action to those who value wilderness. What he proclaimed then, soon after his first journey into the Upper Koyukuk country, applies equally today to the future of the Central Brooks Range and to wilderness in general.

"There is just one hope of repulsing the tyrannical ambition of civilization to conquer every niche on the whole earth. That hope is the organization of spirited people who will fight for the freedom of the wilderness."[16]

Reading Bob Marshall's account of his explorations of the Upper Koyukuk region of Alaska, and sharing with him his enthusiasm and joy at the great beauty, magnificence, wildness, and adventure he experienced, will, I hope, lead to a deeper understanding of the present tragedy and ecological irresponsibility in arctic Alaska, and of the compelling reasons for preserving the wilderness of the Central Brooks Range.

GEORGE MARSHALL

January 6, 1970

[16] "The Problem of the Wilderness," *Scientific Monthly*, XXX (February, 1930), 141-148.

Introduction to the First Edition

Now when I was a little chap, I had a passion for maps. I would look for hours . . . and lose myself in all the glories of exploration. At that time there were many blank spaces on the earth, and when I saw one that looked particularly inviting on a map . . . I would put my finger on it and say, 'When I grow up I will go there.'—Joseph Conrad, Heart of Darkness

ROBERT MARSHALL WAS FASCINATED BY BLANK SPACES ON maps and was drawn to them from an early age. However, the exploration of these areas meant more to him than an expression of nineteenth-century romanticism or physical adventure or discovery. It meant, in addition, experiencing the freshness of the world in all its elemental strength, mystery, and timeless beauty. It took on its highest form for him in areas where there was no record of any earlier visit by civilized man and which, in all likelihood, he was the first human being to behold. It meant remoteness and space where he could roam alone, or with a few congenial companions, free from the environment of modern mechanical civilization. Exploration formed the structure for his deep need for the enjoyment of wilderness with its adventure, its many-faceted aesthetic experiences, its space, its sense of freedom, and its opportunity to search in wild places for what is basic in life.

While the boyhood dreams of "a blank space of delightful mystery" of Conrad's character became "a place of darkness," Bob Marshall's were fully consummated. His joy at discovering the arctic wilderness among the dramatically magnificent mountains, canyons, and rivers of the Koyukuk drainage of the Brooks Range north of the Arctic Circle in Alaska was matched by his pleasure in coming to know intimately the sourdoughs and Eskimos who comprised the remarkable civilization which existed on its borders. Bob found in both the wilderness and in this frontier community some of the essentials of freedom of the human spirit for which he fought and which seemed so lacking in the twentieth-century world of the nineteen-thirties.

Four months after his fourth and final trip Robert Marshall died of a heart attack on a train between Washington and New York. During his thirty-nine years, he had become a leader among those foresters who advocated the more widespread practice of forestry to stop forest devastation, and who insisted that forests should be administered in the public interest, with a planned consideration of their multiple uses, including wilderness preservation. He contributed important studies to technical forestry and forest policy. He was also an advocate of social reform and civil liberties. Through his writing, organization, administration, and exploration, he became an outstanding leader in his time of the movement to preserve sizeable remnants of different types of wilderness. Of special importance were his vital interpretations of the continuing significance and necessity of wilderness.

"Bob" Marshall, as he was always referred to, was born January 2, 1901, in the brownstone house in New York City which our family occupied for more than thirty years. Our father, Louis Marshall, was a prominent constitutional lawyer, a leader in Jewish affairs, fighter for minority rights, humanitarian, and conservationist. All members of our family as a matter of course went through college and graduate school and into a variety of the professions.

Winter activities for Bob centered on our house and, from the third grade through high school, on the Ethical Culture School. However, the best quarter of each year, the summer months with their greater freedom and joy of living, were spent at Lower Saranac Lake in the Adirondacks. Here Bob's ability to observe and appreciate nature in its myriad forms, his woodcraft, and his enthusiasm for exploration were nurtured and grew as his skills and horizons developed. Climbing the hill from the lake to our house, thoroughly knowing each segment of the sourrounding trailless woods, penetrating the distant regions of the Adirondacks, and making first ascents among the high peaks prepared him for the more extensive wilderness of the West and Alaska.

When he was fifteen, Bob decided to become a forester so that he might spend the greater part of his life in the woods he loved. He attended the New York State College of Forestry, was graduated in 1924, received his Master of Forestry degree from Harvard University in 1925, and his PhD. from the Johns Hopkins Laboratory of Plant Physiology in 1930. He joined the U.S. Forest Service in the summer of 1924 and was on the staff of the Northern Rocky Mountain Forest Experiment Station 1925–1928 with headquarters in Missoula. Here and in the forests of Idaho and Montana, he met a variety of new people and overcame his boyhood shyness. He became an avid reader in many fields of literature and science, and did his first serious, disciplined writing. He also found time to satisfy some of his need for wilderness on long week-end hikes in various forests including the region in the Flathead and Lewis-and-Clark national forests, now known as the Bob Marshall Wilderness Area. He was especially enthusiastic about his work at the experiment station and above all the opportunity for forest research in the field with its "delightful contrasts between the mental adventure of science and the physical adventure of life in the woods." [1]

Bob served as Director of Forestry of the Office of Indian Affairs in 1933–1937. Under the new Indian law and the leadership of John Collier, Bob helped integrate the preservation and utilization of Indian forest and grazing lands into the rebuilding of tribal life on the principle of self-government, and helped raise Indian standards of living. The U.S. Forest Service established for Bob the position of Chief of the Division of Recreation and Lands in May, 1937, and he occupied this post until his death in November, 1939. Under his leadership, a system of wilderness areas in Indian reservations and the national forests was created. He also developed projects to make certain other parts of the national forests more accessible to low-income groups.

During these years Bob spent about half his time in the field and half in Washington, D.C. He felt that this was necessary for good administration. It was also a good way of life for him because he enjoyed people just as much as the wilderness, and needed both. He had a splendid sense of humor, great gusto, and infectious enthusiasm; he thoroughly enjoyed living and made everyone about him feel the same way. Dancing and bringing his friends together for good conversation gave him equal pleasure. He delighted in introducing controversial issues and encouraging the expression of conflicting points of view. His forthrightness and moral courage exerted a healthy influence on the liberal ferment of the nineteen-thirties as well as on the course of forestry and conservation.

Bob's writings for the most part were related to one or another of his activities. His subject matters included the Adirondacks, the fields of Alaskan exploration, wilderness theory and preservation, forest policy, technical forestry, and sociology. Two books and ninety-six

[1] Letter, August 20, 1928.

shorter writings were published during his lifetime.[2] Six more of his manuscripts have been published since his death, and there are plans for the publication of others which recently have come to light.

II

Bob had planned to take a leave of absence during January, 1940, from his post as Chief of the Division of Recreation and Lands of the U.S. Forest Service so that he might bring together in a book his Alaskan journals and letters. Each of these had been published previously, but, with one exception, they had only been distributed privately to friends. These papers, which Bob had arranged in order for editing, were discovered only recently in a file which had been in storage for several years. They comprise the basis for this book.

The journals and letters fall in three groups. The first consists of the "Journal of the Exploration of the North Fork of the Koyukuk by Al Retzlaf and Bob Marshall," published in large part in *The Frontier*.[3] It includes Bob's first reconnaissance map of the North Fork and recounts Bob's first summer of discovery of arctic Alaska in 1929. Omitted from it are accounts of his back-packing trips that summer of five and eight days up the Hammond and Chandalar rivers and his Hammond River trip of 1931.

The second comprises a series of letters written from Wiseman, during Bob's second visit to Alaska, in 1930–31. Addressed to his family and friends,[4] they were mimeographed and distributed privately by our sister, Ruth Marshall Billikopf. Bob's purpose in returning to Alaska was to continue his study of tree growth at northern timber line, to make further wilderness explorations, and to know thoroughly and understand the people of the Wiseman area who seemed so happy to him. Those parts of the letters which describe the life and social customs of this community were used, along with his other observations, as the basis for his book *Arctic Village*, published in 1933.[5] It was a Literary Guild selection and became a best

---

[2] See George Marshall, "Robert Marshall As a Writer" and "Bibliography of Robert Marshall, 1901–1939," in *The Living Wilderness*, XVI (Autumn, 1951), 14–20 and 20–23; and George Marshall, "Bibliography of Robert Marshall: A Supplement," *ibid.*, XIX (Summer, 1954), 31–35.

[3] *The Frontier: Magazine of the Northwest*, XI (Missoula, Montana: January, 1931), 162–175.

[4] Letters from Wiseman, Alaska, processed and privately distributed, 1930–1931.

[5] *Arctic Village* (New York: Harrison Smith and Robert Haas, 1933), 399 pp., illustrated; also Literary Guild selection for June, 1933; also in Penguin Books (Hammondsworth, England: 1940), 176 pp.

seller. It was hailed by explorers and sociologists, and by those who gained a further understanding of the, then, depression-ridden world through reading the "biography" of this frontier civilization.

The second group of papers also includes the diaries of Bob's wilderness trips during the summers of 1930 and 1931 and his intervening winter trips. On these adventures, he added greatly to his knowledge of the Koyukuk region and became increasingly enthusiastic over its wildness and beauty.

The third group of journals includes "Doonerak or Bust" and "North Doonerak, Amawk and Apoon," which recount Bob's 1938 and 1939 explorations [6] and which were printed and distributed privately.

Bob's first trip to Alaska in 1929, was the fulfillment of a long-time ambition, dating back to boyhood, to see this wild and far-off land. As early as 1924, after graduation from the New York State College of Forestry, he requested that his first U.S. Forest Service appointment be in Alaska. However, because he wished to do graduate work in forestry, he was unable to commit himself for the long time that the Alaska district required.

Soon after returning from his second trip to Alaska, in 1931, Bob wished to go back. He contemplated a trip for the summer of 1933 around the headwaters of the Koyukuk, to be followed by about three months around Wiseman working and studying Eskimo life; and during the winter 1933–34 he would spend a month with the Alatna Eskimos and then cross the Brooks Range by dog sled to Point Barrow. In July, 1934, he would continue by boat to Harrison Bay and after about a month there among the Eskimos would "walk back to Wiseman before the snow came." He calculated that it would take him about fifteen days from the mouth of the Anaktuvuk River across the Arctic Divide to Wiseman.[7]

However, these plans were set aside when Bob became involved with working on the Forest Service's historic report, "A National Plan for American Forestry," [8] and in writing his two books, *The People's Forests* [9] and *Arctic Village*. Following this came his appointment in the Office of Indian Affairs which made further extended trips impossible. Still, he dreamed about returning to the upper

[6] "Doonerak or Bust. A Letter to Friends About an Arctic Vacation," privately printed in 1938, 36 pp.; and "North Doonerak, Amawk, and Apoon. Another Letter to Friends About Arctic Exploration Between June 23 and July 16, 1939," privately printed in 1939, 31 pp.

[7] Letter, March 15, 1933.

[8] U.S. Forest Service, "A National Plan for American Forestry," U.S. Congress, Senate Doc. No. 12, 73d Congress, 1st sess., 2 vols., Washington, D.C., 1933.

[9] *The People's Forests* (New York: Harrison Smith and Robert Haas, 1933), 233 pp.

Koyukuk and the Arctic Divide. In March, 1937, he wrote to Ernie
Johnson, the companion of his explorations in 1931 (and, again,
1938): "I can't think of anything more glorious than to be on the
trail with you again and exploring some more of what still remains to
me the most beautiful country I have ever seen. . . . There is still
much exciting country to explore there and it would be too bad not
to take advantage of it."

And on May 28, 1937, just after he transferred from the Indian Office to the Forest Service, he wrote to Ernie:

"I keep thinking constantly of those glorious 76 days we spent together out in the wilds of the Koyukuk drainage. I have never spent
happier days in my life. In many ways the greatest one day I have
ever spent was the day we snowshoed up to the very head of Clear
River and looked down over the top into the Hammond River watershed. The thrill of that look into unknown country and the thrill
of being the first people ever reaching the head of a great river, are
things that stand out forever in a person's memory."

At last, after almost seven years of waiting, Bob returned to arctic
Alaska in August, 1938, when he obtained leave of absence from the
Forest Service for his third trip. Nine months later, in June, 1939,
this was followed by his fourth, and last, journey.

Bob's letters from Wiseman in 1930–31 and his two Doonerak
booklets in 1938 and 1939 evoked great enthusiasm among those who
received them. Readers who expressed appreciation included Supreme Court Justices Oliver Wendell Holmes and Benjamin M.
Cardozo. The latter wrote to Bob:

"I find it hard to put into words the pride and pleasure that came
to me from your narrative of Alaskan life.

"First and foremost there was pride. To think that a tenderfoot like
me should have been set down on your list of the favored few to
whom the narrative was to go — well, that was a thrill as intense as
the vision of a nearby grizzly, with the added advantage that it could
be enjoyed in the quiet of my home without risk to life and limb.

"But the pride wasn't all. There was pleasure too. If any one has
the knack of a literary style more vivid and genuine than yours, I'm
sure I don't know who the happy man or woman is. I suspect that
being close to nature, as you have been during these many years,
has an influence, in the end, even on one's choice of words. One no
longer has any patience for thoughts or for phrases that are not genuine and honest. And how deftly you blend the concrete and the abstract. 'Every mountain was covered with snow, every peak showed
a clear white edge set against a pure blue background. Almost

everything in life seems to be at least somewhat blurred and misty around the edges and so little is ever absolute that there was a genuine satisfaction in seeing the flawless white of those summits and the flawless blue of the sky and the razor edge sharpness with which the two came together.' I call that fine.

"I'm glad you have had so glorious a time. How I'd hate it all, much as I love to read of it! I'm glad in even greater measure that you thought of me in those icy wastes. Don't stay away too long, but give me a glimpse of your radiant presence and a sample of your racy speech." [10]

Bob spent a total of two hundred and ten days exploring the wilderness on his various trips to the Arctic. Each one unfolded a larger section of the Koyukuk drainage—turbulent rivers, northern timber lines, dramatic canyons and waterfalls, great precipices, glaciers, mountain peaks, and ever new aspects of the wilderness with its timelessness and space. The successive mapping of the greater part of these regions, much of which had never been seen before by man, formed at once an objective and a record of accomplishment. After he had returned from his second trip in 1931, the U.S. Geological Survey published his "Sketch Map of Drainage in Northern Koyukuk Region, Alaska" and issued it with his Bulletin *Reconnaissance of the Northern Koyukuk Valley, Alaska* in 1934.[11] A short time before the completion of this map, Bob wrote from Baltimore on May 4, 1932: "My map of the Koyukuk country . . . will cover the entire drainage of 15,000 sq. miles, of which 12,000 or more than twice the area of the Adirondacks, have previously been a total blank."

The map of 1932 includes 137 names of geographic features never before used on any map. "Whenever possible," Bob wrote on July 27, 1933, "I took the old and well-established names of the region, many of which although they had been in use for over thirty years had never been recorded. There are, however, dozens and dozens of mountains, creeks, and lakes which had never been named." These names were officially approved by the U.S. Geographic Board in 1932.

Bob further filled in and improved his map of the northern Koyukuk drainage on the basis of his explorations of 1938 and 1939. He published his improved maps in his two Doonerak booklets. The maps in this book are based on his maps of this region.

A great deal of Bob's mapping and tying in of geological points

---

[10] Letter to Robert Marshall, November 28, 1930.

[11] "Reconnaissance of the Northern Koyukuk Valley, Alaska," *U.S. Geological Survey Bulletin* 844-E, pp. 247–256; illustrated with a sketch map of the drainage of the northern Koyukuk region by the author, 1934.

was done on mountain tops. Climbing was one of Bob's greatest joys. A recurrent theme in his writing is the manner in which Mount Doonerak and the distant peaks of the Arctic Divide attracted him and fired his imagination. He took great pleasure in the ascents themselves and what happened along the way. When he failed to reach the summit he showed his usual objectivity toward his relation to the superior power of natural forces. Views from the summits were deep spiritual experiences. His joy was complete when, standing on some peak never before climbed, he beheld the magnificence of a wild, timeless world extending to the limit of sight filled with countless mountains and deep valleys previously unmapped, unnamed, and unknown.

During the course of his explorations, Bob climbed at least twenty-eight peaks in the northern Koyukuk region. Practically all these were first ascents.

Bob's enjoyment of mountain tops was matched by his excitement at his discovery of great U-shaped, glacial valleys of the North with enclosing mountains and tempting side valleys waiting to be explored and followed to some unknown divide.

The announced scientific purpose of his early expeditions—the study of tree growth at northern timber line—served as a further inducement to Bob to seek out the maximum number of river valleys in the region. In each of these major valleys he made increment borings and other observations at timber line and at various distances to the south. These seem to substantiate his theory that "the northern timber line in Alaska is not the result of unfavorable environment for tree growth, but simply of the fact that there has not been time since the last ice sheet receded for the forest to migrate further north." He read a preliminary (unpublished) paper on his studies, which he called "Observations of a Peripatetic Ecologist in Northern Alaska," to the Laboratory of Plant Physiology at Johns Hopkins during the winter of 1929–30. In it he presented some tree-growth data on what he called "latitudinal," "altitudinal," "aquatic," and "pyrogenous" timber lines. Although he found that the size of trees diminishes toward timber line as altitude increases and as they approach the point where the ground becomes too moist for tree growth, he found that the size of trees does not diminish as they approach the center of old burns and as they approach the northern timber line. He had various tables and graphs worked up on the basis of more complete data after his return from the Arctic in 1931 and even had some work done on it as late as 1939. However, with his busy life and many interests, he never found time to write up and publish his final data.

III

Had Bob lived to prepare *Arctic Wilderness* for publication, he would probably have included summaries of his beliefs on four interrelated questions which throw light on the viewpoint he brought with him to Alaska and the conclusions he drew from his adventures. They are the nature and importance of wilderness, the value of solitude in the wilds, the significance of exploration in the twentieth century, and the future of Alaska. His feelings on these subjects are stated in part, or at least are implicit, in this book. However, because these ideas are based on journals and letters, they are not stated as explicitly as in some of his other writings quoted below.

Exploration, map making, mountain climbing, and studies of tree growth and Koyukuk civilization were special objectives of Bob's trips to Alaska. However, above all it was his love of wilderness with its unique physical and spiritual pleasures, and its great sense of space and freedom which drew Bob to Alaska in the first place and which drew him back whenever he could arrange to go. Bob expressed his feeling of the need for wilderness most completely in an article, "The Problem of the Wilderness," which he wrote before his first trip to the Arctic, and published in the February, 1930, issue of *Scientific Monthly*.[12] In it, he wrote:

"Adventure, whether physical or mental, implies breaking into unpenetrated ground, venturing beyond the boundary of normal aptitude, extending oneself to the limit of capacity, courageously facing peril. Life without the chance for such exertions would be for many persons a dreary game, scarcely bearable in its horrible banality.

"The sheer stupendousness of the wilderness gives it a quality of intangibility which is unknown in ordinary manifestations of ocular beauty. These are always very definite two- or three-dimensional objects which can be physically grasped and circumscribed in a few moments. But, in Emerson's words, 'the beauty that shimmers in the yellow afternoons of October, who ever could clutch it?' Anyone who has looked across a ghostly valley at midnight, when moonlight makes a formless silver unity out of drifting fog, knows how impossible it often is in nature to distinguish mass from hallucination. . . . A fourth dimension of immensity is added which makes the location of some dim elevation outlined against the sunset as incommensurable to the figures of the topographer as life itself is to the quantita-

[12] "The Problem of the Wilderness," *Scientific Monthly*, XXX (February, 1930), 141–148.

tive table of elements which the analytical chemist proclaims to constitute vitality.

"Another singular aspect of the wilderness is that it gratifies every one of the senses.

"In the wilderness, with its entire freedom from the manifestations of human will, that perfect objectivity which is essential for pure aesthetic rapture can probably be achieved more readily than among any other forms of beauty."

The theme of solitude and self-reliance is stated nowhere as vividly by Bob as in an unpublished review he wrote in 1934 of Jeanette Mirsky's history of Arctic adventure, *To the North*. Bob said:

"Perhaps the most important impression which all these tales of the Arctic will leave upon the reader's mind will be the great sense of isolation. These adventures were splendid largely because the men who enjoyed them were able to live in a world completely cut off from the normal world of men. There is something glorious in traveling beyond the ends of the earth, in living in a different world which men have not discovered, in cutting loose from the bonds of world-wide civilization. Such life holds a joy and an exhilaration which most explorers today cannot understand, with their radios and aeroplanes which make the remotest corners of the world just a few days or even hours away in distance. Modern mechanical ingenuity has brought many good things to the world, but in the long list of high values which it has ruined, one of the greatest is the value of isolation."

Bob's views on the values to be derived from twentieth-century exploration were expressed in part in a letter written March 1, 1935, to Melville B. Grosvenor of the National Geographic Society. Commenting on Grosvenor's remarks about an explorer who had done air-photo reconnaissance before entering a region on foot, Bob wrote:

"My own belief, which I realize the majority do not share, is that most exploration today is not of material value to the human race in general but is of immense value to the person who does it. Its value to the individual is in the thrill of adventure and in the fact that exploration is perhaps the greatest aesthetic experience a human being can know. The unexplored areas of the world are becoming distinctly limited. Consequently, since they are capable of giving such superb value to human beings, it is desirable that the possibility of exploration be prolonged as much as possible.

"I do not believe that one man can get any more pleasure looking over 10,000 square miles by airplane than he could by exploring 500 square miles on foot, yet in doing the former, he would be robbing nineteen people of the inestimable thrill of first exploration. Further-more, I feel that one of the great values of exploration is in pitting oneself without the aid of machinery against unknown Nature. When you use machinery to get the jump on Nature by making her reveal some of her secrets in advance, it seems to me a little bit like peep-ing at the end of the book to see how the plot will come out.

"In holding this view, I do not feel the least bitterness or animosity toward those who do not."

Bob's recommendations for the future of Alaska were influenced by his warm feeling for the people he met in Alaska and for the values of their frontier life. They were also influenced by his gen-eral public-welfare and national-planning outlook in contrast with the outlook of those who wished to "develop" Alaska for the benefit of land speculators and a variety of promoters. Taking everything into consideration, both for the benefit of the United States as a whole as well as of the people of Alaska, Bob concluded that the develop-ment of Alaska's resources should be retarded, and that some, espe-cially those in the northern, wilder part of Alaska, should be left un-disturbed.

He commented in 1937:

"If Alaska were to remain primarily a great reservoir of resources, largely untapped at present, but available for future use, it would seem as if that balance which should be a major feature of sound planning would best be realized. Over most of the United States, the prevalent attitude has been that the greater the development of natural resources, the greater the public welfare. Allowing a resource to remain as it had remained for millions of years was considered antisocial. . . . Many invaluable resources have been depleted dis-astrously. In Alaska the dominant development policies of the United States should be balanced by a policy of preservation. After all, re-stricted use at worst will only continue for a while longer the con-servation of geologic ages." [13]

However, it was particularly the recreational resources of Alaska on which Bob concentrated his attention. He expressed his opinion succinctly with some passion in 1938:

"When Alaska recreation is viewed from a national standpoint, it becomes at once obvious that its highest value lies in the pioneer conditions yet prevailing throughout most of the territory. There are millions of people who feel that difficult means of transportation and primitive conditions of environment are basic to the highest out-

[13] "The Development of Alaskan Resources Should Be Retarded," an unpub-lished manuscript.

door values. Such people have found that these pioneer values have been largely destroyed in the continental United States. In Alaska alone can the emotional values of the frontier be preserved.

"Because the unique recreational value of Alaska lies in its frontier character, it would seem desirable to establish a really sizeable area, free from roads and industries, where frontier conditions will be preserved. Fortunately, this is peculiarly possible in northern Alaska, for economic and social reasons. Economically, the population is so scattered that airplane transportation is the only feasible means of mechanical conveyance, and auto roads could not possibly justify their great cost. At the same time, the country is far too remote from markets for successful industry. Sociologically, the country of northern Alaska is inhabited chiefly by native populations which would be much happier, if United States experience is any criterion, without either roads or industries. Therefore, I would like to recommend that all of Alaska north of the Yukon River, with the exception of a small area immediately adjacent to Nome, should be zoned as a region where the federal government will contribute no funds for road building and permit no leases for industrial development.

"Alaska is unique among all recreational areas belonging to the United States because Alaska is yet largely a wilderness. In the name of a balanced use of American resources, let's keep northern Alaska largely a wilderness!" [14]

The great world changes during the past two decades have resulted in increasing threats to the continuing possibility of experiencing the enjoyment of extensive wilderness, solitude, nonmechanical exploration, and frontier conditions which Bob prized so highly. However, one can hardly help but have a deeper appreciation of these values and a sense of their abiding importance as one follows Bob Marshall on his trips.

GEORGE MARSHALL

1956

[14] "Comments on the Report of Alaska's Recreational Resources and Facilities," in U.S. National Resources Committee, *Alaska—Its Resources and Development.* U.S. Congress, House Doc. No. 485, 75th Congress, 3d sess., Appendix B, p. 213, Washington, D.C., 1938.

Acknowledgments

GRATEFUL ACKNOWLEDGMENT IS MADE TO THE LITERARY Guild of America for permission to use a part of Robert Marshall's article "Adventure, Arrogance, and the Arctic" published in *Wings* (May, 1933), and to Random House for permission to use several paragraphs from Robert Marshall's *Arctic Village*.

Very special thanks and appreciation go to Max Knight of the Editorial Department, University of California Press, for his meticulous care, skill, and sympathetic understanding in the final editing of the entire manuscript of *Arctic Wilderness*. His able assistance was indispensable to the process of combining a series of journals into a book.

Acknowledgment is made to the Robert Marshall Wilderness Fund for its aid in connection with the publication of this work, and to Margaret, Olaus, and Donald Murie of The Wilderness Society, for their preliminary work on the manuscript and the main map.

The photographs were taken by Robert Marshall during his trips.

All maps have been redrawn and redesigned by Walter B. Schwarz, Berkeley.

G. M.

Contents

Illustrations

MAPS

1 The North Fork of the Koyukuk

THE STORY OF THIS BOOK LOGICALLY BEGINS IN NEW YORK when I was eleven years old and in bed with pneumonia.[1] To keep me from jumping around, somebody read me a story by one Captain Ralph Bonehill entitled *Pioneer Boys of the Great Northwest*. Thereafter I reread *Pioneer Boys* from one to three times every year for the next ten years. It was a splendid narrative of two lads and their fathers who accidentally joined the Lewis and Clark Expedition and went through the glorious adventures of the most thrilling of all American explorations. My ideology was definitely formed on a Lewis and Clark pattern, and for a time I really felt that while life might still be pleasant, it could never be the great adventure it

[1] Pages 1 to 4 are an adaptation of Robert Marshall's article "Adventure, Arrogance, and The Arctic," published in the Literary Guild publication *Wings*, May, 1933.

might have been if I had only been born in time to join the Lewis and Clark Expedition. It was years before I came to reflect that had I been born at that time, I would probably have been bumped off by the Indians or have died of typhoid fever, before I was twenty-five.

At the same time that I was exploring in my imagination an uncrossed continent, I was engaging in actual explorations. My family used to go to the Adirondacks every summer from the middle of June to the middle of September. Up there I was privileged to explore the mighty tract bounded by the Forest Home Road, the Knollwood Road, Lower Saranac Lake, and Fish Creek—an immense expanse, about three-quarters of a mile by three-eighths of a mile, in which one could, with diligence, occasionally get beyond the sounds of civilization. This almost trailless area was a real wilderness to me, as exciting in a different way as the unexplored continent which I had missed by my tardy birth.

About the time that my quarter-square-mile wilderness began to seem a little tame, I was gradually deciding to become a forester. I didn't have the remotest idea what forestry was, but had vague notions of thrilling adventures with bad men, of lassoing infuriated grizzlies, and of riding down unknown canyons in Alaska. When I actually became a forester, I found life much more filled with keeping the meat at the fire camp from becoming flyblown, discussing the merits of various volume tables, measuring to the tenth of an inch the diameter of pine trees, and crawling over acres of ground on my hands and knees to count the number of seedlings which had germinated following logging operations. Most of these activities, I joyfully recall, were either interesting intellectually, stimulating physically, or full of delight aesthetically. Some of them had all three merits. But nowhere was there the adventure of Lewis and Clark.

Then I began to rationalize. I said to myself that mental adventure and physical adventure were in reality the same thing. The days of physical adventure were over. Consequently, people of an adventuresome disposition would have to substitute for the joy of exploration in untraveled lands the joy of exploration into mental continents. This exploration might take the form of scientific discoveries, of original philosophic contributions, of the creation through some artistic medium of a new form of reality. In any case, the characteristics were the same as in old-fashioned exploration, involving breaking into untrammeled terrain, venturing beyond the bounds of normal aptitude, stretching oneself to the limit of capacity, and occasionally facing peril. That was certainly what Pavlov, William

James, and Proust did, the peril part of the formula being, of course, mental instead of physical.

Nevertheless, this logical reasoning did not satisfy me. Superficially I became reconciled to the notion of mental exploration, but subconsciously (and not so terribly far subconsciously at that) I knew that I wanted the other. Consequently, when this "subconscious" wish rose above the surface, I determined to take a two-month fling at real exploration by spending the major share of the summer of 1929 in what seemed on the map to be the most unknown section of Alaska. At that time I had the notion that exploration should have a social justification. So I pretended to myself that the real reason for this expedition was to add to the scientific knowledge of tree growth at northern timber line. However, at this time of writing, four years later, no article has appeared yet on tree growth at northern timber line.

After this first expedition, I was so badly bitten by the bug of exploration that I determined to go back for a second spree, this time for some thirteen months, from August, 1930, to September, 1931. Meanwhile I had developed a new rationalization—I was going to study "civilization in the Arctic." With this second excuse I fared better at least in one respect—it materialized in the publication of *Arctic Village*.

An excuse for exploration no longer seemed necessary to me, however, after my return from this second trip. I frankly acknowledged that the justification for exploration in modern times must be found primarily in what it contributes to the personal happiness of the explorer rather than in what it may add to the well-being of the human race.

Undoubtedly the western pioneers of the nineteenth century did benefit mankind by opening a sparsely settled country to the enjoyment of millions of people. There are many monuments erected to the pioneers throughout the country which state in effect: "By their heroic sacrifices those that came after them have been enabled to lead happier lives." If one grants that the lives of those who came after are happier than the lives of the Indians, such statements are essentially true.

Today, explorations are necessarily confined to the remotest nooks of the world where few would conceive of settling. As I see it, Peary's discovery of the North Pole, Amundsen's journey to the South Pole, Byrd's junketing in Antarctica, or the impending ascent of Mount Everest do not make the road of humanity as a whole the least bit happier. In fact, one could argue, the net result of these activities is to make mankind a little poorer because when an exploration is made there is that much less possibility left in the world for others to experience the joy of exploration in hitherto unknown regions. The justification, if one is needed, for present-day exploration, therefore, is almost exclusively the selfish one of giving oneself the exhilaration of that most glorious of all pastimes, setting foot where no human being has ever trod before.

The summer of 1929 gave me for the first time the long-sought opportunity to visit Alaska and to explore a region which had been mostly a blank space on the map. The section which I chose for this purpose covered some 15,000 square miles at the headwaters of the Koyukuk River, a major tributary of the Yukon, in the neighborhood of the Arctic Divide in the Brooks Range, north of the Arctic Circle. (See maps, on pages 34, 35; also end map.)

This was vacation time for me between my two years at Johns Hopkins where as a forester I was working for my doctorate at the Laboratory of Plant Physiology. To add a scientific purpose to my primary objective of wilderness exploration, I decided to make a study of tree growth at northern timber line.

It took me two weeks to travel from my home in New York by train, steamer, and twisting railroad to Fairbanks, metropolis of Alaska, where railroads and highways ceased. Al Retzlaf, who was to be my partner on my summer's adventure, met me at the depot. He had been recommended to me during the winter by the Alaska School of Mines where he was taking a short course. He had lived in different parts of Alaska for the past eight years prospecting, mining, and doing some hunting. Now he was interested in prospecting in an untouched field. He was three years my senior, being thirty-one, was slightly blonder than I, and a trifle taller, being just over six feet. He impressed me from the start with his energy, competence, and willingness to do whatever needed to be done.

We decided to start our wilderness journey from Wiseman, a gold-mining settlement on the Middle Fork of the Koyukuk. As our time was limited, we thought it best to fly there. In 1929 plane travel was still something new in interior Alaska. Noel Wien had made the first daring flight to Wiseman only four years before. And now planes flew there only irregularly, less than once a month. After a half week of waiting for clear weather, I had my introduction to flying. We flew from Fairbanks on July 22 in a seven-passenger Hamilton cabin plane, a one-engine affair with an average speed of about one hun-

dred miles an hour, which Wien piloted with great skill and without
a good map.

As we crossed the foot of the Yukon Flats it was the weirdest sight
imaginable to see a whole panorama speckled with little, sparkling
patches of water—gleaming ponds that represented the cut-off channels of the old river which at one time or another wandered over the
whole expanse. At one point we flew but 200 feet above the ground
through a high pass. At another, we frightened three caribou which
galloped wildly around, terrified by the mysterious disturbance of
their silent haunts.

After circling the field twice, we landed in the wide canyon at
Wiseman. As we dove and banked, the whole normal world disappeared. On one side, the earth came right up toward us; fields seemed
to be on walls. On the other side, the valley dropped over a precipice.
A crowd of about twenty people met us, greeted us like old friends,
helped us carry our luggage the half mile from the field to the roadhouse and gave us all sorts of information about the country. The
roadhouse was a one-story log structure with the usual north-country
peaked roof. Like other roadhouses in Alaska, it served primarily
as a shelter in winter to dogteam travelers; in addition, it combined
the functions of hotel, restaurant, bar, banquet hall, dance floor,
store, and major social center of Wiseman. Martin Slisco, the roadhouse proprietor treated us like brothers and even lent us shoes for
the dance which they staged specially for us at the Pioneer Hall.
There, five Eskimo women and twenty men, of whom about half
danced, were present. With the day still bright at midnight despite
rain, with the long-yearned-for Arctic actually at hand, with the
pleasant Eskimo girls as partners, with the queer old-fashioned steps
which the prospectors had brought into the country at the start of
the century, with friendly strangers smiling and welcoming, and with
little Eskimo kids having hopping races with me—that evening seems
today a dear, half-remembered dream.

We spent the next two days around Wiseman buying supplies,
making preparations for our trip, and talking with many people.
While Al fixed pack saddles and harness, I ascended two principal
neighboring peaks, took increment borings of several trees, and discussed topography with the old-timers. The views showed rugged
country as far as the eye could see, even though low clouds cut off
the highest mountains. None of the old-timers I spoke with had been
at the North Fork of the Koyukuk River and the adjacent Brooks
Range, which we were to explore.

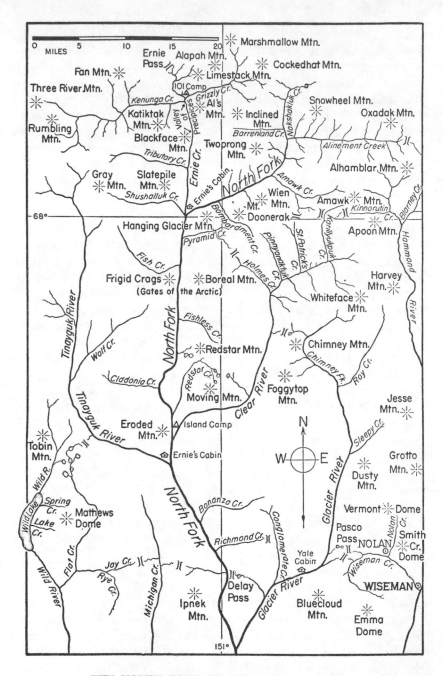

THE NORTH FORK OF THE KOYUKUK RIVER

I also made the acquaintance of arctic mosquitoes while boring spruce trees. These insects were terribly thick; at one time I counted forty-three between my waist and neck including my arms. With hat and mosquito net rendering my head, face, and neck inaccessible to them, and gloves and gauntlets protecting my hands and wrists, and all the rest of me covered with normal clothing, I really was not bothered except when I occasionally had to remove my gloves; but I could see that anyone caught in this country for several days at the height of the mosquito season without special protection would surely be killed.

On the morning of July 25, we left Wiseman for twenty-five days of exploration. Al led the spirited and strong Brownie, I took the docile and weak Bronco—horses we had rented from fat Jack Hood, farmer and teamster of Wiseman. Brownie carried 175 pounds, Bronco 150. In an intermittent rain we followed the dirt road for seven miles to a smaller gold-mining settlement on Nolan Creek. Here, Ed Marsan, one of the miners, who first came to Alaska in the gold rush of 1898, insisted that we go no further that day. We could not decline his and his wife's hospitality.

After lunch I climbed Smith Creek Dome just back of Nolan, which the Nolanites scale every June 22 to see the midnight sun. It afforded a fine view of wave after wave of mountains stretching northward nearly to the Arctic Divide. All peaks were barren, most of them gray or greenish, except those to the east and northeast in the Hammond and Dietrich River countries which were a reddish brown. To the south the mountains were slightly lower but just as barren. Looking northward again, I suddenly realized that probably not a single one of the hundreds of mountains before me had ever been climbed.

Two other settlers who were digging for gold on Nolan Creek, Charlie Irish and Jesse Allen (who lived most of the year in Wiseman), drew maps, showed us pictures, and explained as much about our planned route as anyone could who had never been over it in the summer. Apparently, only five white men had ever been up the North Fork as far as the point where Clear River—an eastern branch of the North Fork—empties into it: our host Ed Marsan who had reached the Clear River in 1907; Charlie Irish and Jesse Allen who had hunted there the previous winter with another miner and woodsman, Kenneth Harvey; and Ernie Johnson of Bettles the most famous trapper of the North Fork, who had trapped there several winters and even built himself several winter huts in the region, including one at the North Fork–Ernie Creek junction. The latter creek was named after him after I came to know him on a later trip. There was no record of anybody having explored Clear River, except for a short stretch above the mouth, fifteen miles at the most. The Tinayguk River, however—a western branch of the North Fork—had been visited many times by people traveling to the Wild Lake mining camps.

From Nolan we headed west for Pasco Pass, about five miles away, aided at first by wood roads, but later gave up looking for them. We crossed much burned territory, found an old cabin in the pass, and descended the steep hillside to a flat between two ponds. There we had our first taste of arctic sedge tussocks. These curses are tufts mostly of cottongrass, which gradually build up out of the swamp, the younger plants growing out of the dead remains of the earlier ones. As they grow larger, they also grow wider so that they are much bigger on top than below, becoming more or less mushroom-shaped. They get to be eighteen inches high, some even higher. They are very topheavy, and when you step on them they are almost certain to bend over and pitch you off into the swamp. When you try to walk in the swamp, you have to step over these high humps, and sometimes they grow so close together your foot catches in between. Three-quarters of a mile of this seemed like five, and at one place we were afraid we could not get the horses through. We were to find later that this was easy compared with some places on the North Fork.

Near the west end of the western pond, we struck an old sled road which led south to Glacier River (a North Fork eastern tributary) and across toward the Charlie Yale cabin. Yale, an old hermit prospector, for ten years had lived alone in this cabin, eight miles over the hill from his nearest neighbor on Nolan Creek. For ten winters, every night his lonely light shone out on the snow with never a soul around to see it. I have camped more than a hundred miles from the nearest person, but this never seemed to me to be half so lonely as this cabin, where a human being sacrificed ten years of social intercourse for the sake of a fortune he never attained.

On the way to the cabin, Al pulled a stunt I had never seen before. In a small brook he spied a grayling, grabbed the shovel, and by a quick thrust caught the fish in its middle, pinned it against the bottom and cut it in two. It tasted nice for lunch.

We rested the horses for four hours at the abandoned old cabin, now filthy, but a haven from the mosquitoes. When we left the cabin, we left the last trail behind. We continued in our—temporarily

—southern direction, descending Glacier River five miles, crossing it twice. On one occasion, Al demonstrated his skill as a fisherman in a more conventional way. "Just a couple of minutes," he said, "and I'll catch those two grayling in that pool for our dinner." And within two minutes Al had cut a pole, tied his line to it, and landed both fish.

That evening we camped at the ruins of another old cabin. Our mosquito-proof tent was a great blessing. This was the first night I had ever slept entirely comfortably in the mosquito season. The swarms were thick, but our tent was designed perfectly, with its attached canvas floor and funnel-shaped door, which could be sealed by pulling two strings. After we had killed the forty or fifty mosquitoes which had entered while we were getting in, not one disturbed us all night.

We descended Glacier River for a further mile to Conglomerate Creek, coming in from the north, where Al fished a couple of hours and caught thirty-five grayling, while I made ecological observations. These studies which I made frequently during the course of our trips, included, in addition to the investigation of tree growth, the study of smaller plants, and noting of slope, soil, moisture, and elevation factors. Among other things, I measured the temperature of the soil on the surface and at a depth of six inches, and the depth at which the ground was frozen. I also recorded daily maximum and minimum air temperatures.

Our fishing and observations concluded and the horses rested, we left Glacier valley, swung west, crossed Jack Delay Pass and reached the North Fork of the Koyukuk, which we followed north, traveling alternately on the hillsides above the river and on the gravel bars. We made camp on the side of a hogback between the mouth of Richmond Creek and the North Fork, and after pasturing the horses, pitched our tent in a cluster of fire-killed spruce.

The small cooking fire which we built on the moss started racing away through the dry lichen, peat moss, and dead blueberry bushes. We had to trench all around the fire to make it safe. I dug down from six inches to a foot without hitting mineral soil, but it was so wet down there that the fire could not spread. Ordinarily in this country, despite its long winters, bogginess, and rain, there is a great fire hazard.

A limestone bluff rose 400 feet sheer from the river about a mile ahead. We had to keep to the hillside above it all morning. We dropped down to Bonanza Creek for lunch and let the horses feed for three and a half hours. Al fished; I took pictures and enjoyed the magnificent, rough mountain scenery of the North Fork on a perfect afternoon.

We started again at six in the evening and struck five miles of exceptionally tough travel. We had to pick our way over and through sedge tussocks almost all the time. The last mile, despite the hard work, was very cold; it felt as the Arctic should feel.

When we reached the river bars at eight-thirty and the sun dipped behind the high western mountains, every hardship and discomfort was forgotten in the presence of rugged mountains sprayed by the soft light of evening, and the turbulent river rolling wildly from the unexplored north.

We made camp among the gravel bars of several sloughs, about 600 feet from the river. Here was the best horse feed we had found; some grass, but mostly *Equisetum*. The sloughs were all cut up with moose tracks.

It became very cold in the night, dropping below freezing. At nine in the morning small puddles of water were still covered with ice.

The river was filled with broad bars of coarse stone on one side or the other, or in the center. In places the stones, which were as large as six inches in diameter, gave way to gravel, sand, or oozy mud. Above the bars—or above the river itself when the bars were submerged by high water—were cut banks from three to eight feet high with only occasional gradients traversible by horses. The principal trees growing in the flats above the banks were cottonwood, but there was also willow, alder, and some white spruce. Back of these flats were successively higher terraces, flat or gently rolling, interspersed with occasional low ridges. They were covered almost completely with sedge tussocks. Their only tree growth was white spruce, dwarf birch, and rarely white birch. The footing on the terraces was abominable, but there was no brush to fight. Just above the river the footing was good, but the brush fierce. The river bars were good in both respects, but never continued for long. No matter which way we went, we were in trouble.

We alternated all morning from bar to brush, making about three miles an hour on the former and half a mile per hour in the latter. At one place, we had to cut a path for an eighth of a mile through a jungle of fallen cottonwood and live alder. It took us an hour and a half to make this eighth of a mile.

In the early afternoon, we reached the mouth of the Tinayguk River. Tinayguk means moose in Eskimo. We stopped for lunch at a place where we were afraid to hobble the horses for fear they would break their legs, so we tied them to trees. The mosquitoes were a pest, but by crawling inside our tent we were able to eat quite comfortably though somewhat cramped. Just as we were ready to start we saw a big black bear. Al took two shots at 1,200 feet, but missed.

As we continued along the North Fork, we hit three miles of the worst sedge tussocks we had yet encountered. It was mount up and fall off and stumble and sink into mud above your shoe tops and drag the horses and, in general, wear yourself out. Finally we spotted a mile of easy bars and descended to the river. We camped early at a lovely island at the junction of the North Fork and Clear River. It was separated from the peninsula formed by the rivers by a shallow slough. On this island we found the only passable horse feed of the day. Back of it, across the main channel of the river, rose a 3,500-foot mountain, with ravines and ridges which were covered by dark green spruce below and a thousand feet of gray rock to cap the summit.

After a rainy day in our island camp, we spent one of those days on which most everything goes wrong and yet the net result is as good as if everything had happened perfectly.

It started all right. We got breakfast, broke our two nights' camp, cached 25 pounds of food in the branches of a cottonwood, packed, and were away before nine. It rained a little in the morning, but by eleven cleared into a fine day.

For three miles things went nicely as we walked along Clear River; but then we came to the foot of a canyon, where the river boiled between precipices which came down steeply to the water's edge. It seemed impossible to get the horses through, so we decided to try the left-hand hillside. As we progressed we had to rise continually because the walls of the canyon kept rising. After three miles we obtained a superb view of the upper end of the canyon where the river raged between giant cliffs for ten miles. Although there are probably a couple of hundred canyons as fine as this scattered throughout the North American continent, there was an indescribable joy at viewing this bit of perfection and a great thrill at the thought that we were surely the first white men who had ever gazed upon it.

The steepness which added so much to the grandeur of the canyon made a descent into it with horses impossible. As we continued, our hillside route grew rougher. We scouted for ways down, but without avail. After another mile we had to rest the horses, so we ate lunch. During this pause, Al found a snail in the dry bed of a recently receded glacier—a surprising place. I bored several spruce trees and found the exceedingly slow growth one would expect.

A mile after resuming our journey, our hillside route became so rough that we didn't dare take the horses a step further. We decided to try, instead, for the summit of the hill on the side of which we were traveling. At this point we were probably 1,200 feet above the water and about 1,300 feet below the peak. We reached the summit, but only after nearly losing the horses several times in the soft underfooting. There had been large landslides on the sides of this mountain which accounted for our naming it Moving Mountain.

The view from the top gave us an excellent idea of the jagged country toward which we were heading. The main Brooks Range divide was entirely covered with snow. Close at hand, only about ten miles air line to the north, was a precipitous pair of mountains, one on each side of the North Fork. I bestowed the name of Gates of the Arctic on them, christening the east portal Boreal Mountain and the west portal Frigid Crags. To the east and southeast also stretched range after range of unscaled mountains, less wild than those to the north. Directly below us to the northeast was a low pass connecting the North Fork with Clear River. Across it were several cliffy peaks, including a strange mountain of which we had been told in Nolan, whose top is covered by a design in the shape of a five-pointed red-colored star, which I was to explore on a later occasion. We could see three of the star's points.

In the pass were about half a dozen ponds, which emptied into the North Fork, except one which flowed into Clear River. We decided to descend to the single Clear River pond and camp there for the night. In the morning we would cross over to the North Fork, giving up for the present our plans of further exploration of the Clear River, because of our difficulties with the horses.

We descended rapidly to within half a mile of the pond. Here a few spruce trees seemed to furnish the most eligible site for a camp. The rest of the country for miles around was treeless, the feed poor, the water some distance away, and the mosquitoes intolerable, but we stopped because the horses were tired after this strenuous day.

The ground was so rough that we thought we could take a chance and leave the horses without hobbles. We thoroughly enjoyed the evening in this barren land as we cooked supper. As usual we ate inside the tent, because to have lifted our mosquito nets long enough to consume our meal outside would have been agony.

After supper, stretched out in that luxurious ease which can only follow a hard day, Al regaled me with stories of moose hunts. He had just killed his third or fourth when we noticed that the horse bell had stopped ringing. We crawled from the tent—it was still full daylight. The horses were nowhere to be seen. Following tracks, Al ran up the mountain at breakneck speed in the direction from which we had come. Twenty minutes later he was back leading the two renegade horses, after having chased them nearly a mile. This time we hobbled them.

While the sun was setting far to the north, Al fished unsuccessfully in the little pond below and I collected a few snails, until we chanced to look up the mountain and saw the horses disappearing again. A wild dash by both of us followed. After a mile of heartbreaking sprinting over sedge tussocks, we got above the horses, caught them, and led them back to camp. The mosquitoes had been so bad, and brush to scratch on so lacking, that the horses had simply been driven crazy and had run away, hobbles and all. We realized we could not stop here. So at ten-thirty we broke camp and started for the North Fork, eight miles away.

That journey was an unforgettable experience. It never got really dark, though at midnight it was distinctly dusky. We were both just tired enough to be in a placid mood of resignation to punishment. But the punishment did not come; the going was relatively good. Only at a few creek crossings did we have trouble, and on one soft side hill where Bronco, whom Al was leading, went down in the muck. I thought for a moment he was lost. But Al talked to the excited animal just as one would speak to a baby, and, while calming it down, took off the pack. Meanwhile, under Al's directions, I led Brownie safely across the ooze. Then, together, we pulled Bronco out and brought him to dry land. We repacked him—the sixth time that day.

The remainder of the night passed peacefully. The red glow of sunset moved from the west to the north and then around to the east. We passed numerous gray ponds. Once at about one o'clock in the morning we came to a pond bigger than the rest. At the water's edge a large bull moose stood outlined in the dawnlight against a hillside covered with a pale yellow mat of reindeer moss. The pink eastern sky mingled with the black of scattered spruce trees in the reflection in the water.

At two o'clock we reached the North Fork, just as the sun was tipping the high peaks to the west. Over Boreal floated a single pink feather. We soon found a fine place for the horses to feed, with plenty of brush on which to scratch. They were quickly unpacked and turned loose, and very shortly thereafter the tent was up. Finally we were enjoying our long-deferred slumber.

We slept off our night's debauch until ten, and spent the remainder of the morning doing minor jobs in a leisurely manner. At one o'clock in the afternoon we started up the North Fork again, following bars virtually all of ten miles. We waded the river a dozen times, the water being from a foot and a half to three feet deep and always quite swift.

As we advanced, the mountains became more and more precipitous until finally they culminated in the Gates of the Arctic. Here on the west side of the valley a whole series of bristling crags, probably at least a score, towered sheer for perhaps 2,000 feet from an exceedingly steep 2,000-foot pedestal. From a similar base on the east rose the 4,000-foot precipice of Boreal. This mountain rose straight up for almost 6,000 feet. Between these two stupendous walls, the valley was probably two miles wide, consisting mostly of dry gravel bars.

Fortunately this gorge was not in the continental United States, where its wild sublimity would almost certainly have been commercially exploited. We camped in the very center of the Gates, seventy-four miles from the closest human being and more than a thousand miles from the nearest automobile.

We left the Gates at ten-thirty the next morning and proceeded upstream. In one four-mile stretch, the stream forked into six or eight channels, forcing us to wade continually. At another place, we cut through a spruce forest in which many trees exceeded twelve inches diameter at breast height—at four and a half feet above the ground. One measured more than fifteen inches and was about 60 feet tall, an amazing tree for so far north as the Sixty-eighth Parallel.

We had lunch opposite the mouth of a creek coming in from the east. It cut into a deep gulch surrounded by a whole series of pyramid-shaped mountains. Consequently we called the stream Pyramid Creek. From our lunch place we had a superb view of the Gates—Frigid, a couple of jagged needles protruding from a pyramidal base; Boreal, just a great wild-looking tower of rock. On the north side of this mountain, just under the east peak which is probably the highest one, was a large hanging glacier. From every view we had of this mountain—which included every side except the east—it seemed impossible to climb.

After lunch we continued upstream for three miles. Here the river forked into two branches of almost identical volume. One, after twisting a little to get through a small canyon, continued into a broad valley which ran in a northerly direction, just as the one we were following had run for thirty miles. The other turned sharply to the east and entered a chasm between some very high mountains. We climbed a low ridge between the two, and after a little consideration concluded that the one which bent to the east was the main river ("upper North Fork"), while the one that continued straight north was Ernie Creek. If this *was* really Ernie Creek, it came in some seven miles too soon, according to what Irish and Allen had told us at Nolan.

We camped between the two rivers on a spot with a view which, we felt, certainly could match the finest in the world. All around, along two great valleys, rocky spires rose toward a heaven of white cumulus clouds drifting through blue. There were more impressive-looking mountains than I had ever seen concentrated in one place. They were so peaked that half of them appeared unscalable. Close at hand were a few spruce trees, many acres of bright yellowish reindeer moss set in sphagnum, and down to the left a marshy meadow with brilliantly green grass.

The next day was hot and muggy. The thermometer rose to 80 in the shade; in the sun it must have been more than 90. Puffing up the rolling hills on the west bank of Ernie Creek, we both felt more as though we were in the Tropics than the Arctic—except for the sedge.

Five miles above the mouth of Ernie Creek we saw the last spruce. Six miles up we found the most satisfactory horse feed since we had left the island camp, so we decided to stop even though we had covered only six miles.

After lunch I set out to climb the mountain rising directly back of us. Al had a headache and stayed in camp, but he caught twenty-four grayling in twenty-five minutes including one which was twenty inches long.

My mountain rose about 3,500 feet above camp. It was just one great pile of loose slate heaped up in spots to the very steepest possible angle of repose. At places I had to proceed carefully to avoid starting a landslide which would carry me down a couple of thousand feet. The final ascent was along a knife-edge ridge of crumbly rock.

The view from the summit was the finest yet. The hour and twenty minutes I spent on the top of Slatepile were easily worth the entire journey to Alaska. In every direction rose mountains higher than mine. I seemed to be on a pedestal in the center of a great towering amphitheater with precipitous and lofty walls. There was variety as well as grandeur. To the southeast were three ragged giants with great glaciers near their summits. One of the three, Boreal, together with the craggy Frigid, bounded the great Gates of the Arctic to the south. Westward against a clouded sun, six massive black needles projected into the sky, a great black basin at their feet. Northward about fifteen miles away was the Brooks Range, least jagged of the visible mountains, but higher than any and capped with snow. Through a notch I could see rocky mountains beyond on the arctic side of the divide. They appeared entirely barren. In the same direction I could look into the head of Anaktuvuk River, though the pass to it (later named Ernie Pass) was hidden by an immense rock looking like Gibraltar, but more than twice as high. I could also pick out the route we were to follow on the morrow.

I descended by way of a gulch on the other side of the mountain which we could see from camp. I ran into great thickets of a new species of willow with lanceolate and very shiny leaves, saw one black bear and one sheep, each about half a mile away, and reached camp in forty-five minutes from the summit.

When I returned, Al had a delicious dinner ready without a thing fried, according to my preferred diet. It included fish chowder, puree of peas, boiled vegetable mixture, and fresh biscuit.

The following morning we pushed up Ernie Creek, sometimes keeping to the stony river bed, sometimes among the willows, sometimes on the rocky or slightly soggy hillsides. The river ran quite rapidly, dropping perhaps 125 feet to the mile. About noon we entered a canyon through which the water poured with great fury. We forced ourselves and the horses up the channel and were in continual fear that they would slip and break their legs on the great boulders. The river made a Z going through this canyon. When we reached the upper arm, it leveled off again and ran smoothly for several miles through a level-floored canyon. We ate lunch on the west side of the valley right under that Gibraltar-like precipice which had been visible ever since we had passed through the Gates. (It was later to be called Blackface Mountain.) At this point the main North Fork–Ernie Creek valley, which had been running strictly north since Tinayguk River emptied into it thirty-seven miles below, bent gently to the left.

Beginning at the bend and for five miles upstream, to a point where Ernie Creek splits into three forks, the valley was bounded by high, dark, and dangerous-looking precipices, surpassing, in my estimation, the grandeur of Yosemite. We called it the "Valley of

Precipices." On the west side, black cliffs of brittle slate towered into the air for 2,000 or 3,000 feet from a thousand-foot steeply sloping base. The strata were tilted at all angles, sometimes dipping north, sometimes south, and occasionally running nearly horizontal. On the east side of the valley, the mountains were less abrupt, but rose for about 3,000 feet with strata tilted at thirty degrees. These immense boundaries of the U-shaped canyon stretched with only four narrow breaks on the east side where chasms cut in the softer rock lead back to lofty cliffs and great peaks of tumbled conglomerate. Wherever the soft strata crossed the skyline they had crumbled away leaving hard serrations which added to the jaggedness of the scene.

After five miles of this austere grandeur the Valley of Precipices came to an end and Ernie Creek forked into three branches. We followed up the northeast one for another mile to the foot of a deep canyon where we found excellent horse feed.

Here, a hundred and one miles from the closest human being we made camp, on August 4, among bleak surroundings. There was just dwarfed and tangled willow in the river bottom—no timber nearer than thirteen miles. The lower hills were sparsely covered with herbs and occasional willows, the higher ones were bare rock, and the main Brooks Range—which we could see up the channel—had white grottolike cliffs, capped by whiter snow.

As we reached camp we heard several loud peals of thunder, but saw no lightning. We cut as long sticks as we could from the willows and twisted them together and bound them into poles six feet high. With these and the large rocks which abounded we put the tent in fine shape.

This was lucky, because the next day a wind lashed a cold downpour against the tent for twelve hours. We cooked only breakfast and supper—it was too soaking to make a fire for lunch. The thermometer hovered between 51 and 55 all day, but the penetrating wind and the barren country made it seem 20 degrees colder. However, we were quite comfortable all day in the tent which was as waterproof as it was mosquitoproof. All day, that is, except for a sensational two-hour forenoon diversion.

Immediately after breakfast Al started out in the drenching rain for the west branch of Ernie Creek to pan for gold. I sat comfortably in the tent reading Meredith's *Diana of the Crossways* to the beat of the rain on the canvas. Suddenly I heard the horses snorting and saw them dashing hell-bent toward the tent, hardly hampered by their hobbles. I ran out with sugar and succeeded in mollifying them enough to halter them, but they were still terribly agitated. I thought they might have stepped into a hornet's nest or smelled a bear. Suddenly Bronco gave a tremendous leap, tore completely out of my grasp, and started like fury down the valley. Brownie tried to follow, but I managed to cling to him though I could not stop his progress. Then, looking up to the hills 100 feet above camp and perhaps 600 feet away, I saw an immense, whitish-brown humped mass taking strides toward camp—a grizzly. A moment later a smaller one appeared in the background.

I managed to halt Brownie at the tent long enough to snatch up the gun which lay near the door, but he continued dragging me down the valley toward Bronco, who had paused in crazed disturbance, waiting for his comrade. Meanwhile the bear kept approaching the tent, the horses kept growing more agitated, and I was being dragged farther from home and possessions. I could not take aim at the bear without dropping the halter and losing Brownie, so I shot from my waist without aiming, still holding the halter rope tightly. I thought I would scare the bear, but the shot must have echoed, because the grizzly seemed to imagine it came from behind him. Anyway, he proceeded with doubled speed toward the tent. Now I knew there was no choice but to let Brownie go and shoot in earnest. I hit the bear, but not fatally and he turned around and retreated into the hills. The other bear had already disappeared.

The next job was to catch the horses, and this was not so easy. They were wild, and galloped away toward the three forks, dragging hobbles and halters with them. By dashing as hard as I could over some rocks too rough for them and wading through the river I managed to get below them. They stopped, but when I tried to approach they charged by me with a force no human power could stop. By another short and desperate dash I managed to get below them again. Then I waited shivering in the chilling driving rain for the steeds to calm down. Finally after half an hour Brownie was composed enough to approach. I got hold of his halter again, but Bronco I could not touch. I started back for camp with Brownie, anxious to return and make sure the bear had not come back. I trusted Bronco to follow. He did not, but I felt one horse was better than none. An eighth of a mile from camp Brownie, still frightened, refused to budge a step closer to the scene of his terror. I was prepared for another long, cold wait. But to my joy Al appeared about a mile away, coming down the west branch of Ernie Creek. He saw Bronco, who had by this time calmed down enough to be caught, and joined me. With this augmentation of forces, Brownie regained a little courage and we proceeded together to camp from which we had departed so abruptly an hour and three-quarters before.

Al had, on another occasion, picked up some interesting-looking rock samples at the east branch of Ernie Creek and planned to have them assayed in Fairbanks. But this time, on the west branch, he reported no trace of color. He had seen a series of cascades which tumbled from a lofty basin for 1,500 feet, the lowest one with a 200-foot drop. The top of this magnificent fall could be seen from camp.

A cold rain fell practically all next day, and it became very uncomfortable in this beyond-timber camp. A tremendous volume of water came down our fork of Ernie Creek.

I read Krutch's *Modern Temper*, made ecological observations in the flat around camp, tried unsuccessfully to dry clothes by a dismal fire between showers, and took an afternoon walk to view the falls of the west branch of Ernie Creek. I got soaked and saw little. When I came back, I found that Al ingeniously had inside the tent rigged up a cooking stove, made of five candles and a one-pound tea can.

The day was dismal and soggy. The only excitement came when part of a mountain fell into the main branch of Ernie Creek about two miles below camp. The noise upset the horses, scared as they still were from the previous day's adventure. We decided to leave camp in the morning if it kept raining. We were afraid the rivers might rise so high that they would cut us off and prevent our return.

The weather showed great promise of clearing the next morning so we decided to remain one more day. Al stayed in camp, while I made a try for the Arctic Divide.

I set out up the northeast fork, which we named Grizzly Creek because of our recent adventure. The mountains were covered with clouds and they never became fully visible for more than brief intervals all day. Intermittently the sun broke through and a blue sky briefly appeared but there was more rain than sun. Despite the unfavorable weather, I had a wonderful day.

I passed two miles of roaring Grizzly Creek cutting through a slate canyon. Near the end of the canyon a gulch came in from the south with one sheer 200-foot waterfall, and hundreds of feet of cascades. I continued along Grizzly Creek. A mile beyond the mouth of the gulch, on the left side of Grizzly Creek, a very deep canyon cut back to the Arctic Divide. I thought I might get to the divide by following the canyon, and started out, but returned to Grizzly Creek, when I found it to be a box canyon ending in steeply precipitous cliffs. The lower part cut deeply through slate and was filled with sandstone and igneous boulders which apparently were continually tumbling from the giant peaks above the canyon.

I continued further along Grizzly Creek. As far as I could make out, the main Arctic Divide was set on a base of slate and capped by limestone with occasional igneous intrusions. The top part exhibited steep cliffs of 1,500 to 2,000 feet for most of its course, but there were places where it had been eroded down into barely ascendable talus slopes. Big sections of the mountain top had broken off from time to time, either leaving shattered fragments all over the lower mountain side, or else remaining as tremendous chunks bigger than bungalows. I measured one—it was roughly box-shaped, 20 feet high and 45 by 40 feet at the base.

Four miles above camp Grizzly Creek forked. One branch doubled back in a broad valley and went due south. It was overhung by one great glacier, and one slender cascade, probably a thousand feet high, which I was to visit on my way back. The south fork came plunging in leaps of 50 to 100 feet from mountains half hidden by mist. The deeply cut north fork seemed to continue for miles.

I gave up hope of getting to the divide by following streams and determined instead to climb directly to the top of a great tabletop mountain to the west which we had seen intermittently for many miles of travel up the Koyukuk North Fork. (We later named this mountain Alapah, meaning cold in Eskimo.) It was stiff climbing up a talus slope almost too steep for repose. Near the top I had to be careful not to dislodge any of the great boulders which seemed all posed to plunge down the mountainside. Just below the table were thousands of great, squarish projections sticking up in the air like sore thumbs—an unforgettable garden of rocks.

On the summit I was worse off than Moses, because he at least got one glimpse of the promised land, while all I saw of the country north of the Arctic Divide was fog and, for an instant, two barren, snow-clad peaks in the shifting mist.

My tabletop mountain also had a little snow on it. The last thousand feet were entirely devoid of vegetation except lichen. The last vegetation to be seen on the way up had included arctic willow, a pine avens, sphagnum, a sedge, two lichens (*Letharia* and *Dactylina*), arctic sandwort, and *Cassiope*.

I took my return trip to our Grizzly Creek camp over the same route which I had taken going up, except that I added a trip of two miles up the broad valley of the thousand-foot slender cascade and the overhanging glacier. Another amazingly wild spot. In fact, the farther north one goes from the Gates of the Arctic, which had seemed the ultimate in primitiveness, the more jagged the country becomes.

Back at camp Al and I spent a rainy night. It promised to clear in the morning, and the sun actually came out intermittently. On August 8, we decided to return to Wiseman. We broke camp leisurely, allowing things to dry in the process.

Ernie Creek was a raging torrent, but we managed to ford it just above the spot where it is joined by Grizzly Creek. The five miles through the Valley of Precipices were easy going and we hit a three-mile-an-hour pace, at the same time enjoying to the full the great, dark crags which towered on both sides of the valley.

At the southern end of the Valley of Precipices we stopped for lunch. Al went fishing, but the water was so deep, swift, and muddy that his success was meager.

It was impossible to follow the swollen Ernie Creek south of the Valley of Precipices as we had done on the way up. Instead we followed the rocky ridges east of the river. Soon they became so rough that we could proceed only at distinct peril to the horses' legs, but there was no other choice. When, after a couple of miles, the rocky going ended, we were worse off than before. What had been passable though difficult stretches of sedge tussocks on the way out, were now discouraging morasses after the three days' downpour. The facile travel of the river bottom and the easy crossings from one good shore to the other were barred to us. For nine interminable miles we picked our way through sedge tussocks and mud into which we sank ankle-deep; pulling the horses across bogs through which they had barely the strength to wallow; making laborious detours to avoid other spots too soft to risk with the horses; fighting for four hours against the toughest footing; and having continually the task of more or less dragging the horses after us. Finally at six o'clock in the evening the mud ended, as we crossed a high ridge which came down from a mountain northeast of the junction of Ernie Creek and the upper North Fork—the part of the North Fork upstream from the junction.

It was a beautiful mile down to this junction through an open spruce forest dotted with several pretty little ponds. We walked over soft carpets of reindeer moss, sphagnum, Labrador tea, and club moss. The reindeer moss (*Cladonia*) was bright cream colored and delicately textured like the finest lace. Everything was softened by the evening sunlight which shone through a lofty notch in the ragged skyline to the west. When we arrived opposite the meadow where we had left our horses six nights before, near the junction, we camped on a sandpile, still on Ernie Creek, less than a mile north of its confluence with the upper North Fork.

Al decided to stay in camp next day and do a little fishing, bake bread, prepare other food requiring more time, and keep an eye on the horses. I set out to explore the upper North Fork. Despite the high water, I was able to go most of the way along bars or at the edge of the river. At a few places I had to climb over high banks, and now and then fight short, severe battles with dense alder and willow brush.

The flooded upper North Fork was turbulent and seemed to be unfordable. Leaning trees from cut banks extended over the water and framed shifting vistas of gray mountains, which looked exceptionally wild as a strong wind blew low-flying black scuds across their summits. On either side of the broad U-shaped glacial valley, tremendous rock masses rose into cloud-capped peaks. The highest and most rugged were to the south, forming the two easterly of the "ragged giants" which I had observed from Slatepile Mountain. These great mountains rose probably 5,000–6,000 feet above the valley floor. They were topped by hanging glaciers and sheer precipices. The most westerly of these two mountain masses I called Hanging Glacier. The easterly one was a towering, black, unscalable-looking giant, the highest peak in this section of the Brooks Range. For the moment I called it Matterhorn of the Koyukuk, although it looked less ascendable than its celebrated Swiss namesake. Two years later I renamed it Mount Doonerak and calculated its height at 10,100 feet,[2] based on observations I made with barometer and hypsometer; the name Doonerak I took from an Eskimo word which means a spirit or, as they would translate it, a devil. The Eskimos believe that there are thousands of dooneraks in the world, some beneficent, but generally delighting in making trouble. On my trip up the Alatna River two summers later, I heard more about these dooneraks and their importance to the power of medicine men.

As I walked for hours beneath the stupendous grandeur of these colossal mountains, I felt humble and insignificant.

Although the mountains to the south of the river were most striking, the great rock masses to the north, some of them with precipices of a thousand feet, were even more marvelous. Two good-sized unnamed streams which cascaded into the upper North Fork

[2] Mount Doonerak was shown with an elevation of 10,000 feet on government maps as late as 1945. Soon thereafter, the U.S. Geological Survey reestimated its height as 8,800 feet and on its 1956 Wiseman quadrangle as 7,610 feet.

from this (northern) side emptied from gorges which looked tantalizingly interesting. But there was no time to explore them.

Following further the upper North Fork I reached a forking, about eleven miles above its junction with Ernie Creek. It was one o'clock by now. I measured a spruce of more than eleven inches diameter at breast height, yet just a mile beyond was the last timber. The spruce was about 20 years old. Twelve hundred feet back was a stand of 70-year-old trees; 800 feet back some 130-year-old ones; and still another 1,000 feet back some 170-year-old ones. This stepladder arrangement, together with the fast growth of the most northerly trees, seemed to indicate that it was not the severe climate which kept the forest from moving farther north, but simply that there had not been time since the recession of the last glacier for the seeds to blow farther. A white spruce would probably have to be 50 years old before it bore seed, and these would not be apt to blow more than 1,000 or 1,200 feet. Then there would have to be another wait of 50 years until these new trees matured seed before there could be another advance of the forest.

I continued up the river, passing under a great cliff, and turned back about two miles above the upper forking. While I was returning the sun came out, and Mount Doonerak became completely visible. Far down the valley it was storming violently, giving a curious cloud effect.

On either side of Mount Doonerak were deep gorges. The upper —between it and Wien Mountain—had a fair-sized creek which broke into a great silver plunge of several hundred feet. The lower gorge was a narrow cleft which divided Mount Doonerak from Hanging Glacier Mountain. This cleft I determined to explore. A quarter-mile climb up the bottom of the U-valley brought me to the mouth of the cleft. This I followed for a mile and a half between frowning, almost overhanging walls till I came to an enforced halt when precipices rose on every side. Marvelous waterfalls were plunging down on every side. I was continuously in their spray, so narrow was the chasm. Some were just small trickles of water, others were good-sized streams. In this mile and a half I counted thirteen falls with an estimated drop of 200 feet or more, and innumerable smaller cascades. This, to be sure, was an abnormal condition caused by the rains of the past few days and their melting effect on the two hanging glaciers. I returned to camp at the North Fork–Ernie Creek junction still with the overwhelming impression of that unique experience in my mind.

When we started downstream next morning we found that the

heavy rains of the past few days had so swollen the upper North
Fork that it had cut a new channel. Instead of joining Ernie Creek
about three-quarters of a mile south of our camp, as it had done
on the way up, only a small slough now entered at this point, while
the main stream came in three miles farther down.

It was cold, damp, and completely overcast during lunch, and
about as dreary as one could imagine with the black, frowning Gates
and the barren bars surrounding us. As we started again, the rain
commenced and continued the rest of the day. It hardly mattered
because the afternoon was just one river-wading after another. We
must have waded up to our thighs half a dozen times and to our
knees twenty-five or thirty times. Part of the way we followed side
sloughs. The North Fork was so deep and swift that the risk of
drowning was very real. Since we could not get across, wherever
the river cut against the east bank we had to take to the hills and
tug the horses through the soggy moss. This made a lot nastier
going than even the continual river wading. At some places we had
to follow perilous side slopes almost too steep for horses. At one
point Al, returning from an inspection of a game trail, reported
"some of the moose went ahead and most didn't, but we'll try it."
We emulated the minority and got through. Thus, between soak-
ings in the river and fatiguings in the moss we covered ten miles
until wet to the skin, tired, but in excellent spirits, we pitched our
camp in pouring rain in the very spot we had pitched it at two
o'clock in the morning after our all-night march. It was so wet that
we had to split logs to get dry wood, and we were forced to start
the fire under the shelter of a tarpaulin; but we had a wonderful
supper, wrung out our clothes, and retired for a comfortable rest.
It poured all night, but the tent was dry and the sleeping bags warm.

Next morning, the rain stopped just long enough for us to cook
breakfast and break camp; but by the time we resumed our march,
the rain resumed too. We struck two miles of easy going along
river bars, then took to the hills for six miles, and kept high up above
the river on ridges covered principally with reindeer moss, sphagnum,
Labrador tea, sedge, and dwarf birch. We had frequent fine views
of the winding river; but of the mountains we saw only their bases.

We stopped for lunch in a queer pit, the basin of a dried-up miniature lake, about two hundred yards across. The shoreline was plainly
apparent all the way around. In the center were large stones so
evenly sorted by size that, as Al remarked, they looked as though
someone had been there with a sifter.

Shortly after resuming our travels we passed three lakes, one with a large flock of ducks. A hundred yards beyond, we came out on the river which we followed near its edge through spruce, cottonwood, and willow to our island camp of twelve days before at the junction of Clear River and the North Fork.

We found the island camp an island indeed. We reached it by wading through what formerly was the shallow slough which separated it from the peninsula between the North Fork and Clear River and had now become a good-sized, though shallow, pond. The North Fork, easily fordable on our trip north, was now a wild river, uncrossable except by boat or raft. Clear River had risen three feet, and was now a raging torrent. We wondered how we could get across. Our old ford had become impossible.

The streams had become so high and dirty that we could not fish any more. Fortunately we found our cache intact. After supper Al reconnoitered up Clear River for about a mile to find a possible ford. He reported that wading was absolutely out of the question. A raft would be the only possibility. We could take ourselves and our equipment over that way and drive the horses across, but it would be risky at best. Our only other possibility would be to wait two months for cold weather, when the river would go down and we could ford it; but we had only five days of normal rations and only a fighting chance to get a moose. Of course, we could barbecue the horses!

Our nearest neighbor was forty-nine miles away. Gloomily we went to bed.

At three in the morning I awoke from the noise of rushing water. It was raining hard when I looked outside and, much to my surprise, I discovered that the water in the quiet slough next to camp had risen almost to the fire, and had become a strong, churning current. I moved the cooking pots back to what I thought was a safe place, commented casually to Al on the phenomenal rise of the water, and hurried back to bed. Moved by my report, Al took one sleepy look out of the tent and immediately was all consternation.

"Hurry, get up," he shouted, "we've got to get out of here quick. The main river's cutting back of our island and if we're not damn fast we'll be cut off from everything."

I thought he was exaggerating, but one look at his grim countenance and feverish haste in dressing made me change my mind, and I started putting on my clothes with all speed. It was now about three-thirty. Al, dressed first, grabbed the halters and started after the horses, calling for me to hurry and pack things. In a few minutes he was back, even more agitated.

"It's too late to pack the horses. It may be too late even if we carry the stuff ourselves, but we've just a chance. Water's up to my thighs already and cutting out the bottom. We've got a few minutes at best. Never mind the little things. Just pack up the tent and bed rolls, but for heaven's sake hurry. I'll take this box."

And away he went with his little packsack on his back, a heavy box of food on one shoulder, and the ax.

I continued the packing at breakneck speed, appreciating the danger, but strangely enough I felt quite calm. Al was back again before I had finished with the tent. He started across again with my big packsack, the gun, and the extra harness. When he returned a third time I had the tent done up.

"Just about time for one more load," he shouted, taking up the other box of food and the tent. But the load was too big and he had to drop the tent. I followed with his bed roll which also contained many stray items. We got across safely, though the water was nearly to our waists and just about as swift as we could stand. We immediately turned back, Al to pick up what was left around the camp and I to pick up the tent. I recovered it, deposited it on shore, and returned halfway into the water to relieve Al, staggering under a clumsy load, of his bed and some pots while he continued with the saddles, tarps, and shovels. It was four o'clock when we had led the horses across too and reached the safe shore for the last time, just thirty minutes after Al's alarm. Ten minutes later the channel was absolutely impassable for any human being. Had we slept even a little longer, we would have been caught on a tiny island covered only with willows and half a dozen slender cottonwoods, with no game, and food for only five days.

Some time during the excitement it had stopped raining. We set up camp again at what we believed to be a safe distance from the river on the highest spot of ground we could find, but it barely gave us a four-foot margin. I walked down once more to the edge of the river in the grim, gray light of a cloudy morning, and watched the mad torrent raging. Man may be taming nature, but no one standing on the bank of the North Fork of the Koyukuk on this gray morning would have claimed that nature is conquered.

We went back to sleep for three hours, then, before breakfast, back-tracked up the North Fork half a mile to where the day before we had seen some felled spruce logs by the ruins of a very old cabin. We found, to our delight, that these logs were sound enough for a raft. This helped us decide that our only hope of escape from our trap between the unfordable North Fork on one side and Clear River on the other was by raft.

We returned to our refugee camp for breakfast. It had definitely started to clear, which made the situation a little more cheering. After breakfast we reconnoitered two miles up Clear River for a possible place to drive the horses across. There was none, and the river had run completely wild. It was split into three or four different channels, each impassable. It seemed almost as big as the North Fork, and much swifter. We estimated its speed as fifteen miles an hour, the North Fork's as about twelve. On the way back to camp we scared up a moose cow and calf. Al did not have quite enough time to get a shot and felt badly about it.

We now set out for the old logs which we were going to use, and started the construction of a raft. "We" means really Al, for his was the plan, the skill, and half of the unskilled labor. He was very much a hero today, because of the morning dash to safety, where perhaps he saved both our lives, and because of his ready plan for a vessel, which we hoped would free us from our dilemma.

We first cleared out the brush and small trees from the area in which we planned to build our raft. Then we cut two skids sloping to the edge of the water and laid nine 16-foot logs across these, alternating-big and small ends at each side. They formed the foundation for the raft. Al deftly notched each log so that there were four grooves running the width of the raft, one above and one below at each end of the logs. Into these grooves we fitted stout, green spruce poles, two on top and two below, and by lashing them firmly together with rope we hoped to provide a firm binding for the raft. The upper two poles were augmented by two shorter, parallel poles holding the center, attached by six 6-inch spikes which we found at the old cabin, and by additional rope.

We laid a platform of smaller logs on top of the last two shorter poles in order to provide a dry place for our goods, bound these in place with three more poles at right angles to the smaller logs of the platform; finally we lashed two more logs across the front and back ends of the three poles, in order to have something to brace ourselves against when poling the raft. We also cut three slender 15-foot poles to use for guiding the raft. For lashing the raft together, we used both sling ropes, five tent ropes, and one strong extra rope. For mooring it, we used two lash ropes.

We completed the raft the following noon after a final two hours of high-tension work. She seemed strong enough to hold together against the buffeting of an ocean, but one unavoided submerged tree or rock would inevitably tip her over in that terrific current, and our chances of swimming out would be slight indeed.

How I felt can be seen by the following entry in my journal: "August 13, 1929. Yesterday's beautiful weather is gone, and it is pouring once more. It is a case of now or never while the relatively low water due to yesterday's dryness still holds. We will shove off the raft as soon as we can. This may be the last thing I ever write."

However, everything turned out differently than expected.

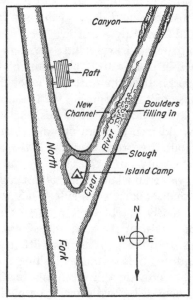

As soon as the raft was finished, we took the horses to the tip of the peninsula between Clear River and the North Fork and tried to make them swim Clear River to the mainland on the east side of the North Fork, but they refused, returning to us in great terror.

This entirely upset our plans, for our only other choices were (1) to leave the horses, (2) to wait for a lowering of Clear River despite the fact that our rations were now reduced to four days, (3) to tow the horses behind the raft, which in that shallow water and terrific current would have augmented the already great hazards of our voyage.

We started back up Clear River in a desolate way, still harboring the hope that we might by some hundred-to-one chance find a ford for the horses. And actually we did. About a quarter of a mile from the mouth, the terrific current of Clear River was cutting a new channel and filling up the old one with a wall of boulders so that it looked as if we could, with difficulty, cross it. Meanwhile the new channel was not quite deep enough to bar us.

Al tried the crossing, found it just passable, and decided that if we rushed we could still make it before the new channel was too deep. We ran with the horses most of the way back to the raft, to which we had transported our entire equipment in the morning. It was all ready for loading. In a great rush we unlashed the ropes from the raft, reassembled the packing outfit, and packed the two horses. Within an hour we were back at our ford. We crossed the torrent in a great semicircle of about two hundred yards. At the worst place the new channel was three feet deep and raced along at about eight miles an hour. By walking with the current, bracing ourselves for all we were worth, and using the horses for support, we barely managed to get across. Several times we were swept off our feet, but by clinging to the halters were able to regain our footing. Within five minutes we stood on the far shore, miraculously escaped from our flood-lined trap. An hour later we would in all probability have been too late; an hour sooner, we would have been too early.

We proceeded downstream two and a half miles along a high beach and pitched camp in the rain, which had continued since morning, on a flat, three feet above the river. It was a cold, soggy night and a wild camp still many miles from our nearest neighbor; there were hardships ahead, but freed from our nerve-wracking plight we felt cozier and jollier than if we had been housed in a modern steam-heated apartment.

The rest of our return trip to Wiseman we continued following approximately the same route which we had taken on our way out. On one occasion we heard part of a mountain across the river tumbling with a thunderous noise—the effect of the only recently receded glaciation in this geologically young country. At Jack Delay Pass we saw two moose—a lone cow, and a calf. They were quite close and tame and we could have shot them easily, but we did not want to waste a moose just for the one or two meals we still had ahead of us. During the last night I was awakened by splashing and looked out of the tent to see a moose calf crossing Glacier River.

Opposite Yale's cabin, Al caught the first fish since the flood. After our meal, we checked our food supply and found that after twenty-three days all we had left was eight ounces of salt and four ounces of tea!

When we struck the Nolan-Wiseman road late that afternoon, the last real hardship was over. At the top of the long grade from Wiseman Creek to the Middle Fork we saw our first human being in twenty-two days. Pete Dow, a hard-bitten cynical sourdough of thirty-two arctic winters, was standing beside his tent and greeted us enthusiastically. He told us there had been speculation during the past few days whether we would come back.

At seven-thirty in the evening, on August 16, we drew up in front of the roadhouse at Wiseman. A whole mob of people came out and welcomed us warmly, held the horses, and helped us unpack. Jack Hood, the owner of Brownie and Bronco, was there, too, grinning from ear to ear. They had been kidding him and saying that we had probably crossed over to Point Barrow and run off with the horses. Martin Slisco, the roadhouse proprietor, was more warm-hearted than ever; he kept slapping us on the back and laughing, and reiterating how relieved he was that we were back. There were many questions about the mysterious upper North Fork, which were very pleasant to answer. Martin soon had a delicious dinner ready, with caribou liver the *pièce de résistance*. We gorged ourselves, but then we had been traveling on pretty light rations for several days.

Adventure is wonderful, but there is no doubt that one of its joys is its end. That night, sitting in a dry room by a warm fire, we felt a pleasure unknown to anyone who has not experienced days on end of cold and soggy travel. Later, lying in bed with no rising rivers, no straying horses, no morrow's route to worry about, we enjoyed a delightful peacefulness.

2 The Arctic Divide

TWO THINGS DREW ME BACK TO ALASKA THE FOLLOWING summer. First, my introduction to the wild and beautiful country of the North Fork and the Arctic Divide made me restless to see more of it, especially since there were large parts of it left which had seldom if ever been seen before by man. Second, my meeting a number of the white and Eskimo people who lived on the borders of this remote region left me with a sense of their vivid character and with the impression that they were the happiest folk under the sun. I wished to know them better.

I met Al Retzlaf again in Fairbanks and we flew from there on August 25, 1930. "We" included Clara Carpenter, 22-year-old Wiseman schoolmarm returning from a visit to the "Outside"; her big brother Lew, a Wiseman miner; Robby Robbins, the pilot; Al, myself, and two goldfish which Clara was transporting to brave the arctic winter.

Robbins had been to Wiseman only once before. The entire region north of the Yukon was so inadequately mapped that it was easy to get lost. When we came to the place where the Jim River, South Fork, Middle Fork, North Fork, and Wild River come within a few miles of each other and all head in the same general direction, we did not know for a while which was which. It wasn't like being lost in an automobile where you can stop and study the map at leisure. Here we were moving at a hundred and ten miles an hour over a wilderness without any landing field nearby, and with a map mostly composed of blank spaces. Fortunately, Lew soon picked out Wild Lake, for which we were heading, and simultaneously Al and I recognized some of the topography of the North Fork which we had explored the summer before, so Robbins banked her sharply and we returned to the Middle Fork of the Koyukuk which we had mistakenly crossed.

The welcome in Wiseman was overpowering. The moment I stepped from the plane Martin Slisco threw both arms around my neck; 7-year-old Willie English, one of the Eskimo boys with whom I had hopping races last summer, jumped up and kissed me; old Pete Dow nearly pumped my arm off, his face cracked with smiles; and then came all the rest, every soul in town, Eskimo and white.

I spent the next two days chatting happily with the people I had known only fifteen days the year before, but who acted like life-long friends. They were eager to pour out reports about the events of the past year to someone to whom they were not stale stories and who was also genuinely interested in them. So I heard over and over, from a dozen different friends, each giving a slightly different slant, of past year's chief events in the life of the community—of the great lawsuit between Dubin and Hyde; of Dan Aston blowing out his brains during the dark days; of John Laane leaving Emma Creek last August on a forty-day prospecting trip to Blue Cloud and disappearing without a trace; of Captain Rowden clearing out with several thousands of unpaid debts; of the poor year in the diggings; of the exceptionally cold winter; of the sensational ice jam when the river broke up in the spring.

Most of the time in Wiseman, however, Al, Lew, and I spent preparing for our four-week trip to the Arctic Divide. Four weeks are not very long for an exploration compared with the two and one half years of the Lewis and Clark Expedition or Stefansson's five years on the arctic ice; but when you do not expect to meet a human being for even four weeks, when you have to be prepared for both winter and summer weather, when your work is going to be botanical, ecological, geographical, photographical, and mineralogical, there is a surprising amount of essential preparation. If you forget one little thing, for instance a whetstone, it may cause you days of inconvenience, if not worse.

The personnel of our expedition included two partners, one employee, and two horses. The partners were Al Retzlaf and myself. Al had brought back some rock samples from just south of the divide on Grizzly Creek last year and had them assayed in Fairbanks. They had run so high in gold that a promoter from Texas had backed Al to the extent of fifteen hundred dollars to investigate further the potentialities of the region.

I had as my major ostensible objective again the laudable study of tree growth at northern timber line, as my minor ostensible objective the study of the geography of the great unexplored headwaters of the North Fork of the Koyukuk and the preliminary mapping thereof (see map, page 6), and, as my by far most important though not advertised objective, gaining the absolutely unassessable thrill of just looking at superb natural beauty.

We planned to spend about two weeks in this great thousand-square-mile wilderness of the North Fork headwaters, just south of the Arctic Divide, and a week or so more traveling to and from it. In this tract of land the closest point to civilization was seventy-five miles from the nearest human being while the farthest point was a hundred and fifteen miles away. As we could not very well backpack four weeks' worth of varied equipment, we hired, as last year, Jack Hood's two horses to pack us in. Because it was late in the year for feed and would be a nuisance to look after the horses while we were reconnoitering, we decided to take a man with us to bring them back as soon as we reached our base camp on Grizzly Creek. All the way out we would leave food caches in small trees where animals would not disturb them, so that on our return journey we would not have to be bothered toting much food.

The man we hired was huge Lew Carpenter, 6 feet 3 inches tall, weighing 235 pounds, 48 years old. Lew had a reputation as a man hard to get along with but, as usual, I found that if one forgot the reputation and treated the man decently he was a fine companion. He was most genial during the trip, enlivened several evenings with excellent yarns, did more than his share of the work, and never grumbled despite numerous hardships.

On our first day out we again merely followed the road seven miles from Wiseman to Nolan Creek. Here we spent the late afternoon and evening visiting. An old couple, Mr. and Mrs. Pingel, gave us lunch and a sumptuous dinner. Mrs. Pingel was a former mis-

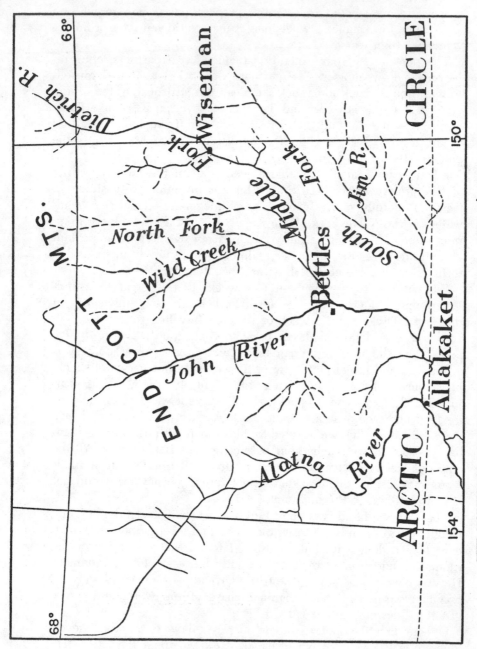

THE NORTHERN KOYUKUK DRAINAGE BEFORE THE AUTHOR'S EXPLORATIONS

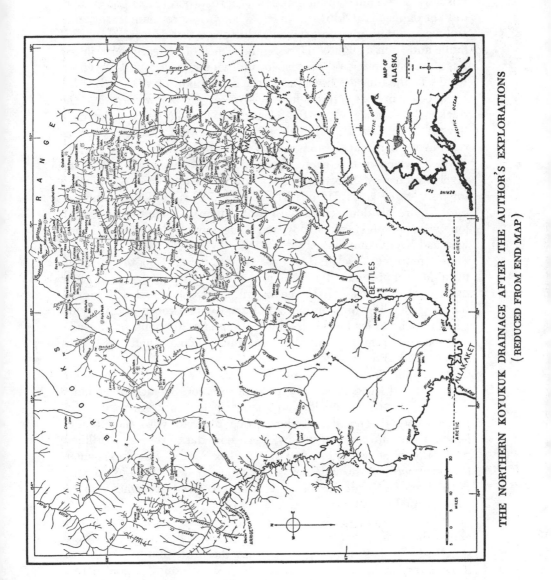

THE NORTHERN KOYUKUK DRAINAGE AFTER THE AUTHOR'S EXPLORATIONS
(REDUCED FROM END MAP)

sionary with a rare sense of humor. After dinner she hitched up her dog with its pack harness and started for Wiseman to attend to some business. Seven miles of mud and a dark road before she got to town did not daunt her. Old man Pingel, who was more than seventy and still worked with pick and shovel in his cut every day, played on his fiddle and spun a slightly misty reminiscence of his early days in the Far North: storming White Pass in mid-winter, boating up the virgin waters of the Stewart River, seeing a companion clawed and bitten by a bear, breaking through overflows at 60 below, crossing the trackless wilderness from the Chandalar to Coldfoot in the dark days of December. He relished particularly in the memory of a courageous woman school teacher who made the crossing with him.

We all went up to George Eaton's, an old bachelor, to spend the night. Eaton was almost as old as Pingel and had been prospecting for thirty-three years. He put Al and Lew in his bunkhouse and got me to share his double bed with him. Then he talked from ten till long after midnight, the steady, rambling monologue of an old man who had lived alone too long.

Next morning at seven-thirty we set out for our month's vacation from the rest of humanity. Eaton and Pingel postponed starting their day's work long enough to see us off. Al went ahead and picked the route, leading Brownie. Lew followed with Bronco and his gun. I had nothing to lead but carried my gun and a 30-pound pack, walking sometimes in the middle, sometimes behind, and sometimes going ahead to reconnoiter.

During the first four days out from Nolan we followed the same course Al and I had taken the previous summer. Scenically the chief difference was that the valleys, instead of being dark green and light green where the needles of the spruce blended with the broader leaves of cottonwood and willow, were now dark green and brilliant gold. Along the valley of the North Fork of the Koyukuk, which extended without turning for many miles, it was glorious to look down from some promontory over this bicolored sea walled in by snow-capped mountains.

The third afternoon, as we were laboriously leading the horses above the bluffs opposite the mouth of Tinayguk River, we were startled by a voice shouting to us from the other side of the North Fork. I ran down to the bank and saw a man poling a boat across the stream. In a few moments he landed and introduced himself as Ernie Johnson. He had a friendly open face and the springing stride of a woodsman. The slight accent of his speech betrayed his origin from Sweden. I had heard frequently about Ernie, most illustrious hunter and trapper of the Far North, a sort of Daniel Boone among the pioneers of this arctic frontier, unanimously admitted by the exceptionally competent woodsmen of the Koyukuk to be their superior. Although Ernie spends practically all his time in the woods, and is alone most of his days, he is not an anchorite by preference but merely because he seldom can find anyone to share his difficult life.

When Lew and Al reached the river's edge, Ernie fairly insisted that we go no further that day. So we pitched our camp a little way upstream among the willows, hobbled the horses and left them to feed, and crossed the unfordable North Fork in Ernie's boat. All the while his four dogs barked furiously. At the river's edge Ernie had a comfortable and spacious tent, with a Yukon stove and a bunk built in. Back about a hundred yards was his winter cabin (like all winter cabins, no good in summer because the dirt roof leaked in rain) and a cache for his food, snowshoes, sleds, magazines, and the like.

While Al fished and Lew started supper, Ernie wanted to show me the Tinayguk. He thought we might see a moose so we took our guns, but Ernie talked such a blue streak that any moose within rifle range must have pulled out of the district before we came near. We talked principally about geography and compared notes on our observations in the country at the head of "Ernie Creek" which probably no white man but he, Al, and I had ever seen. Ernie told me of low passes leading from one drainage to another, pointed out some of them to me from a hill we climbed, explained about sloughs which cut off tedious passages over sedge tussocks. It was the vital information of the wilderness.

He also told me about his life. He had been born in Sweden fifty years before, and had come to America when he was sixteen. He became a carpenter and, after living in Minnesota and some other states, joined the stampede to Kuskokwim in 1904. He had not been outside of Alaska since. Although he had come north on a gold rush, he had also been drawn by his love of the woods in this greatest wilderness of the continent. Here he spent all but about two weeks in the year out in the hills, away from the "cities" of Wiseman (population 103) and Bettles (population 24). These populations do not even represent the number of people living permanently in each of these centers, but the number who come regularly to their stores to trade. Bettles was Ernie's base town where he had a cabin and sometimes a garden. He trapped and hunted, averaging a yearly income of about twenty-five hundred dollars. "I can make better money as a carpenter," he said, "but I am staying out here because

I like it among these ruggedy mountains better than anywhere else in the world."

Ernie and I hit it off fine from the start and before we got back from our hour-and-a-half "hunt" it was practically arranged that we were to make an exploration of the upper Alatna River country next July—a country which Ernie described as "the most ruggedy I've ever seen in all Alaska."

After supper Ernie took us back to our camp. He seemed loath to say good-bye. He was to float downstream next day toward Bettles, while we were to move up, but for one night the only two camps in thousands of square miles of wilderness were just across the river from each other.

Next day we traveled north in an intermittent rain which turned into snow during the afternoon. A fierce wind howled from the north and we had to push ourselves against it as we crossed the high ridge where the river takes its big loop to the west and back again. Here Al dropped behind to fish in a lake about which Ernie had told us, and caught thirty-five grayling in as many minutes. They gave pleasant variety to our menu. When we made camp that night after seven it was snowing hard and we were chilled through. It seemed like anything but the right time to be setting out on an exploration of the Arctic Divide.

But next morning we were awakened by the sun shining through the tent. We rushed outside to find a crystal-clear day. There was not a cloud in the sky. Every mountain was covered with snow, every peak showed a clean white edge set against pure blue. Almost everything in life seems to be at least somewhat blurred and misty around the edges and so little is ever absolute that we felt a genuine exultation in seeing the flawless white of those summits and the flawless blue of the sky, and the razor-edge sharpness with which the two came together.

In the whole sparkling panorama the most exhilarating sight was the view due north toward what the summer before I had christened the Gates of the Arctic. Ten miles away rose the two gigantic white posts, Frigid to the left towering 4,000 feet above the valley floor, Boreal to the right jutting up more than 6,000 feet. Between them was a deep gap about two miles wide through which the wintry summits of the Arctic Divide could be seen twenty-five miles beyond.

All day we traveled up the floor of the North Fork valley toward these massive Gates. To avoid the severe going of the side hills we kept to the gravel bars which lay first on one side of the river and then on the other. Thus we were forced frequently to ford the swift and icy current. At one place where the crossing was especially difficult we could only make it by walking on the upstream side of the horses and using them for support. As it was, Lew was almost swept away, and it was an agony to be forced to watch him without being able to lift a finger in aid. We stopped for lunch south of the Gates at Fishless Creek, an eastern tributary of the North Fork, and dried out.

After lunch we continued up the valley of the North Fork. Wandering through the falling gold of the cottonwood and willow leaves would have been joy enough, even without those snow-covered mountains on every side, and our goal of the Arctic Divide far ahead. As we drew closer to the Gates, they appeared more and more bristling with crags. On Frigid I counted twenty-seven separate pinnacles in three miles. Boreal had fewer but they were even more immense.

At the center of the grand chasm we found our camp of last year. Al and I were standing reminiscing by the dead coals of the old fire when suddenly we saw two grizzlies 100 yards ahead. They reared up and looked, but then ran away before we could hobble the horses so that Al might take a shot.

We camped a mile beyond the Gates at Fish Creek, a western side stream of the North Fork, building a big bonfire to dry out. There was a brilliant aurora that night. The thermometer dropped to 24 next morning, with the weather sparklingly clear. We traveled eight miles upstream to the junction of the North Fork with Ernie Creek and made camp for the day at noon. I spent the afternoon snapping pictures in every direction, for whichever way one looked rose majestic summits. There were so many unexplored chasms, such an infinitude of barely scalable mountains, that a person could spend many summers tripping from this center and still have fresh territory to explore. I predicted to Al that there would be a summer hotel here within not so many years. It certainly would make the most ideal mountaineering center.

Ernie Johnson had a cabin near here, about a mile above the junction, surrounded by a good stand of spruce. One tree I measured was sixteen inches in diameter at breast height, and about sixty trees per acre ran ten inches or more, notwithstanding the fact that the northern timber line was only four miles away. Near the cabin Al and Lew fixed up a cache with food supply for four days, while I bored into, and made growth measurements on, a dozen trees.

The next day was also perfect. There wasn't a cloud in the sky from morning to night. It was 27 when we got up while a fierce wind howled from the direction of the North Pole. By eight-thirty we were on the march, facing the harshness of the wind, but it was harshness easy to face with a warm sun shining and snow-capped peaks rising on every side. Behind us was that mammoth range comprising Wien Mountain, Mount Doonerak, and Hanging Glacier, and—farther south—Boreal Mountain, a lofty snowclad boundary to the vision. To the west were all the piled-up mountains which culminated in the pinnacles of the Six Darning Needles. North, as imposing as ever after a year of memories, was the 3,000-foot Gibraltar-like cliff which marked the entrance to the Valley of Precipices. And beyond its stupendous dark face, a little to the right, the snow-covered peaks of the Arctic Divide.

After lunch we proceeded up that superlatively precipitous gorge, the Valley of Precipices. So steeply did the cliffs to the west rise that by one o'clock the valley was shaded as in the evening.

As we trudged up this great gorge of the north, we lost all sense of time. It was like waking out of a sleep when we suddenly burst into full light and found that the sun, shining down the gentler valley of Grizzly Creek, was still four hours high.

A mile farther we stopped at our 101-mile camp of last year, so named because we estimated we were that far from the closest neighbor at Nolan. It was rather a blow to find that bears had dug up the cans I had buried so carefully the year before, but it gave Al, who has the true prospector's indifference to the sight of old tin all over the landscape, a great laugh. Al and I immediately set to work rustling enough dry wood from the meager willow growth to serve us a few days. The last spruce was twelve miles behind. Lew fixed a site for the tent. By six o'clock we were all settled in our remote home. The sun dropped behind the mountains to the west and it was immediately very cold.

A week of explorer's heaven followed—the sort of thing a person of adventuresome disposition might dream about for a lifetime without ever realizing it. Each day I set out to climb some fresh peak or explore some fresh valley. Often, as when visiting Yosemite or Glacier Park or the Grand Canyon or Avalanche Lake or some other natural scenery of surpassing beauty, I had wished selfishly enough that I might have had the joy of being the first person to discover it. I had been thrilled reading Captain Lewis's glowing account of the discovery of the great falls of the Missouri. I yearned for adventures comparable to those of Lewis and Clark. I realized that the field for geographical exploration was giving out, but kept hoping that one day I might have the opportunity for significant geographical discovery. And now I found myself here, at the very headwaters of one of the mightiest rivers of the north, with dozens of never-visited valleys and hundreds of unscaled summits still as virgin as during their Paleozoic creation.

The first day in this heaven was blessed with perfect weather. Lew decided to stay over one day and hunt Dall sheep. These white animals are about the size of a big deer, but with shorter legs. The rams have massive coiled horns and the ewes have slender spikes which curve back. Except for their color, they look like bighorn. They are found on the steep rocky mountains north of the towns; their meat is a favorite in the region.

Al was going to prospect near camp, where he had picked up his gold-bearing rock the summer before. I wanted to take advantage of the weather to climb one of the highest peaks on the Arctic Divide, the summit of which was about four miles from camp.

The ascent commenced over gently rising, sod-covered slopes at the bottom of Grizzly Creek valley, but after five hundred feet I found myself among huge conglomerate boulders over which I had to pick my way with care to avoid smashing an ankle. In a little basin among the boulders I scared out three sheep. Above the conglomerate came a slope of yellow rock fragments so steep that I was continually starting juvenile landslides; I could not climb more than seventy-five steps without stopping for breath. But when I reached the top of this incline I could see from the course of the streams that I was on the very divide. Above me rose the last thousand feet of my mountain, just a gray stack of limestone. So I called the peak Limestack Mountain.

The view from the summit showed a myriad of wildly thrown together mountains rising from deep valleys, cut up by great clefts and chasms, their bases resting in green vegetation, then rising into rocks—stratified at times and chaotically tumbled at others—culminating in unbroken snow, and framed always by the pure blue of the sky. The number of mountains was bewildering. I could pick out Blue Cloud, sixty miles to the south, but from it to the summits far north toward the Arctic Ocean there was not one among all the hundreds of peaks I could see which to my knowledge had ever been climbed or even mapped.

I spent more than three bright hours up there on top of the continent, looking in every direction over miles of wilderness in which, aside from Lew and Al, I knew there was not another human being. This knowledge, this sense of independence which it gave, was second only to the sense of perfect beauty instilled by the scenery on all sides. My time on the summit was spent by first giving myself to an enjoyment such as another person might experience listening to Beethoven's Fifth Symphony played by some dreamed-of super-Philadelphia Orchestra; I then took pictures and made sketch maps of the topography in every direction. I had to be careful on top because though the side from which I had climbed Limestack was gentle enough, the opposite side fell off vertically for about 1,500 feet.

When I got back to camp Al was cooking supper and a sheep was hanging from a tripod. He had been prospecting for two hours and had come to the conclusion that his kind of rock occurred only sporadically in the conglomerate. Then he saw a sheep moving along the skyline on the mountain across Grizzly Creek. He grabbed the gun, rushed up the mountain, which rises perhaps 2,000 feet above camp, and when almost on the summit came upon a band of a dozen sheep. He knocked over two easily enough, then aimed at a third about 200 yards away and killed him too. He brought one to camp, leaving the other two behind, to be picked up later. That evening we consumed heaped platefuls of fresh lamb stew.

It was eight o'clock and almost dark, when Lew dragged in packing the hide and several big chunks of steaks of a grizzly bear. He had crossed to the arctic side of the divide and tramped for hours without seeing a fresh sign of sheep. Just as he was about to turn back he saw on a ledge of rock above him a grizzly, pacing back and forth like a tiger in a cage. The bear did not see him. Lew detoured, came above the bear, and ended his pacing by a couple of shots.

Next morning Lew pulled out with the horses, his bear skin, most of the sheep, and all our superfluous equipment, including the 8 by 10 tent which we had been using. This left us with a 5 by 7 tent, with room for little besides ourselves. Consequently, Al and I packed our stuff about 300 yards up the valley where an overhanging schist bluff furnished fine shelter for everything we could not take into the tent. It also protected us from the north wind. Al rigged a fly for the tent from an old tarp and we soon had the new camp set up in a way we felt could withstand the worst the Arctic might bring.

In the afternoon we climbed to the summit of the mountain on which Al had killed the sheep. We took choice cuts from the two Al had left behind. We also opened their stomachs and found that the sheep had been feeding exclusively on reindeer moss and sphagnum. Though the perfect weather had ended, and the sky was heavily clouded, the air was still very clear, the mountains just as wild from here as from the divide. If we did not have as extensive a view as I had the day before, from here we could see the divide itself, about two miles away airline across the valley of Grizzly Creek. The divide was capped by a limestone palisade from a thousand to two thousand feet high and extending for about five miles. It did not show a solid front, but a vast series of columns chiseled out by the uneven weathering of the limestone. From the grooves between the bases of the columns, the crumbled limestone debris spread out in fan-shaped formation for another 1,500 feet of elevation. The bottom five hundred to a thousand feet of the valley might have been the bottom of any glacial valley except that there was no vegetation larger than dwarf willows.

We could look right over low Ernie Pass in the Arctic Divide at the head of Ernie Creek, into the headwaters of the Anaktuvuk River which flows west and then north by way of the Colville River through three hundred miles of wilderness to the Arctic Ocean. Here, however, the Anaktuvuk ran through a broad, gentle valley. It looked greenish-brown and so peaceful it might have been some Montana valley—the Gallatin, Deerlodge, Missoula, or Bitterroot valley—except that the snow-covered limestone crags beyond were too rugged even for Montana.

We returned to camp by a rocky, unexplored hanging valley on the east side of the mountain and the steep south wall of the Grizzly Creek canyon.

Next day, despite an intermittent drizzle, we followed the middle of the three main forks of Grizzly Creek to its source. Just before we came to the first fork, five and a half miles above camp, the river flowed over a solid bar of bedrock. This, Al informed me fervidly, was a prospector's dream, because if there was any gold at any point above, some of it would surely be washed down and lodge in the crevices of the rock. It was in just such places that all great historic strikes had been made. Why, holy mackerel, if this were Bonanza Creek or Eldorado Creek in the Dawson country, one claim would yield several millions. It was glorious—but unfortunately after Al had panned for half an hour he did not raise enough gold to fill one tooth of a rodent.

A mile above the first fork the middle branch came in from the right, tumbling down in 200-feet high cascades from a lofty valley just below the clouds. We headed up this fork and soon were climbing great steps of basaltic rock. This giant stairway rose 200 feet, then suddenly ended, and we found ourselves in a strange, flat valley from which the glacier had departed so recently that the stream had not yet had time to gouge out the valley floor. This perfectly flat bottom was about 400 feet wide and covered with gravel and small rocks which had shattered as they had tumbled from a black mountain to the right, the crest of which was lost in fog. But partly hidden in the mist we could discern huge boulders which seemed to be just poised to fall on us. As we followed the valley for half a mile more, until it turned at almost right angles, there was again the delicious feeling of exploring untrodden ground and a half spooky sensation that some supernatural phenomenon might lie just ahead.

But if this half mile seemed unearthly, what lay around the bend seemed even more so. Here was absolutely nothing but dull-colored rocks—conglomerate rocks, basaltic rocks, limestone rocks, schist rocks, even one granite rock from God knows where. For all we could see the whole cosmos might have been rock and fog. We had felt below that we were heading the advance of mankind into the valley, but here we were leaving life itself for there was not the faintest sign of any animal existence in this rocky world and not a single bit of green vegetation—nothing but a few dry, black lichens desperately clinging to the dry black rocks.

At the head of the valley was what seemed from the distance to be a great dam. When we reached the base we found it to be solid conglomerate bedrock about 60 feet high. We climbed up the face which was so steep that we could barely make the grade and found ourselves at the end of our valley, almost on the Arctic Divide and almost in the clouds. Looking down the valley through the fog we could make out the lower slopes of many other jagged mountains, always leaving a suggestion of mystery where they were cut off by the clouds. There were many spectacularly deep gorges, often separated by only narrow ridges. Every one of these chasms would have been a celebrated scenic wonder in the world accessible to tourists.

The following day we set out from camp in the opposite direction to follow Ernie Creek's west fork to its source. About a mile above the mouth of this stream a series of cascades dropped down from a hanging basin on the left; together these falls were about 1,500 feet high, including one which plunged down straight 200 feet. This far Al had been the year before, panning gold; this far Ernie had hunted sheep; but beyond, all was untraveled ground.

For about six miles, going was surprisingly easy. The river cut through well-worn slate mountains, meandering now to one side of the valley, now to the other, then curving around a high, flat-topped mountain (Katiktak Mountain). Suddenly we found ourselves in a recent glacial valley flanked on the south by a series of knife-edge ridges. Their black igneous faces rose more than a thousand feet sheer from the valley floor, while between them were deep hanging gorges high up above the main valley, sending down waterfalls. One slender fall must have been five hundred feet high. Across the valley, in complete contrast, the mountains sloped quite gradually without any deep gorges cutting into them.

We followed the broad, rapidly rising valley floor for three miles. Here the river dropped in great leaps for a quarter of a mile through a canyon which it had cut in the rock. We separated at this point, Al to pan for gold, I to explore the head of the valley. I climbed steeply along a ridge northwest of the canyon, obtaining a glorious view down the valley whenever I turned. Far below to my left the river was tumbling its initial two miles through a deep V-gorge. Across it a mountain rose almost straight up for probably 2,500 feet. Its face was a patchwork of black rock and white snow. Chunks of rock were continually breaking off and rumbling down into the valley, so I called that peak the Rumbling Mountain.

When I crossed the highest point on the ridge, I could look down into a big glacial cirque forming the very head of the west fork of Ernie Creek. The floor of the cirque was covered with gravel and mud, but, amazingly for this region, with scarcely any rocks. To my right nestled a tiny lake, probably 200 by 400 feet in size, bluish-green in color. At an elevation of 6,000 feet, this little water spot was perhaps the loftiest body of water in the whole Brooks Range.

Beyond the cirque was a low, curving ridge which I took to be the Arctic Divide. It was about 800 feet above the cirque and the slope was not too steep, so I decided to clamber up. About half way, I heard a noise like an explosion above me and looked up to see a big rock, probably six feet across, plunging down the mountainside in my general direction. I started to run, but slipped and sprawled flat. When I looked again, it seemed to be coming straight for me and it was too late to move. For an instant it was like a horrible nightmare I used to have about semiannually in childhood, of a great rock about to crush me and I being unable to move. I lay just as flat as I could, knowing that chunks like this, as they go bounding down the mountainside, hit the ground only now and then. Fortunately the spot where I was lying was neither now nor then, so I was soon on my way once more, a bit shakily, to the top of the ridge.

It *was* the Arctic Divide! About 300 feet above me was a low mountain at the very head of the cirque, and I climbed it easily. From its summit to the east and north I had perhaps the most impressive view of my life. The great knife-edge south wall of the valley extended in a semicircular front for eight miles from the Rumbling Mountain to Katiktak Mountain. Within these eight miles I counted ten different knife-edge ridges, each faced with a giant precipice where it broke off into the main valley, each rising two or three thousand feet from the gorges which separated it from the neighboring knife-edge ridges. These gorges lay about a thousand feet above the valley floor, where the river meandered back and forth with many old channels marking the valley with varied patterns.

I named this remarkable valley and the river which drained it Kenunga, which is Eskimo for knife edge, thus presumably putting myself in the same shady class of nomenclators as the poet Charles Fenno Hoffman who, nearly a century before, had taken the Seneca word Tahawus and placed it on a mountain the Senecas had never seen.

To the southwest, about two miles along the divide on which I stood, was a very high mountain (later named Three River Mountain) which I imagined must be at the junction of the major rivers, the Anaktuvuk, North Fork, and John. I decided to climb it, even though a cap of fog rested on its summit and the way seemed exceptionally precipitous. I followed the ridge for a gently rising mile to its base, then swung over to the north side and scaled its very jagged summit by some stiff rock work. The fog was so dense that I got very little view, but topographically I was able to verify my surmise. The southeast face of the mountain was a sheer precipice 1,500 feet high, dropping into a snow-filled hanging valley. I descended into this high valley, but not by the direct route, and then dropped down another thousand feet by a frozen cascade to the very head of Kenunga Creek. From here I hastened back to Al. We returned the ten additional miles to camp without event. That evening we feasted on fried tenderloin of wild sheep and grizzly-bear stew with potatoes, vegetables, and dumplings.

Our last three days in Paradise I want to mention only briefly. On the first day we followed the east fork of Ernie Creek, Grizzly Creek, for 3½ miles to a deep gorge cutting back between the limestone pinnacles of Alapah and Limestack. For a mile we climbed up along the sides of this gorge which came down too steeply for comfortable walking. Then the slope tapered off and we found ourselves in a great amphitheater about a mile long and nearly half a mile wide. It was capped by pillars of limestone 200 to 1,500 feet high, the bases of the upper rows of pillars resting on the capitals of those beneath. Below the pillars were steeply sloping banks of limestone debris where the spectators might have sat, to see the creek tunneling under permanent ice or cutting through a chasm twenty feet deep and only four feet wide. There were not even dried lichens here, let alone spectators—only snow and crumbled limestone and, above that, precipices of the same rock.

The next morning it rained so much I stayed in camp studying

Spurr's *Geology* and reading *Anna Karenina*. After lunch, when the rainfall temporarily ceased, I set out to explore the hanging basin above the series of waterfalls near the mouth of Kenunga Creek. When I had climbed the 1,500 feet to the top of the falls, I was surprised to find myself in a gently rolling valley which might have been set down without anachronism in the Adirondacks or even northern Massachusetts. This other side of the mighty west wall of the Valley of Precipices was only a hillside. I climbed it easily without stopping for breath, and from the summit of the mountain marveled at the contrast between the overhanging view into the Valley of Precipices, 3,000 feet below to the east, and the gentle slope of an agricultural country dipping into the hanging basin on the west. Only the very head of the basin, covered by a permanent icefield, could be called "rugged." While following the valley up to this icefield, I saw ten unfrightened sheep looking placidly at me.

The last day a high fog settled down and we could not see more than fifty yards from the tent. I continued reading my books. Later the fog lifted, and by four o'clock, chiefly for exercise, we set out to walk to the center of Ernie Pass, about three miles to the north. The route to the pass was over gently rising, sod-covered hills which afforded easy walking. The center of the pass was more than a mile wide without a steep climb on either side. Just before the pass, one of the forks of Ernie Creek flowed in from the right, with great velocity. It cut through a wild canyon which looked interesting enough to follow. It was gentle scenery compared to what we had seen, yet brown slate and schist bluffs rose a hundred feet from the edge of the water. Miscellaneous rocks were heaped besides these bedrock formations, including limestone and conglomerate which had slithered down from the divide. But most the rubble—brown diorite, diabasic porphyry, and black diabase—had obviously been carried by the glacier.

Returning to camp I started an experiment to throw light on the validity of my theory that the northern timber line in Alaska is not the result of unfavorable environment for tree growth, but of the fact that there has not been time since the last ice sheet receded for the forest to migrate farther north. According to my theory, the spruce stands eventually will extend to the Arctic Divide and cross over into the sheltered valleys north of the divide. If this is so it should be possible simply by sowing seed to extend the timber line far north of where it now is. So I collected spruce cones about four miles south of the last timber, extracted the seeds, and sowed them on two plots of ground on Grizzly Creek, twelve miles north of the present timber line. One plot was covered with the natural vegetation of sphagnum, reindeer moss, *Dryas octopetala, Salix arctica, Carex,* and a plant the Eskimos call Angowuk—undoubtedly *Arctostaphylos alpina.* On the other plot I scraped away the vegetation and sowed the seeds directly on the black soil. If successful, this experiment constituted an advancement of the timber line of about 3,000 years according to my estimate of spruce-migration rates. I did not know then that I was to return to this spot seven years later to check on the results.

On the morning of our eighth day below the Arctic Divide, it was still raining, our tent was beginning to leak, and the prospects of clearing seemed so remote that we decided to pull out. We shouldered what we fortunately thought were 60-pound packs apiece—later they turned out to weigh 70—and started down the long seventeen-mile grind to the mouth of Ernie Creek. Before starting we ditched a week's food supply, including 8 pounds of sugar which nearly broke my heart, and took with us only 12 pounds of this most concentrated food. The packs felt so heavy at first, especially to Al who had less experience in back packing than I, that when after two hundred yards I let out a loud cheer at the completion of one one-thousandth part of our journey home, Al answered with a disgusted grunt. We stopped about three times per mile, sitting down always on a sloping bank or rock so that we could rest the packs without removing them. Shoulders straining, backs straining, heads straining against the headstraps, we scarcely appreciated the grandeur of the Valley of Precipices. On the whole the going was fairly good; but the last five miles, through clumps of sedges, made a substantial installment on the required payment for our one week in heaven.

We pitched our tent near Ernie Johnson's cabin at the Ernie Creek forks and used his stove for cooking. The cabin at this season was too damp and dirty for sleeping. As it alternately rained and snowed the next day we stayed close to camp, but I spent much of the time making growth measurements and stand tables in the timber adjacent to the cabin.

The following day we were off before seven for a two-day exploration of the upper North Fork—Al's exploration to be largely by pan and shovel, mine by map and camera. We took no sleeping bags or tent, planning to "siwash" out for the night—to camp Indian fashion without equipment. Thus we had very light loads, just my photographic and Al's prospecting equipment, a little food, a pot and frying pan, and the gun.

We covered the eleven miles above our starting point in about four hours, and reached a large stream coming in from the east which I later named Amawk Creek, meaning wolf creek. The scenery was superb—

on the left a high gray stone ridge cut by six deep gulches; on the right
the multipinnacled summits of three mountain masses rising 5,000–
6,000 feet above the valley floor and divided by two great gorges. In
the center, the upper North Fork, as it twisted back and forth across
the valley, was in continual foam. We picked a campsite about half
a mile above Amawk Creek, and, after an abbreviated lunch, continued on our way, Al to pan and I to explore.

Near our campsite, the upper North Fork turned toward the north.
Straight gray stone walls rose steeply on either side of the valley
through which the river had cut. After five miles, I reached a second
sizable stream coming in from the east, which a little later I named
Alinement Creek. From this point the upper North Fork continued in
a northerly direction for several miles to the Arctic Divide. I gave this
northern extension of the upper North Fork the name Nakshakluk
Creek, meaning creek of the blocked pass, because a mile upstream
it issued from a deep canyon which blocked the way.

Near the mouth of the junction of Nakshakluk and Alinement creeks,
where I was standing, Charlie Irish of Nolan and Ernie had been hunting before. Apparently no human being had been up Alinement Creek,
however, which flowed in from the east; so I determined to explore it.

A mile and a half brought me to a small permanent icefield. I slipped
across, then passed a little knoll, and suddenly found myself five hundred feet from a band of seventeen sheep. They ran up the mountainside while I snapped three pictures. As I continued up the valley I
observed that the north divide consisted of the unusual group of almost equally high peaks in perfect alinement which I had marveled
at from Limestack. They were a little more than a mile apart, and
there were seven of them in the ten miles between Nakshakluk Creek
and the final fork of Alinement Creek. Below each rocky, snow-capped
summit, a deep gulch with a heavy flow of water descended. These
numerous breaks in the topography added excitement to the exploration of this unknown river, for it was always a mystery as to just what
would be in the deep draw ahead.

Although, on the whole, the valley of Alinement Creek was much
less precipitous than the Valley of Precipices or the Grizzly or Kenunga
Creek valleys, the country was enough on end to suit the most ambi-
tious climber. Best of all, it was fresh—gloriously fresh. At every step
there was the exhilarating feeling of breaking new ground. There were
no musty signs of human occupation. This, beyond a doubt, was an
unbeaten path.

Then for a short distance I wished it were a lot more beaten. The
river kept boiling down the narrow valley, now sharp up against one

steep side, now flush against the other. Occasionally I had to leave the bed and climb over high cliffs. But usually I could pick my way around at the base. At one such place, where a schist ledge came down straight to the edge of the river, the rock near the base had fragmented and I could use its right-angled cleavage for a precarious footing.

There was a stretch of about forty yards which totally absorbed my attention as to how to place my feet. When I looked up, my heart stood still, as the books say. About 150 feet ahead were three grizzlies. This may seem like a long distance to a catcher trying to throw a man out stealing second, but not to a man faced by three bears, eleven miles from the closest gun, hundred and six from the first potential stretcher bearer, and three hundred from the nearest hospital. As in Goldilocks, the first bear was small, probably a two-year-old, the second was of medium size, the third appeared like two elephants plus a rhinoceros. They reared up, one after the other, from little to gigantic, just like so many chorus girls going through some sprout in sequence. They stood for a moment and then got down on their four legs and disappeared into the willows.

I continued upstream. As the water from each deep gulch was subtracted from the volume of the main creek it became noticeably smaller. When I finally came to the last forks, only a little brook was left. Here, virtually at the head of the upper North Fork, I reluctantly turned around.

I made the fifteen miles back to Al and our siwash camp at a four-mile-an-hour clip. The feeling of striding through untrammeled terrain was only a little less keen than going out. It had cleared, and the spectacle at the Nakshakluk Creek forks was one of wild grandeur. Downstream, framed by the cliffs where the river cut through Graystone Ridge rose a jagged rock wall more than 4,000 feet high and three miles long. Directly across Nakshakluk Creek rose the paired pinnacle of Twoprong Mountain, each prong jutting straight up into the sky. Upstream was the dark canyon from which Nakshakluk emerged, and across the canyon appeared massive Inclined Mountain, with its dark, tilted strata. The Alinement peaks, one after the other, seemed alive as the late afternoon sun played queer pranks around their snowy tips, while real life was added to the scene by five sheep feeding on one of the low, grassy hills near the forks.

When I reached our camp I found that Al had made the best possible preparations for a cold night without blankets. He had cut willow and spruce boughs to lie upon, inclined slightly toward the fire, and had collected a great quantity of dry wood. In addition, a delicious macaroni and vegetable dinner awaited me. The night passed as nights without blankets usually do when there is no cut bank to reflect the fire's heat. We were alternately roasting and chilling, with little sleep, but beyond that, not too uncomfortable. At two o'clock in the morning a fairly strong wind came up followed by snow. By half past five we started, but visibility was so limited that we realized further exploration for the day was useless and returned through a heavy snowstorm to our camp near Ernie's cabin. We just stopped once to examine the deep gorge separating Doonerak from Wien Mountain. A big creek came out of it, seemingly leaping from the clouds in two sheer falls of 500 and 200 feet. The upper fall was the largest and most impressive single plunge I have seen in northern Alaska.

Had the weather been even tolerable the next day, we would have climbed Hanging Glacier Mountain. But it was storming all around us, showed no indications of clearing, and it seemed to be time to get out. We shouldered our packs, now reduced to 65 pounds each, and started on the long trailless trek to Wiseman, ninety-one miles away.

Our seven-day journey back to civilization can be summarized in three words—damn hard work. These could not, however, be repeated ninety-one times, once for each mile, because there was a vast difference among the miles. Some, along gravel bars, we hardly noticed. Others were such, that it seemed ridiculous anyone of his own free will should put himself to such grinding effort. Opposite one gulch it took us fifty-five minutes to make half a mile. We were forced to proceed along a very steep side hill, where even without pack a person would have had a hard time worming his way through the tangled alder thickets. With brute strength we simply tore our way through the brush. There was also a very difficult stretch where the river takes a great loop to the west. We had to climb uphill for four miles through sedge tussocks and over half-frozen moss into which we would sink to our ankles at every step. It was snowing steadily that day, which made our rests chilly and uncomfortable and our footing very slippery. As I looked dimly through the storm up the North Fork, frozen along the banks and completely surrounded by the snow-covered landscape, I was ready to believe that this really was the Arctic. The worst going was at Jack Delay Pass. Here the sedge tussocks were so high and grew so close together to make walking between them impossible. But it was also impossible to walk on top of them for any distance, because they would roll over, plunging us off into muck. This would happen about once in every twenty steps and as we took about two thousand steps to the mile I think it conservative to say that at least a hundred times in each of three endless miles we would find ourselves sitting on the ground, a 65-pound pack anchoring us firmly in the mud, with an overhanging cliff of sedge formation nearly waist-high towering above us. We would grit our teeth, gather energy, and pull ourselves up the necessary three feet—only to do it all over again within the next twenty paces.

Nevertheless, there was genuine exhilaration in triumphing over the toughest conceivable travel. Tired we would be, but never worn out; difficult as the going was, we always had plenty of reserve. It was the kind of stimulation I had received earlier in my life from such varied activities as climbing the five slashed summits of the Adirondack's Dix Range in one day with my brother George and our friendly Adirondack mountain guide Herb Clark; racing through twenty-nine stormy Idaho days out of thirty in November, 1927, to finish a program of experimental work, coming home from the woods each night soaked through and then doing office work until long after midnight; staying up forty hours without sleep on a water-relations study at Johns Hopkins; or suddenly, after hard concentrated study, getting a glimmer of the significance of the quantum theory. I could give many other examples but the principle is always the same. It is the great stimulus for mental and physical adventure alike—simply the joy of triumphing over something which is difficult to accomplish.

There were two pleasant half-day interludes on our homeward journey. In the first we climbed the Redstar Mountain, fifteen miles south of the junction of the North Fork and Ernie Creek. This mountain had excited our interest on every one of the three previous occasions when we passed it, because it was capped by a red, star-shaped blotch, probably 2,000 feet across. We had been too rushed or too wet to stop before, but this time, despite snow flurries all around, we determined to investigate the source of this brilliant coloration. The ascent proved very easy, about 2,500 feet in elevation and four miles in distance with only the last 400 feet steep. We found that the entire top of the mountain as well as the tops of the higher peaks immediately north, were an igneous upthrust, the only one we had seen in this vicinity. The red, a vermilion, was only superficial, the interior of the rock under its coating being a steel gray. Much of the vermilion substance, all pulverized, was scattered in the rock crevices and over a large area. What it was mystified us as much as ever. Al picked up some of it for analysis at the Alaska School of Mines in Fairbanks.

The second interlude came when I shot a moose on the afternoon after we left the camp near Ernie's cabin. The first shot, at about 700 feet, tore off a hind leg, and the rest was simple. Like the Indians, we made camp where the moose died, dressed him, and cached most of the meat—I planned to return with a dog team, when the first snow came. We cooked a feast which included the tongue and two huge T-bone steaks. The moose was a young bull which Al estimated to weigh about 450 pounds dressed. Shooting the moose gave me a dual pleasure. First, I never tasted more delicious meat than that we enjoyed at every meal for two days. Second, when in the future certain of my friends would chide me for being a reluctant nimrod and when it would be too complicated to explain that a living wild animal is more beautiful to me than a dead one, I would be able to elevate my nose a trifle and remark: "Oh, deer (or elk, or goats as the case may be) seem too tame after moose."

The last night out the thermometer dropped to 15. The following day it remained cool all morning and we did not perspire while staggering up the steep mountainside to Pasco Pass. Once through it, our last real difficulty was over, and the remaining eleven miles to Wiseman were downhill. We reached the house of the Pingels on Nolan Creek in time for a noon dinner, after a most hearty reception. We spent most of the afternoon around Nolan, telling our tales, hearing the latest news and enjoying the company of other human beings, after four weeks of wilderness. After 101 trailless miles of back packing, from Grizzly Creek to Nolan, the seven miles of road to Wiseman seemed easy, even though excessively muddy. I sat down flat once. When we hit the last mile from the foot of the big hill into Wiseman we were going strong and struck a four-mile-an-hour pace into town. Everybody dropped around to the roadhouse that evening and it was very pleasant to talk with our friends. Very pleasant too it was to find seventeen letters awaiting me.

Thus ended a glorious trip. I had not felt the slightest eagerness to get back to civilization. There had been much hard work, but never any real discomfort and we had traveled efficiently. It had been just an active unexciting trip physically, but the most thrilling in aesthetic pleasure.

Our record of exploration included the ascent of six until then unclimbed mountains, three of them on the Arctic Divide; the visiting of three major unexplored valleys and six minor valleys, gulches, and chasms; and the mapping of forty-two miles of until then untraversed valleys.

Our scientific record included the study for growth of six stands of timber, the laying out of four sample plots to determine the size of trees and number per acre; the launching of an experiment testing tree establishment beyond timber line; the collecting of rock samples which we brought back for identification; and the opening of animal stomachs to determine feeding habits.

We had prospected six creeks and had found gold in none of them; and we had seen a black bear, two moose, seven grizzly bears, and three score sheep.

Our personal statistics included the carrying of packs and leading of horses for two hundred sixteen miles, side-tripping with light packs for a hundred and seventy miles; the killing and partly eating of three sheep, one moose, and one grizzly bear; the catching and enjoying of one hundred and twelve grayling; and the gathering of delicious blueberries and cranberries.

I should like to conclude the account of this trip with a few words about my partner. Although we had no important interests in common aside from this particular journey, Al was considerate, affable, and eager to help me in accomplishing my purposes. He was the most resourceful person imaginable. He could do everything from patching up the split hoof of a horse to repairing my camera. He was better than I in every one of the many activities of our trip except for walking, back packing, mapping, and photographing. He did twice as much work around camp as I did, yet never even hinted that he was doing more than his share of the work; nor was he disgruntled that my objectives were entirely realized while his ended in total failure.

Jesse Allen, author, and Nutirwik at Canyon Creek camp

Wiseman, 1931, from across the Middle Fork of the Koyukuk River

Wiseman with the roadhouse (first building, left)
and the author's cabin (third building)

Bettles, main street

Ernie Creek with Hanging Glacier Mountain (left)
and Boreal Mountain (far right)

Al Retzlaf

Kenneth Harvey

Verne Watts

Ernie Johnson

"Mushing"—lower Clear River

The Arctic Divide in winter

Boreal Mountain

Snow wall at the head of Clear River

Kenneth Harvey and Jesse Allen at Snowshoe Pass

Gravel bars of the John River

Eskimo children at Wiseman

Ekok and family gathering wood

*The author's dendrograph—a device
to measure tree growth*

Method of packing dogs

Going up the North Fork of the Koyukuk River by boat

Mount Doonerak

Gravel bars of the Hammond River

The author on North Doonerak

Harvey (wearing mosquito net) and "Moose" in Pinnyanaktuk Creek valley

The Arctic Divide

Cockedhat Mountain as seen from Limestack Mountain

Mount Apoon from Amawk

Nutirwik (left), Kenneth Harvey, and Jesse Allen
at Bombardment Creek camp

Arrigetch Range

3 Mushing

WHEN WE RETURNED TO WISEMAN FROM OUR TRIP TO THE
Arctic Divide, Al went back to Fairbanks and I settled down for the
winter of 1930–31 in a log cabin close to the Wiseman roadhouse.
This was my headquarters while studying the unusual, independent,
and exciting life of the Eskimo and white man of the northern
Koyukuk region. Scarcely a day went by without five or six people
visiting me. During the year, every person around Wiseman, except
one three-month-old baby and one Eskimo woman who could not
speak English, spent several hours with me in my cabin. I got to
know these friendly people further by visiting them in their homes,
sharing their meals, attending dances at the roadhouse, and taking
trips in the nearby countryside. I also paid about a dozen visits to
the neighboring gold-mining centers and to the more remote mining
camps and cabins.

In the course of visiting some of the outlying camps during the winter months, I was introduced to "mushing"—winter travel in the Arctic. Despite the hard labor mushing is one of the genuine joys in the life of most Koyukukers.

In addition to a number of shorter trips, I had the good fortune to go on two longer winter wilderness journeys—one up the Middle Fork of the Koyukuk; the other up Clear River and over to Wild Lake. (See end map.)

Early in November, Jess Allen and Kenneth Harvey invited me to join them on a ten-day trip to help them haul back eight sheep they had shot in the autumn and cached near the head of Dietrich River, the east branch of the Middle Fork, some sixty-two miles from Wiseman. Jesse, at 51 and despite the loss of his right arm just below the elbow in a mining accident seventeen years before, was one of the outstanding hunters and rifle shots of the region. He was tall and lanky with early white hair, bushy eyebrows over deeply set eyes and a face lined with wrinkles. He and his wife were living in Wiseman. He was probably the most widely read and most liberal person in the Koyukuk region. He was completely free from prejudices and any feeling of superiority toward the Eskimos, and so understanding of the difference in their philosophy of life from that of the whites, so tolerant and patient with any of their shortcomings in terms of white *mores*, that they trusted him more than any other white man in Wiseman. He first came to Alaska in 1901, the year Harvey and I were born. His home originally was in West Virginia.

Kenneth Harvey, usually addressed by his family name, was a bachelor and, at 29, one of the youngest and physically most vigorous men at Wiseman. His jovial round mustached face, topped by a shock of black hair, went well with his broad-chested, stocky, strong frame. Like most white men of the upper Koyukuk, he mined gold for a living, but was also an enthusiastic and excellent hunter. In addition, he was the leading mechanic and watch repairer of the region, having learned both trades by correspondence course. He had grown up in Ohio as one of the ten children of a migratory worker, who never knew the meaning of security. He first came to Alaska in 1922 and to Wiseman two years later. He and Jesse had become good friends and went together on a month's hunting expedition every autumn.

It was a sparkling clear morning that Jesse, Harvey, and I set out on the trail to Hammond River. The sleds were nearly empty so we made good time, Jesse and Harvey with five dogs each to pull them, I with four. We stood on the rear runners, holding the handle bars for support, and though we averaged only seven or eight miles an hour, with perhaps a maximum of fifteen miles when we struck the downhill stretches in a spray of dry snow, so close were we to the ground that we seemed to be hurtling over the trail. We tore along aisles between dark green spruce trees, were brushed by the willow branches and the evergreen leaves of the Alaska tea, followed the rhythm of the legs of the huskies as they beat on the pathway, had time to look up at the mountaintops and note the constantly changing outlines they cut against the deep blue sky, and felt ourselves to be a part of the world through which we were traveling. This sled riding was in complete contrast to riding in an automobile, where you are you and the landscape is the landscape and never is there any merging of the two.

We spent the afternoon and night at a small gold-mining center near the junction of the Hammond and Dietrich rivers. The next morning at eight o'clock, before the first streak of dawn, we set out up the Dietrich River, following the course of the river. Our three teams followed each other in single file, Jesse and Harvey as the experienced mushers breaking trail, and I as the greenhorn bringing up the rear. In spite of the hard going and the softness of the dogs we covered more than twenty miles that day, and pulled up by two-thirty in the afternoon at a little cabin just below the mouth of Bettles River. Straight across the Dietrich River, scarcely a mile away, was a horned pinnacle which jutted more than 3,000 feet into the air. Beyond the mouth of Bettles River was an even loftier mountain with a precipice wall several miles long and more than 1,500 feet sheer.

Next morning we were up shortly after five to start breakfast, and by eight-thirty, still before the first daylight, we were once more on the move. It was a day spent alternately walking along in front of the dogs on the easy stretches, helping them pull on the hard ones, and detouring cautiously around the frequent overflows of the river.

Overflows are among the greatest hazards of winter travel. When it gets very cold the streams at places freeze to the bottom, and this dams the oncoming water which had been flowing under the ice. The water is backed up until it finds an outlet by way of some crack or air hole and flows out over the top of the ice. The colder it is, the more numerous are the places where the river freezes to the bottom, and consequently the more it overflows. The fresh water soon glazes over so that it looks like firm ice. Unless you are very careful you will break through. If you are wearing shoe pacs and the water does not go over their tops, you are all right; but if it does go over the tops or if you are wearing moccasins which become immediately soaked, you must stop at once to build a fire and dry out as fast as possible. Most people who lost their feet in the north country and many who froze to death have had their catastrophe start on an overflow.

Shortly after two in the afternoon the sun disappeared behind the high limestone crags to the west, and the temperature dropped so rapidly that we started thinking about camp. We had left behind the area where an occasional cabin may be found, so we set up a tent and chopped spruce bows to cover the snow. We had a good stove, and we could make the inside of the tent as warm as any steam-heated apartment if one of us would spend an hour or two cutting wood. By the time we had everything done—dogs tied, tent set, boughs cut and spread, stove blocked up and stove-pipe pieced together, wood cut, ten gallons of water melted, supper cooked, supper eaten, dishes washed, dog feed cooked, cooled, and given out, clothing brushed off and hung up to dry, holes and tears sewed— four or five hours of steady hustling had passed. We stoked the stove full of wood before we crawled into our sleeping bags around ten o'clock, but the fire was burned out in a couple of hours, so that by morning the tent was as cold as the outside air.

It took a dash of fortitude to crawl out of the warm bag and start the fire, but once it was going the tent speedily warmed. A couple of hours sufficed for us to cook and eat breakfast, break camp, pack the sleds, hitch up the dogs, and be on our way. The weather was perfect, the going was good, and we could observe the whole pageant of a mid-winter arctic morning growing out of a mid-winter arctic night. It was full starlight when we started, heading straight on the course toward Polaris. After half an hour the black sky began to turn gray, and the unbelievable arctic brightness of the stars slowly faded. The gray became faintly blue, and then a single snowy peak in the northwest showed a tip of pink. So gradually that you could hardly notice it advancing, the pink spread from peak to peak until all summits to the north and west were colored. The pink kept creeping down the slopes, changing imperceptibly in color, until all at once you noticed that it had vanished, and that the mountainsides were bathed in a golden spray—craggy peaks, snowfields, dark spruce timber, everything. Then suddenly, at high noon, after journeying a whole morning in the shadow, there was a wide bend in the river, and we drove out into the sunlight.

We reached our destination on the Dietrich River that afternoon shortly after one o'clock. The cached sheep had not been disturbed and were ready to be loaded for the downstream journey on the morrow. It was getting constantly colder, and we could not work hard enough to keep warm while setting up camp. We had to stop fre-

quently and thaw our feet and hands by the fire where the cornmeal
was cooking for the dogs. But by five-thirty all chores were completed
and we retired to the well-heated tent for supper and relaxation. The
thermometer dropped that night to 40 below zero, but this merely
seemed to accentuate the snugness of our solitary habitation.

That evening of November 10, I thought of my friends on the Outside who were spending the night comfortably in steam-heated rooms
in the heart of steam-heated cities. We spent that night scarcely less
comfortably near the Arctic Divide, though the thermometer dropped
to 40 below and we had only a thin canvas shelter. But ours was a
single oasis of warmth and comfort in thousands of square miles of
freezing wilderness. That same night, eight miles to the south and
unknown to us, Albert Ness of Wiseman, trying to reach us on a mercy
mission, was forced by darkness to stop and shiver through a misera-
ble night by an inadequate siwash fire.

That night also marked the tragic end of Martin Slisco's cousin, Leo
Slisco. Broke, sick, just over his second divorce, he had determined to
come to Wiseman and start life again. When he reached Fairbanks
the authorities jailed him a month for disorderly conduct while under
the influence of dope and refused to allow him to come to the Koyukuk
by plane. He therefore set out over the three-hundred-and-twenty-
mile trail from Nenana. There was a roadhouse eighteen miles out.
Leo apparently had gone seventeen of them after it became dark.
It was very cold. Inadequately clothed, unused to the north country,
dissipated, cold horror must have seized him when darkness came
without his reaching shelter. He probably felt that he had traveled
much more than eighteen miles and must surely be on the wrong
trail, that his only hope for life was to return. When only one mile
from shelter he wheeled around and backtracked. Next morning they
picked him up by the side of the trail in a sitting posture, frozen stiff.
Like so many others, he had only sat down to rest for a minute which
became eternity.

On the morning of November 11 Harvey set out straight up the
mountain opposite our camp in quest of more sheep. Jesse Allen and
I started upstream to use the opportunity and do some exploring. We
had only gone a mile and a half when Harvey came running up with
the news that Albert Ness had just driven into camp, with a message
for Jesse to return to Wiseman at once because Mrs. Allen was seriously sick.

This emergency had been met by the community in a way typical
for this frontier. It was essential to get Jesse. So Ed Marsan volunteered his dogs and sled, and Albert Ness volunteered a week of his
time and set out after us. As mentioned, he had to siwash out one

night in the bitter cold. But all this was considered merely the normal neighborliness of the frontier; Albert expected no thanks and would have been indignant at any offer of money.

It was too late for Jesse to start back that day. But next morning he was off before daylight, and with six dogs making his empty sled fly down the river he reached Wiseman the same night.

Albert Ness stayed with Kenneth Harvey and me to help us haul the sheep meat to Wiseman. But before we returned, I set out again for the divide between the Koyukuk and the Chandalar to the east, another major tributary of the Yukon. The two streams were but three-quarters of a mile apart and were connected by a very low pass rising only 50 feet above the Chandalar valley and five hundred feet above the Koyukuk. It was bleak and windswept this frigid mid-November afternoon and, with the thermometer still below 30, snapping photographs with a cut-film camera was a chilly pastime. But there was a joy in sliding on the ice of the Chandalar, a joy in seeing the Arctic Divide to the north, lit by the last sunlight of the short afternoon, and especially an exhilaration in coasting five hundred feet into the Koyukuk.

On the way back to camp I stopped at the last timber. With much pressure and at the price of numerous shivers and some profanity I bored nine different trees. The ages and distribution of the timber gave welcome confirmation to my theory on the advance of the northern timber line. When I got to camp I just had time before darkness to cruise a quarter-acre sample plot in the heavy timber surrounding us. It may be disconcerting to those who hold the commonly accepted theory of a stunted northern timber line to learn that just a mile and a half away were trees 18 inches in diameter at breast height.

It took us six days to return because the loads were so heavy that we had to double-haul more than half the distance, that is, split the load and haul twice over the same ground. It was hard work, but the nights in camp were very pleasant.

Conversation covered a wide variety of subjects ranging from Houdini, to Albert Ness breaking through the ice, to local geography and mining, to genes and heredity, to what fine people the Eskimos are, to agnosticism and religion, to Jefferson and Hamilton, to life in the Koyukuk being happier than life Outside.

When we returned to Wiseman, we learned that Mrs. Allen was still seriously ill. Jesse was badly broken up over it. A few days later she was sent to Fairbanks by plane to receive competent treatment.

4 Wintertrip into New Country

THE WHOLE TRIP, YOU MIGHT SAY, STARTED OVER AN ARGU-
ment. The issue was whether Clear River, one of the three main
tributaries of the North Fork of the Koyukuk, headed against the
Arctic Divide. Since nobody was ever known to have been even close
to its source, the discussions were entirely conjectural based on knowledge of adjacent drainage. The vote of those who hazarded an opinion was four to four, with Ernie Johnson the leader of the believers
in the Arctic Divide origin, and I the chief opponent of this viewpoint. When Ernie had been in Wiseman over New Year's, 1931,
he had suggested we should resolve the doubt by following the river
to its source when the days grew longer in March. This would also
give him an opportunity to seek new hunting grounds. I had more
work planned already than I could possibly ever accomplish, but the
chance of following an unknown river to its source in mid-winter

seemed more important than anything else. Besides, the trip would give me an opportunity to study timber line on another major drainage, and thus make my investigation more complete. I thought we could well tie in a visit to the gold-mining settlements at Wild Lake where Ernie had friends; we could mush to the lake after our exploration of Clear River and return to Wiseman via Bettles. (See map, page 6 and end map.) It sounded splendid and I agreed to accompany Ernie.

The community gave us a great farewell dance the night before we were to leave Wiseman. Then, when Ernie's dogs were sick the next day from the medicine he had given them to eradicate worms, there was a second farewell the next night. But even worms have their ends, so on March 6, well danced, we hit the trail and mushed fourteen miles to the old Charlie Yale cabin on Glacier River, which Al Retzlaf and I had visited in 1929.

The second day we mushed twenty hard miles to an old prospector's cabin on Bonanza Creek, which had such a low roof I must have put a permanent dent in my head from constant violent contact. The third day we covered twelve easy miles to a cabin which Ernie had built at the junction of the Tinayguk River and North Fork. There were no remarkable events or scenery on either of these days, yet they left a vivid memory of that world of three pure, unblended colors through which we traveled for sixteen consecutive days of perfect weather—the base of fresh, white snow, the dark, green spruce trees set upon it, and the clear, blue sky as a covering. Everywhere we looked we saw the sparkle of snow crystals where the bright sun reflected from the surface.

Perhaps a word is in order here about our equipment and method of travel.

To begin with, what does a person wear for a mid-winter journey in the Arctic? First, there must be something which will insulate the body and keep the heat in. Second, something, either leather or closely woven cloth, which will keep the wind out. Third, everything must be fitting loosely, especially footwear, so as not to impede the circulation of the blood. Most important, a person must be sure not to wear so much that he perspires, because it is disastrous to get wet. Most people who froze to death in this north country first got wet, either by breaking through overflows or by sweating. Wetness means ice in short order, and no matter how much clothing one has on, it is impossible to warm up with a coat of ice against the body. The only thing one can do is build a fire and dry out before it is too late. Of course, when the temperature is only 10 or 20 below, and no wind is blowing, a little perspiration is no cause for worry.

I wore a suit of medium-heavy wool underwear, an ordinary flannel shirt, a pair of light wool pants, a pair of cotton overalls (to break the wind and keep the snow from sticking to the wool), a sleeveless sweater, one of those closely woven, green Filson cruising jackets, and a light cloth parka over everything. The parka had no buttons, could be slipped over the head, came down a little below the knees, and had no vent to let the wind get through. On one or two fairly cold days—it was never more than 31 below—I wore a caribou-fur parka while riding the back end of my sled. For my head I used a muskrat cap with pieces covering my ears and the sides of my face. There was a hood on the parka which came way over in front, and was a great protection from the wind. On my feet I wore three pairs of wool socks, inner soles, and moose-skin moccasins with eight-inch tops. My hands were protected by anything from wool mittens inside and wool-lined leather mittens outside, to just canvas gloves, depending on how cold it was.

Our method of travel was by dogs. Ernie had one sled with four dogs, I had another with three. Between us we carried about 450 pounds of equipment. Half of this consisted of dog feed, in the form of dried salmon, tallow, cornmeal, rice, and oatmeal.

We used three principal ways of traveling by sled. If there was a well-broken trail, or if we happened to be following a recently overflowed river with fresh ice, we just stood on the rear end of the runners, steering by pressure one way or the other on the handle bars, and let the dogs pull us, except on up-grades where we ran along behind.

If the trail was at all drifted, especially on side hills, it became very difficult to hold the sled on the trail merely by steering from the rear, so we geepoled ahead. The geepole is a stick which protrudes in front of the sled on the gee, or right side, and by pushing on it one way or the other the sled can easily be kept where you want it. While geepoling, depending on how fast the dogs could travel, we walked or ran on snowshoes just in front of the sled and astraddle of the towline by which the dogs were hitched.

If the snow was very deep and soft, the dogs could not get footing and sank to the bottom at every step. Then we had to snowshoe ahead on our smallest pair of snowshoes, working hard at every step packing the snow down so that the dogs could have it a little easier. When the going was particularly bad, we both snowshoed ahead and let the dogs follow. At other times one of us geepoled the two sleds which we coupled together, one behind the other.

At the Tinayguk River cabin, to which Ernie referred as "home" although it was forty miles from the nearest neighbor, we broke up our load. We left about half our food and dog feed for the Wild River part of our journey, storing it in Ernie's cache, a little log cabin built on poles about eight feet high. The poles were girdled part way up by tin to prevent clawed animals from climbing them. In this country with its camp robbers, weasels, grizzly bears, and, worst of all, wolverines, storing food is a problem.

Not so bright and early the next morning we set out for Clear River. It was only four miles to the mouth. Nine miles beyond it Ernie had left a tent when he had gone up about two weeks earlier in a futile effort to find some signs of fur. His old trail had not drifted badly, so we had a relatively easy time. This was fortunate because it gave us leisure to enjoy the Clear River canyon, where, first on one side of the river and then on the other, rock walls rose straight up for one or two hundred feet, bright yellow surfaces mixed with white snow, and capped with spruce trees which grew to the very edge of the cliffs. Al Retzlaf and I had looked down into this canyon in the summer of 1929, when we and our horses climbed the Moving Mountain.

Next morning we broke camp early, taking the tent and stove with us, and continuing up the canyon.

The sky was cloudless and blue, snow sparkled over everything. After ten miles of winding among precipices, the country opened out, and we found ourselves among well-rounded, rolling hills, which did not seem at all like the customary topography of the Brooks Range. Miles to the north, however, some jagged peaks loomed, making the landscape less unfamiliar.

Most of this day we geepoled, but there were some overflowed places where we had the finest riding on the runners. There were also a couple of stretches which had overflowed so recently that they had not frozen yet so that there was a shallow layer of icy water over the solid ice beneath. Here we changed our moccasins for mukluks— waterproof sealskin boots with the fur turned in.

As we progressed upstream the timber became more and more scarce, until we came to a patch which we thought might be the last. Just above it Clear River entered another canyon which blocked the view farther upstream. As we did not wish to make camp among the dwarf willows after dark, we stopped here for the night. The timber was on a bench, 40 feet above the river. It took us half an hour to break an uphill trail a couple of hundred yards to the timber, but the view it gave us, even more than the shelter, made this effort a cheap price to pay.

Making camp in loose snow, several feet deep, in which one sinks practically to the bottom the instant snowshoes are removed, is an interesting experience, at least for one brought up in a civilization where shelter comes ready made.

Our routine in camp was the result of many a night out in the deep snow. We would start with nothing but two bundled sleds, a wilderness in which a shelter had never yet been erected, and more (Ernie) or less (I) personal competence to combine the two into something safe and comfortable. Our procedure generally began by Ernie tramping down with his snowshoes a space big enough to pitch the 9 by 9 tent, with a little extra room to prevent our sinking clear to our waists the moment we stepped outside our tent. Then we usually hitched the tent to trees by ropes at either end of the ridge, and stretched out the wall ropes to trees, shrubs, or specially cut poles, whichever happened to be most handy. Meanwhile I would hack down a green spruce for blocks on which to set the stove, saving the boughs to spread on top of the snow inside the tent. Ernie would cut more boughs, and soon we would forget we were roosting on snow, unless we happened to look under the stove.

Before we started out in the morning, Ernie always filled the stove with shavings, kindling, and dry sticks of wood, so that once it was set up and the stovepipe attached at night, we would have a roaring fire in a few moments. Getting a fire started quickly was most important in really cold weather. Even in relatively mild weather the sooner the fire got going the better, because all cooking had to wait until we had melted enough snow to get the water we required. For melting the snow we used five-gallon gasoline cans, with one side cut out. Each night we used three of them, half full of water, two for cooking dog feed and one for ourselves.

But with melting the snow our nightly task was far from finished. Wood had to be cut. The dogs had to be unhitched and tied to trees. Spruce-bough bedding had to be prepared for them. Then we had to take in our own bedding and spread it out on our boughs. We had to scrape the snow from our socks, overalls, and moccasins, and hang them up to dry. When a little of the snow was melted we started the tea water, and after that the rest of the supper. While we were eating and afterward, the dog feed would be cooking. After supper there would be dishwashing, sewing, repairing snowshoes, and—most tedious of all—crawling, head first, into a sleeping bag to change films in total darkness. When the dog feed was done we would take it outside, pour it into separate pans for each dog, and let it cool. Just before going to bed we would serve it.

This may sound like a lot of work, and actually we were kept busy until ten or eleven o'clock. Nevertheless these evenings were very pleasant. Ernie was a simple but excellent cook, and the meals he prepared added real joy to our life after a day of mushing. The *pièce de résistance* of our suppers was always a pot of boiled meat. Ernie believed it essential for healthy camp life to avoid too much frying, and above all to avoid burned grease. The meat was tender sheep, which Ernie had shot late in the fall. With the natural cold-storage facilities of the Arctic there was no trouble in keeping meat all winter. We varied our suppers by boiling lima beans, peas, dried vegetables, rice, or macaroni with the meat. One potful lasted us for two nights. On the second night it was only necessary to thaw out and heat what was left from the first. The same was true of fruit. We always had a pot of dried apples and cranberries cooked and ready for immediate use. The only fresh cooking necessary for supper on the second night was tea, biscuits, and sometimes rice or macaroni.

At supper and after came the period of leisurely conversation. Ernie had taken along *Kristin Lavransdatter* and Whitehead's *Science and the Modern World,* while I had 1,217 pages of Tolstoi's *War and Peace* (which Ernie had read along with *Anna Karenina* during his last two-month trip in the wilderness). But we were both so busy talking that neither of us read a single page. Ernie had remarkably broad interests, bred from vast reading during thousands of solitary evenings in camp. Our conversations varied in subject matter from midwestern Methodist moral notions of the school teacher and Tolstoi's overworking of the phenomenon of love at first sight to the work of the physicists Albert A. Michelson and Robert A. Millikan and how it tied up with the cosmic-ray theory. The most recurring theme, however, was Ernie's love for the wilderness.

"If I had a hundred thousand dollars today," he said with his slight Swedish accent, "I wouldn't quit this life in the hills. I'd get a little better equipment, and I'd go Outside and get married, but I'd come right back in here again. I know what the life Outside is like and it don't appeal to me. I've lived this free life in here too long."

Referring to a notoriously parsimonious local citizen, he said, "The man was indignant because we opened a can of corn. 'It costs too much,' he'd say. Now there's no sense to that. We're here such a short time and a person can get so much pleasure out of good eating, he's a fool if he don't take that pleasure while he can."

Like the majority of Koyukukers, Ernie was very contemptuous of the modern, high-power publicity explorers like Wilkins, Byrd, and the Roosevelts. Concerning the Byrd Expedition he said: "Jesus Christ, do they call that exploring? Why, they had everything they could ask for except women. That foodstuff they had they could live on in luxury all the time. They don't know anything about hardships. They ought to get out in the hills here where they have to live on themselves, and can't radio for help every time they get in trouble."

Bed for both of us consisted of a heavy, winter sheepskin, as soft as a coiled spring mattress, laid on the boughs. Over this we spread our sleeping bags and crawled in. The stove would burn for two or three hours after we retired, keeping the tent as warm as a house. Then it would gradually chill off to outside temperature, until about five or five-thirty. At that time Ernie, who always slept nearest the door of the stove, would start the fire, while I would crack the ice on the top of the water can and fill the coffee pot. Then we would drop back into our bags for a delicious half hour of dozing while the tent was warming and the water heating.

Our regular breakfast was sheep steaks fried in olive oil (another of Ernie's dietetic hobbies; he is death on lard or bacon grease), hot cakes, coffee, and fruit. After breakfast we would dress for the trail, and if we were moving camp tear down the tent, pack up the sleds, and hitch up the dogs.

On the morning after reaching the timber patch above Clear River canyon, however, we didn't break camp. Not knowing what lay ahead, we determined on a day of reconnaissance. So we hitched up the sleds, empty except for our heavy parkas, a change of footwear for emergency, extra gloves, mukluks, a lunch including a large thermos bottle filled with hot coffee, and my photographic outfit.

As soon as we started, the dogs tore down the 40-foot slope to the river so fast that we had to ride the brakes hard to keep from dashing the sleds to pieces among the trees. We swung out on the clear ice of the river, and started up the dark canyon at a pace of nine or ten miles an hour. The canyon was not very deep, but the walls were so steep that three hours after sunrise it seemed like late evening.

Then all at once we were out of the canyon, at the foot of a great sunny amphitheater, perhaps six miles long and three or four miles wide. The floor was as gently tilted as any agricultural valley might have been. There were scattered stands of spruce timber as far as we could see. On either side mountains rose for about 2,000 feet steeply, but not precipitously, except at the very summits. Only at the upper end of the valley, from which we could see three deep gorges emerging, was there any sign of those incredibly jagged summits which typify the upper North Fork country. It was a peaceful, cheerful valley, all sunlight and flawlessly blue sky and snow.

After a couple of miles we came to the end of the river's overflow. We left the river, and from now on the snow was so deep that we had to plod along on snowshoes, breaking trail for the dogs. It was work, but work filled with delight in the beauty of that bright valley, the increasing wildness of the country ahead, and the mystery of which gorge before us carried the main tributary of this never-followed river. Halfway up the valley, I looked back beyond where our camp lay and was startled by the sight of a rock chimney, about 300 or 400 feet on the sides we could see, rising from the drainage to the east. All the way up the valley we kept looking back at this gigantic rock which bore a striking resemblance to Chimney Rock in the Kaniksu National Forest in Idaho. We called it Chimney Mountain.

If this sight was startling, it was nothing compared with the revelation of fresh grandeur which was awaiting us when we reached the head of the amphitheater. We discovered that Clear River emerged from none of the three gorges we had imagined, but from a hidden valley which turned almost at right angles to the east. I cannot convey in words my feeling in finding this broad valley lying there, just as fresh and untrammeled as at the dawn of geological eras hundreds of millions of years ago. Nor is there any adequate way of describing the scenery, beyond giving the measurements and outlines: Eight miles long, one and a half wide, U-shaped, flanked by mountains rising 2,000–3,000 feet almost straight out of it. I could mention dozens of thousand-foot sheer precipices; I could liken the valley to a Yosemite without waterfalls, but with rock domes beside which the world-renowned Half Dome would be trivial—yet with all that, I would not have conveyed the sense of the continuous, exulting feeling of immensity; of the thrill of seeing gigantic pinnacles on every side overhanging gorges; of the great, white, serrated skyline at the head of the valley, built of towering summits nearly a mile higher than where we were; and of the freshness of the all-covering snow, the blue sky, the clarity and sparkle of the mid-winter atmosphere.

Perfect as this valley seemed from its foot, its ascent unfolded new scenery so magnificent that the first view seemed like only a tourist's glimpse of the real beauty. For into this wide major valley, ten unique gorges debouched. I say unique because every one had a character and individuality which made it stand out unforgettably. In the continental United States every one would be considered worthy of preservation as a national monument.

We ascended the valley for seven of its eight miles, unmindful of the hard snowshoeing, because of the wonder of the unfolding panorama. All the way up the main valley seemed to close in more grandly about us, while new side gorges were continually revealed. First, on the left, we saw a deep valley heading to the northeast of Boreal Mountain, which forms the eastern post of the Gates of the Arctic that we had seen previously from its other side on the North Fork. On the right, a gorge appeared which became lost among the serrated ridge tops. Then came, on the left again, a gorge completely circled by a spectacular series of needlelike pinnacles. Just above it, on the right, a short valley dropped from the lofty rocks. It was two miles to the next valley on the left. This one had the same Yosemite character as the main valley—broad, deep, U-shaped, precipitous-looking mountains rising on either side. Half a mile above it, on the right, a steep creek became visible, flanked on one side by an inclined plateau, on the other by sheer crags. We traveled two more miles until we were practically at the last timber. A mile beyond was the head of the valley, and we could see that four more great gorges entered into it. The temptation was strong to go on to the end, but we knew we would first have to move camp up here if we wanted to reconnoiter this upper country properly. Further, the dogs were getting tired from the hard pull, so we decided it was best to turn back.

The journey downstream supplemented the upstream one, for now we got all that beauty from the opposite approach. If it was, on the whole, not quite as beautiful as facing the other way, there were individual views on the return journey which exceeded the comparable ones on the outward trip. The view of that crag-surrounded gulch was one, and the sight of the great rock chimney all the way down the wide amphitheater was another.

Traveling was now much more comfortable. The trail was well broken, and we could walk or trot easily along behind the dogs while holding the geepole. We had plenty of leisure to enjoy the scenery. After ten miles of this going we struck the ice. We took off our snowshoes, hopped onto the rear runners, and flew the last four miles into camp.

That night was the coldest of the trip. The thermometer dropped to 31 below. But that was what we wanted, for we knew that as long as it stayed cold it would remain clear. And clear it certainly was that morning after breakfast when I climbed a little knoll near camp to take pictures. Every visible object, even though miles away, stood out so sharply and plainly that I felt with the slightest effort I should be able to touch it. There were four distinctly different views from this hill. The one to the north revealed the jagged summits across the amphitheater, that to the south the very opposite type of country—the low, rounded, rolling hills of the middle Clear River. West, across the river, was a great basin surrounded by the high summits which constituted the North Fork and Clear River watershed; it looked like a delightful place to spend a week or two in exploration some summer. But the most exciting view of all was directly to the east where only two miles distant, and hardly any higher than where I stood, a low pass led to—well, where *did* it lead? That was what made it exciting. It had been reported several years before by two trappers who had seen it from a distance, while climbing over the rolling hills to the south. They thought it must lead to the Arctic; we didn't. At any rate, in order to tie up our present mapping with that I had done in 1929 it was essential to find out one way or the other. So we decided that before moving camp to last timber we would spend a day exploring what lay beyond the pass.

It was two easy miles of snowshoeing to the pass, almost on the level. From here we got a glorious view of that crag-flanked creek which entered the upper valley of Clear River. The dozens of needle-like summits which surrounded it were overtowered by a great, black, unscalable-looking peak which we recognized to be Mount Doonerak. This made the first direct tie we had with the geography we already knew.

If the sight of this peak made us feel at home, the view through the pass to the east gave us quite the opposite feeling. We could see that about two miles away it led into a big valley, but we could not tell whether that valley led north or south. If the former it would be the arctic drainage, if the latter either the Hammond River or Glacier River watershed. The fact that there was spruce timber right across the pass and down into that drainage made the solution of that problem all the more exciting, because if it really was the arctic drainage, this would be the first spruce I had seen there (though I had been told of spruce on the Firth River along the international boundary).

We dropped down a gentle grade and snowshoed across a half-mile-long lake, but it was not until we were almost in the main valley that we were sure it definitely led southward and was therefore not a part of the arctic drainage. For a moment I thought I knew just what part of Hammond River we had reached, and then discovered that I did not know at all. We followed down the steeply dropping ice of the river through heavy spruce timber for about two miles, when we came out on an open bench. We got a view for miles down the broad valley, which had none of the jagged surroundings of the upper Clear River and North Fork country. I tried to recognize landmarks which I had seen on my journey up the Hammond River a year and a half before. Finally, however, after considering the surrounding mountains and the terrain, and the directions and distances of points previously marked on the map, we concluded that it was Glacier River. We had supposed that it petered out miles to the south.

After nearly an hour of sketching the topography, we turned back upstream. The rear side of the chimney we had seen from Clear River was towering above us steeply, but not too much on this one face for an ascent. We continued up Glacier River above the pass. The river kept on rising at a sharp grade, all the while diminishing rapidly in size. After three miles we reached the very last trees, and could see a few miles above us the head of the stream. It was too late to make the steep ascent to it. Instead I spent an hour profiting by this unexpected encounter with another northern timber line.

We returned through the pass by the route we had come out. On the way we saw the fresh tracks of three moose which we had scared. Had we needed the meat it would have been easy to go after them. All the way down to camp from the pass we walked toward a glorious orange sunset which by itself would have been enough to make the day a rich one.

Next morning we broke camp and returned up Clear River, in search of its sources, by the trail we had broken two days before. Unfortunately, wind had blown in the meantime and we had to rebreak the trail practically all the way, but the hard bottom already established helped a good deal. There was not the excitement of bursting into new territory which had marked our first venture up here, but the scenery was just as beautiful. Many vistas, unobserved the first time, gave a fresh thrill to this day, including a thousand-foot black cliff hanging over the south side of the valley, which had made no particular impression before, probably because I was looking so eagerly ahead. To enable us to discuss the geography without pointing we gave names to some of the valleys. The first one on the left, northeast of Boreal, we named Holmes Creek after the great jurist, whom we both admired so much, and who was celebrating his ninetieth birthday at about that time. The gorge surrounded by the fabulous series of needled pinnacles, we called Pinnyanaktuk, the Eskimo word synonymous with "absolute perfection of beauty." The gulch which came in at the head of the valley to the left we named Karillyukpuk, meaning "very rugged."

We made camp in deep snow in a thick clump of spruce timber, half a mile below the very last trees. We seemed to be in the center of a ring of towering mountains, which we saw in vistas through the evergreen branches.

Three more days of perfect weather and perfect exploration from the camp followed. Each morning after breakfast we set out on our large snowshoes for a day's journey over uncharted country. Each afternoon, hungry and happy, we returned to a comfortable camp and a royal supper. Each evening after supper I spent a stuffy half hour unloading my day's photographic efforts and loading up for the next day, while Ernie cooked the dog feed. Each night just before retiring we stepped out into the 30-below air to feed the dogs, and to stand around a few minutes watching the colorful waves of the aurora surging and darting across the sky.

The first day we climbed a low mountain at the head of the valley. It was so centrally located that we got a splendid view of each of the four gulches which emptied into upper Clear River. Nothing could exceed the grandeur of the sight down the great U-valley of Pinnyanaktuk flanked on the south by what were almost 2,000-foot precipices, on the north by far higher peaks, so jagged that the skyline for eight miles was a succession of needles. At the foot of the valley the deep drainage of Holmes Creek headed back against the lofty summits of the North Fork. The valley floor itself was checkered with white snow and scattered patches of dark green spruce, which occurred through its whole length on the south-facing side, but was lacking on the cold north slope. The final timber line consisted of a group of five trees, almost at the head of the valley.

In the northeastern corner, at right angles to the direction of the main valley, the largest fork of Clear River, which we had named Karillyukpuk, entered between a solid array of precipice-faced mountains. They rose for perhaps 3,000 feet on both sides of the half-mile-wide glacial valley. These sides were so deep that the sun shone in the valley for only a couple of hours in the morning. Perhaps six or seven miles up we could see that the river bent sharply to the right, but following the direction it had been going was a low pass through which we recognized with delight Twoprong Mountain on the upper North Fork. This gave us another tie with what was already known to us, and provided an excellent check to my crude method of mapping our position by compass shots and estimated distances traveled.

We had not yet, however, accomplished the major purpose of the expedition—to determine whether Clear River headed against the Arctic Divide. We both thought the high skyline a mile beyond us was this divide, but it was too steep to scale in the loose snow—the danger of starting a snowslide was too great. As it was, this little mountain we scaled had made the steepest snowshoe work I had ever tackled, though Ernie assured me it was nothing.

It was still early in the afternoon when we reached camp, so I hiked back up the valley with my increment borer and diameter tape to make growth and diameter measurements on the timber. Boring half a dozen of those frozen trees was more exerting than the whole day's traveling. But the results were most interesting, and while they seemed to corroborate my timber-line theory in general, they made certain modifications necessary too. The most important of these was the severe struggle the farthest trees have with the wind until they become established and can break its velocity and protect the young seedlings. Apparently, in the early stages, the wind for years keeps breaking off the tender tops of the young trees. Finally, perhaps on some rare occasion, the weather is milder at the critical time giving the tops a chance to survive. The trees, after that, grow at a good rate. I found one tree which had taken 52 years to grow the first four and a half feet, while the average time to attain that height in this area was from 30 to 35 years.

Next morning we set out to follow Karillyukpuk—the largest fork of Clear River—to the divide, we hoped, if it did not prove to be too far away, and if there seemed any possibility of scaling up to it. We cut across the bench on the north side of Clear River, and dropped into the canyon where the Karillyukpuk Creek enters the Clear River. Then we snowshoed for miles along the creek, between great precipices which towered 3,000 feet from the valley. Aside from one steep gulch which cut in on each side, these massive rocks enclosed the canyon in an unbroken wall for six miles. I became so accustomed to them that it was hard to realize their immensity until I pictured myself against the base of one of those cliffs, and felt like a beetle on the side of the Equitable Building. I was happy in the immediate presence of nature in its most staggering grandeur, in living intimately with something so splendidly immense that all life seemed trivial in its presence. No doubt too, there was the joy that here was something which mankind with all its mechanical power could not possibly hope to duplicate.

Six miles up the Karillyukpuk we came to the low pass which we believed led to the North Fork. There was an abrupt change in topography. The great sheer cliffs which had bounded the left side of the valley gave way to rolling hills—beautiful in their contrast to those hard, titanic summits. They were cut by deep gulches, all glaciated and filled with blue ice. On the right side the mountains kept rising ever higher, but they were further removed from the valley and no longer quite so precipitous. Ahead we kept seeing one very high, two-peaked summit—Apoon. We could not see on which side of the divide it lay, but we knew that even if it were on the near side we would not have time to reach the divide that afternoon.

The Karillyukpuk Creek which we were following—mostly in the frozen river bed—ran among great boulders, and often cut subsidiary canyons for itself in the floor of the main canyon which embraced the entire valley. Sometimes it jumped down twenty-five feet at a time, giving us quite a task to pull ourselves up the frozen waterfalls. After a while we could see it was making a great horseshoe ahead. We cut off to the left, and started climbing gradually up the rolling hills on that side, heading in the direction a pass must be if there were one. For a long time we plowed steadily up with the barren, snow-covered hillside always before us. Then the grade lessened and we could see mountain peaks jutting above the skyline just in front of us. We quickened our pace, knowing that in a few minutes we would find out whether we could reach the divide or not.

Shortly after, we were standing on what we believed to be the great Arctic Divide. I do not know what may be the supreme exaltation of which a person is capable, but for me it came that moment I crossed the skyline and gazed over into the winter-buried mystery of the Arctic, where great, barren peaks rose into the deep blue of the northern sky, where valleys, devoid even of willows, led far off into unknown canyons. Below me lay a chasm so many hundreds of feet deep it seemed no sunlight could ever penetrate its depths. From its upper reaches, bathed in sunshine, a white pinnacle rose into the air for almost a mile at a slope not less than sixty degrees.

We remained for two hours around the pass, snowshoeing down along a plateau on the other side for a couple of miles to get a better view of the chasm. The pass really consisted of a plateau land, running nearly east and west. It was bounded on the south side by the very high peaks I have mentioned, on the north by those rolling hills which divided it from the North Fork drainage. The plateau was cut deeply on one side of the "divide" by that deep chasm, on the other side by the source waters of Clear River. To the east, we thought we were looking into the Arctic. To the west rose that most jagged of all these northern ranges, the one which separated the upper North Fork from Clear River. It included hundreds of high, forbidding, black crags, and the highest, most unscalable-looking, blackest of all was our old friend, which had previously stood out as a landmark from every other direction, Doonerak.

Later in the year, on a pioneer trip to the head of the Hammond River with Jesse Allen and Kenneth Harvey, I was to discover that, instead of standing on the Arctic Divide this March day in 1931, Ernie and I were standing actually in the pass between the Clear and Hammond rivers. The true Arctic Divide was still farther to the north. I learned this with mixed feelings—it made me win my geographical argument with Ernie concerning the origin of Clear River, but it meant that my exaltation had been based on a misapprehension. Nonetheless, this error could not take away the memory of that moment of intense feeling or of the wildness and beauty of the scene. To commemorate Ernie's and my mistake I gave the name Kinnorutin ("You are crazy") to this pass and the creek which flows eastward from it into Hammond River.

We found it extremely difficult to tear away from this splendid plateau, even when the sun, dropping behind the great, black dome of Doonerak, warned that evening was approaching. However, the prospect of siwashing out beyond timber with the thermometer pressing close on 30 below finally made us abandon all that beauty, and drop back into the upper canyon of Karillyukpuk Creek. We snowshoed with long strides down the precipice-set valley, only stopping long enough to remove our webs and slide down the frozen waterfalls. Our view, as we faced downstream, was so different from what it had been in the morning, that we felt as if we had found another great chasm. When we emerged from the lower end and stepped out into the bright sunlight of the Clear River valley, it seemed also as if we had found a new day, although it was only the ending of perhaps the greatest day of my life.

The next day should have been a great and memorable one; but, following the pleasures of the preceding day, it could not help but seem an anticlimax. Ernie stayed in camp, while I explored the deep, Yosemite-like valley and its creek—later named by us St. Patrick's Creek—which enters the upper Clear River from the north about halfway between Pinnyanaktuk and Karillyukpuk creeks. The valley looked like a replica of the main valley and like it was interrupted by numerous side gulches. It was about ten miles long and headed against a fairly low pass into the North Fork. Each side valley looked like a fascinating field for further detailed exploration. Several of them branched into additional gulches. I could not tell where this process of branching ended because the heads of several subsidiary forks were hidden by great crags.

When I returned to camp, I found Ernie had spent the day resetting the guide ropes on the sleds, cooking up dog feed, and generally preparing things for our departure.

Thus we broke camp swiftly the next day, and by eight o'clock were flying along on the rear runners of our sleds down the old trail we had broken on our way up Clear River.

Once you break a trail, the packed-down snow freezes and gives you a fine, solid bottom on which you, the dogs, and the sled can travel without sinking. Such a trail permits almost ideal going, better than on ice, because the sled slides with almost as little friction, while the dogs can get a much better foothold. Also you do not have to worry about fresh overflows as you would on rivers. However, if you drive off your old trail just a little bit, the runner which gets off sinks out of sight, and probably the next moment the sled will tip, the dogs will howl, and you will cuss. This happened during a four-mile stretch near Holmes Creek, where the wind had drifted the snow just enough to prevent a poor pilot riding the runners from keeping the sled on the trail. I never could keep an automobile for any protracted period on the ridge between two adjacent ruts in a muddy road, and that is child's play compared with putting just the right weight and pressure now on one and now on the other rear handle bar so that the sled turns one eyelash instead of two. So I piloted my load off into the deep snow, now on one side and now on the other; ran up front to help pull it out, ran back, ran front, ran back again, and all the time, most exasperating of all, saw Ernie ahead comfortably riding the rear end of his sled without the slightest trouble.

When the four drifted miles were over, so was the hard going. Thereafter I had an easy day, standing comfortably on the rear end of the sled while the dogs trotted at a steady seven-mile-an-hour clip. What had taken us three hard days to ascend flew by in a single one. Over the snow, out on the ice, through overflows, the dogs jogged in their unvaried gait, while the now familiar scenery of the amphitheater, the Glacier River pass, the great basin, the rolling hills of the middle river, the big bend, and the lower river canyon all passed by. We emerged on the North Fork–Clear River junction, exactly where Al Retzlaf and I had been almost trapped by the two flooded rivers a year and half before.

When we reached Ernie's headquarters cabin at the North Fork–Tinayguk River junction, four miles to the south, we found one red fox frozen in a trap. It was the first Ernie had caught during this winter of unusually poor trapping. We also found that, evidently only a short while ago, a wolverine had dragged away another trap, toggle and all. We further discovered that some animal, probably another wolverine, had stolen from our inadequate cache most of the moose I had shot last fall. As soon as we had unhitched the dogs and had started the water thawing, we took after the wolverine that had run off with the trap. We tracked him across the North Fork and up a mountain on the other side, and finally caught up with him more than two miles from camp. He was making heroic strides up the mountain, dragging a birch log behind him. Although he had an unusually fine fur, I almost wished that he would pull out of the trap at the last moment and get away. Instead of helping him, however, I snapped pictures, thus settling my score with the moose-meat-stealing genus *Gulo*. After the pictures and much ferocious snarling the wolverine succumbed from a .22 bullet between the eyes.

WILD LAKE

Next day we laid off, more or less. We took the sleds in the cabin for thawing out and reorganized our commissary for the second phase of our expedition—a visit to the mining community on Wild Lake. We spent the afternoon breaking trail for five miles up the Tinayguk River.

The following day we loaded the sleds and started out over the same route. When we came to the end of the broken trail, we had to snowshoe ahead of the dogs for seven miles up the Tinayguk River. Ernie expected that we would have ice most of the way, but it was practically all fresh breaking—hard work. An hour before dark, we reached the point where we would leave the Tinayguk. As soon as camp was up, Ernie set out again to break trail up the steep mountainside above us. This was the route we would have to travel on the morrow to cross through the high pass to the west into the headwaters of Flat Creek, a tributary of Wild River. Meanwhile I chopped wood and did the cooking. It was long after dark when both of us finished our tasks.

Next morning we started up the mountainside. It was lucky Ernie had broken the trail so well the night before, because, even with this help, we had to put ropes over our shoulders and pull with the dogs in order to get up the steep incline. From the grade we got a fine view northward into the head of the Tinayguk, which at its northern end runs into higher mountains. We crossed the pass, and then dropped very gently into Flat Creek valley which was full of lakelets, but otherwise as uninteresting as its name. We descended the creek for three and a half miles, Ernie breaking trail, and I gee-poling the coupled sleds.

After we left the creek and headed for the low pass which leads to Wild River about four miles north of Wild Lake, we encountered the toughest mile of traveling of our whole journey. Ernie would snowshoe ahead about a hundred yards, snowshoe back, and snow-shoe out again before I would start with the dogs, pulling with them all the time for everything I was worth. Even then, with seven dogs and one man pulling two not very heavily loaded sleds over a three times beaten trail, we could only go about thirty feet before the dogs would have to puff for breath. It took an hour and a half to cover one mile and climb up perhaps five hundred feet. But we finally reached the saddle and looked down into Wild River.

The drop-off into this stream must have been about eight hundred feet, and it was even steeper than the ascent. The problem now, how-ever, was to keep the sleds from going too fast. We roughlocked the runners by twisting around them the chains with which we used to tie the dogs at night. But the sleds would not stay back, and I had to brake half the way down by leaning on the geepole and bracing my webbed feet in front of me. It was somewhat reminiscent of skiing, and I greatly enjoyed it. But the continual catching of the rough-locks on buried snags I did not. Every time that happened I had to go back and chop them out. With my poor axemanship, on one oc-casion I not only chopped through the snagging stick but also hit the sled runner. Fortunately the steel in the center of the runner was harder than my ax, so I could not chop it all the way through. Ernie, with his rare patience, just sighed "Jesus Christ!"

We made camp by the Wild River. Next morning, instead of turn-ing south for the gold-mining settlements, we decided to add a short sidetrip north to investigate the timber line of one more major river. We had hardly started when we saw the fresh tracks of five moose which we must have scared while setting up camp the night before. The valley seemed to be full of moose, for we saw the new tracks of seven more farther up. We did not see the animals themselves, though I imagine half an hour of effort would have disclosed them.

Timber line was only seven miles north of our camp, and three miles beyond we could see the head of Wild River. Ernie and I spent an hour and a half between making tree measurements and warming our fingers. Even when the temperature is as relatively comfortable as 20 below, counting fine tree rings is a chilling task. They had to be counted on the spot, because the cores extracted from the frozen wood were very brittle, crumbled to pieces, and could not be preserved. On the way back I measured one tree, just a mile from the last timber, whose diameter was more than eighteen inches at breast height.

The following morning we broke camp, retraced our steps and walked south, downstream, for the diggings on Wild Lake. It was four miles of hard trail breaking to the head of the lake, and then two miles of easy traveling across the frozen lake to the Spring Creek mining settlement on the east shore.

The glare from the sun was annoying even with sun glasses. These glasses are essential for all spring-time travel in the Arctic. The combination of high sun and snow can easily cause snow blindness. At this time of year, in the spring, everybody, native and white, wore sun glasses, mostly even around town. The agony of real snow blindness is rare, though a touch of it is frequent. I got a slight dose one day, and it felt like an eyeful of lashes.

At Spring Creek we met the first human beings in sixteen days. Lutey Hope, an immense, 225-pound squaw, rushed out from her cabin to greet us, and threw her arms around Ernie's neck. As I was a total stranger she did not adopt quite such violent methods with me. Nevertheless, she instantly made me feel at home, and immediately I felt as if I had stepped suddenly from the wilderness into civilization.

We spent three days at the lake. It is one of the largest lakes in the Koyukuk drainage—seven miles long and about one and a half wide—and is surrounded by steep mountains which reminded me of the mountains which rise from the shores of Lake Placid in the Adirondacks. But Wild Lake had none of Lake Placid's attractive islands, nor the fine forests which extend from its shores to the mountaintops. On the other hand, Wild Lake had no thickly clustered camps nor noisy power boats.

I made the acquaintance of many new friends, while Ernie renewed old friendships. I spent a day and a half at the two centers of habitation at Spring Creek—with Eli Hanson (a Norwegian), R. H. Creecy (the only Negro in the Koyukuk), and Lutey Hope and her family; and four miles down the lake with Gus Wagner and Hans Leichmann, two Germans who had left their homeland at the turn of the century in hopeful quest for gold.

It was hard to leave the fascinating and pleasant inhabitants of this remote region after only three days. But we had to be on our way, and so, on the fourth morning, we hitched up the dogs and continued on our way over the well-beaten trail to Bettles, fifty-three miles to the south.

It was uphill and down, on the trail and off, run behind or ride, all day long. On the level stretches and gentle down grades we rode comfortably on the rear runners. On the steep down grades we descended in a flurry of snow made by the tightly pressed brake. On all up grades we ran, to ease the effort of the dogs. The only really hard going was on the side hills where the trail had drifted. Then it was a tough job, at least for me, to keep the sled on the trail. But on the whole the going was good, and we struck off thirty-six miles in one run.

We stopped for a couple of hours at a government cabin to rest the dogs and eat a belated lunch. These cabins are small public winter shelters scattered along some trails in Alaska between settlements. After our rest we set out to cover the remaining seventeen miles to Bettles. The first seven miles made delightful mushing over a gentle down grade; there was nothing to do but to stand comfortably on the rear runners, and enjoy the sunset sky, and hum a little to the rhythm of trotting dogs. Afterward came a considerably drifted flat country, so we had to work most of the last ten miles of the day. Although it now became dark two hours later than at the beginning of our trip, we didn't get into Bettles until an hour and a half after dark. There we were greeted by the seven people in town out of a population of twenty-four. At the beginning of the century, Bettles had boasted three hundred inhabitants. Kindly scrawny old Jack Dodds, with his huge hooked nose, presided over the roadhouse of Bettles. He was, in effect, the mayor and medical officer and board of charities of this small community.

We stayed three days in Bettles. On the third day a howling snow storm came from the north. The following morning we set out for Wiseman along the Middle Fork of the Koyukuk in quite a blizzard. But blizzards don't worry you when you travel with the two best dog mushers north of the Yukon. Ernie and I were joined by quiet Charlie Pitka of Tanana, a three-quarter Yukon Indian and one-quarter Russian, who had pulled into Bettles with the monthly mail the afternoon before. It gave me a sense of perpetual youth to see him and Ernie, both past fifty, breaking tough trail in the soft,

freshly fallen snow more easily than most people would walk down
the street, and a lot more easily, I am sure, than their companion
of thirty, when his turn came.

The first day out was hard going every foot of the twenty-three
miles to a cabin at the junction of North Fork and Middle Fork,
which we reached at dark. On the second morning the going was
worse yet, but by afternoon we seemed to have left the most severe
zone of the storm. Our day's run of twenty miles was made considerably faster than that of the preceding day and brought us to
the Windy Arm cabin on the Middle Fork about halfway between
the North Fork and Wiseman. It snowed very little on the third
day on which we traveled the remaining twenty-one miles to Wiseman. We rode the rear runners all the way, except for Charlie, who
geepoled his long sled on short skis, on which he slid along with just
as little effort as though he were riding.

We reached Wiseman in mid-afternoon of the last day of March.
All the kids came rushing out and, as soon as the dogs were tied,
made me put in a more energetic hour giving piggy-back rides, than
were most of the hours on the trail. After having my whiskers duly
pulled, and having told a few stories about the Man in the Moon,
I was allowed to read the mail which had come early in March.
There was a big dance that evening, which, though nearly broken
up by April Fool pranks around midnight, continued gaily until three
in the morning.

5 The Alatna and the John

BY JULY, 1931, THERE YET REMAINED IN THE ARCTIC KOYUKUK drainage a *terra incognita* forty-five by a hundred miles in extent—about equivalent to the area of Connecticut. It was roughly rectangular in shape, bounded on the south by the main Koyukuk and the lower Alatna rivers; on the east by the John River; on the north by the Arctic Divide; and on the west by the Alatna River and its tributary the Unakserak River. The mouths of some major side streams entering these boundary rivers showed on the maps, but aside from this the forty-five hundred square miles were almost as unknown as the geography of the moon. (See end map.)

On our mid-winter trip three months before, Ernie and I had decided to spend the summer exploring this country. In preparation for the trip Ernie had spent several weeks at his Bettles headquarters building a 25-foot long poling boat from spruce lumber which he himself had whip-sawed. To Ernie the building of a boat was a routine activity in the life of the frontier.

The Fourth of July festivities of Wiseman had not quite petered out when Ernie arrived from down river in his brand-new boat, equipped with a ten-horsepower outboard motor. Next to Christmas, Fourth of July is the great gathering time of the year in Wiseman, and isolated miners living as much as sixty miles from town had hiked in for a few days with their fellow men. There was visiting and exchanging of the latest news at many cabins. There was a great shooting contest, in which whites and Eskimos, men and women, seventy-year olds and children participated. The big feature of the festivities, however, was dancing. We started at six-thirty on the evening of July 4, and at eleven next morning four Eskimo girls, Kaaruk, Ashuwaruk, Kayak, and Kachwona, were still going strong; the dance had to end only because all the men were played out. The Eskimo girls were not content even with sixteen and a half hours dancing in their systems. They kept inducing those of us who remained around town to return for a foxtrot or two-step or waltz every few hours during the bright day and the bright night. Even after Ernie and I had the boat loaded for our long journey and hip boots hitched up, they kept pulling us back from the river bank into the roadhouse and making us dance just once more to the phonographic strains of *Look for the Silver Lining* or *The Blue Danube* or *The Utah Trail.*

On the hillside, back of Wiseman, I established a small scientific station to aid me in my study of the northern timber line. As I prepared for leaving I made arrangements to have it attended during my absence. For this chore I found an outstandingly able person in Ekok, the daughter of old Tobuk, patriarch of the Alatna Eskimos. She was married to an Eskimo hunter, had five children, but despite her household duties ran the instruments faithfully and accurately while I was away. The station, in addition to the usual weather instruments, included two which required special skill to handle. The one, composed of five Livingston anometers to measure evaporation, required the daily replacement of evaporated water and its measurement by burette to the tenth part of a cubic centimeter. The other, a dendrograph, was designed to record tree growth so delicately that one could see how a tree grew during the night and shrunk during the day.

Finally, at eight o'clock in the sunny evening of July 5 we shoved off into the Middle Fork and started south on our fifty-day journey.

Compared with all other forms of arctic travel, descending rivers is easy. The current swept us along at four or five miles an hour. Ernie, sitting or standing in the back, and I, kneeling in the front, had merely to give the bottom of the river an occasional push with our iron-tipped spruce poles to keep us in the main current.

There are only two dangers on such rivers—riffles and sweepers. "Riffles" is the term used in the Arctic for shallow places where the water may run at five or ten miles an hour. A "sweeper" is the result of the constant undercutting of the geologically young river banks by the rapid current. This leads to a settling of the spruces, birches, cottonwoods, and willows from the vertical to the horizontal until they finally sweep the surface of the water with their foliage. They are also likely to sweep everything animate and inanimate from the boat if it should get under them.

Neither riffles nor sweepers, however, were dangers to us with the best river man of arctic Alaska in the back of our boat. He shot us through the riffles without ever allowing the boat to get broadside to the current and steered us safely away from cut banks and tangled foliage. Kreeper Riffle, about half way to Bettles, was a landmark to remind me of the blessing of Ernie's rare competence. Here, many years before, a prospector by the name of Dave Kreeper had let his boat get broadside in the current. A weather-beaten slab in a jungle of dense willows on the shore and the name of the riffle were all that remained to keep alive the memory of a gold seeker who never returned.

The major scenic feature along the Middle Fork between Wiseman and Bettles is the canyon of the Koyukuk just below a gravel stretch, called Tramway Bar, where gold in paying quantities was first discovered in the Koyukuk region in 1893. Tramway Bar is a bench 80 feet above the canyon of the Koyukuk River. The origin of its name is not certain, but it is probable that a mining tramway existed here during the early gold-mining operations—a small dump cart running on an overhead cable, frequently used in the region at the turn of the century. In this canyon, queer-shaped rocks in the middle of the stream jutted straight out of the water. We sailed through the canyon in the bright sunlight of three o'clock in the morning, after a gay midnight lunch with Billie Burke and Donald ("Daisy") Wheeler who had been on the quest for gold in the north for thirty-three years; they were spending the summer in camp mining on Tramway Bar.

When we pulled into Bettles at one in the afternoon, it was in complete contrast to that blizzardy morning three months before when we had mushed away. Now not a speck of snow or ice was visible anywhere. The cottonwoods and willows around town were in bright full leaf, and the gardens were luxuriant with lettuce, spinach, cabbages, beets, carrots, and potatoes.

We left Bettles the second day after at two o'clock in the morning with a large accession to our passenger list. Ernie was taking along his four dogs for the remainder of our journey, partly because he had no one to take care of them, partly to help with the work, but most of all because he just liked them. Two of them sat in the back of the boat with Ernie and two in the front with me, when they were not out on the shore working for their passage.

It took the Koyukuk River approximately ninety miles of fishhook bends and oxbows, and flat monotonous scenery to make the thirty-six miles air line from Bettles to Alatna, the next town downstream. It really consists of two towns, Allakaket and Alatna, just west of the point where the Alatna River empties into the Koyukuk. The two towns, three-quarters of a mile north of the Arctic Circle, represent the point where the two extraordinarily contrasted native cultures of the Indians and the Eskimos come together. In Allakaket, on the south bank of the Koyukuk River, live the Indians; in Alatna, on the north bank, the Eskimos.

We found the two towns already over their Fourth of July celebration. The Indians had all pulled out for their fish camps along the main Koyukuk River and the South Fork. The Eskimos had nearly all gone to their fish camps on the Alatna River. Old Tobuk, together with his son Jimmie and several of his grandchildren, had not yet departed. While Jimmie interpreted, I spent one fascinating day with Tobuk, listening to his Eskimo legends, his philosophy of adapting to the ways of the world, and his genial ridicule of the white man's religious superstitions.

Tobuk told me about the "dooneraks" who were something like spirits, but a little less personal, and who were responsible for everything that transpired on earth. There were thousands and thousands of dooneraks, each with different ideas and objectives, often thoroughly antagonistic, and the happenings of the world represented the balance between their innumerable objectives. Some order was brought among their chaotic competition through the medicine men whose accomplishments always came through the dooneraks whom they controlled. The most powerful medicine man in the history of the Kobuk Eskimos was Tobuk's grandfather who had forty dooneraks working for him. The only remaining medicine man among the Koyukuk Eskimos was old Peter Nictune.

"He's no real medicine man at all," said Tobuk laughing. "He's such a bum medicine man it's sure to clear up when he tries to make it rain and I know I am going to get wet when he tries to make it clear up. I guess he's only got one weak doonerak working for him—maybe not that many."

Alatna and Allakaket each had a store. The real center of the two communities, however, was the Episcopal Mission at Allakaket. It was founded in 1907 by Archdeacon Stuck, who six years later made the first ascent of Mount McKinley. The mission consisted of three well-constructed spruce log buildings, one with a modest steeple whose bell summoned children to school on week days and every one to church on Sundays.

This summoning, of course, was a sporadic proposition, and there were long periods when no one was around. Then the two missionaries, Miss Boyes, the trained nurse, and Miss Wilcox, the teacher, would attend to the variety of matters on which their own livelihood depended. They would spend days out in the hills picking berries, tend their gardens, can vegetables, make repairs on their buildings with the generous assistance of any man who might be around, and sew clothing for themselves and the Eskimos. They were kindly, competent ladies, with a good sense of humor, who did not try to force on the natives any more of the white man's schooling or medicine or Christianity than the natives were willing to absorb.

After a couple of days around these Arctic Circle communities, we set out for the source of the Alatna River. Our plan was to take the boat up the Alatna as far as its junction with the Kutuk River, which by air line was only eighty miles from the mouth of the Alatna, but which by the extraordinarily winding river was more than twice as far. For the first hundred miles it twisted in unceasing bends through flat land with no points within vision rising more than 50 feet above the river. The poorly drained soil was generally covered with thick stands of slow-growing black spruce, the largest trees seldom more than five inches in diameter. At a few places where the drainage was better grew some cottonwood trees. Willows were everywhere.

So were mosquitoes. Out on the Alatna River where a breeze was usually blowing they did not bother us much, but as soon as we touched land they would swarm around. Of course we had to keep ourselves completely covered. Nets dangling from broad-brimmed hats kept the mosquitoes away from the face and neck, while canvas

gloves protected the hands. It is remarkable how quickly one becomes adjusted to almost any condition in the woods, and though
in abstract it may sound like a terrible life, in practice one soon
takes mosquitoes for granted.

The current of the Alatna River was slow for the first hundred
miles, probably not averaging more than three miles an hour. We
used three different methods of traveling. Where the river was deep
we let the outboard motor shove us along. At other places we
"lined" the boat up the river, which means that Ernie would stand
in the back of the boat pushing against the bottom with a pole and
keeping it straight with the current while the four dogs and I would
be hitched to the 150-foot rope stretching out from the front end
of the craft and would tug as we walked along the shore. Where
the river was less than three feet deep, Ernie and I would jump
over the side of the boat and pull her along. We wore hip boots
while out on the river.

The Geological Survey map of the Alatna River which Philip
Smith had made twenty years before was a remarkably fine piece
of work. We could follow our course, bend by bend. But even more
remarkable was the free-hand sketch map of the lower part of the
river which Ekok had made for me. She was greatly interested in
my study of tree growth at northern timber line and told me that
when I went up the Alatna I must be sure to look at an amazing
tree growing in one of the innumerable bends of the Alatna River.
In order to help me find the tree she had sketched the lower forty
miles of the river, bend by bend, from memory, and there wasn't
a single bend she had not recorded correctly during this entire
stretch.

Ekok had said this tree was the only one of its sort she had ever
seen. It had cottonwood bark and spruce needles, which immediately suggested a Douglas fir. However, no Douglas fir was ever known
within hundreds of miles of this location. Ernie and I spent more
than an hour looking for the tree but there was no sign of it. We
decided to renew the search on our way back.

A few miles above the place where the tree wasn't, we suddenly
found ourselves in the midst of civilization. On a high bank above
the river was a jaunty Eskimo fish camp with twenty adults chop-
ping wood, repairing fish nets, or caulking boats, and as many children helping with the work or playing. I had not met any of these
Eskimos before, but Ernie knew them well. We spent a lively two
hours chatting and joking with them, and I played hide-and-seek

with the younger urchins of the Kartuk and Napoleon families among their mothers' fish nets which were hanging up to dry. We camped that night half a dozen miles above the Eskimo camp.

For two more days we headed the boat up the serpentine river, traveling in every conceivable direction, never at one time being able to see more than a half mile ahead. It rained intermittently, which made the landscape seem even less exciting than it would ordinarily have been. On the bench above the river where we made our second night's camp was an ancient, rotted traveling bag, probably left there in the 1898 stampede by one of the tenderfeet whose desire for fortune was coupled with such a complete ignorance of the outdoors that he had taken this clumsy equipment into the remote Arctic where he had finally abandoned it in disgust. Here it had lain unobserved, slowly disintegrating for a third of a century.

We reached Helpmejack Creek, a western tributary of the Alatna River. On the low, narrow peninsula where the creek joined the river grew some very large willows. One specimen of *Salix bancolata* was six inches in diameter at breast height and 25 feet tall. Four specimens of *Salix bebbiana* were seven inches through and ranged in height from 22 to 27 feet.

Beyond Helpmejack the surroundings changed. Mountains began to appear on either side, and the endless mud changed in many places to high gravel banks. The current became considerably swifter, averaging perhaps five miles an hour. The creeks entering the river below Helpmejack had not had enough current to distinguish them from the mud sloughs which were on every side.

It rained hard and uninterruptedly during our fourth day. The river wound back and forth from one side of the valley to the other. We traveled steadily from eleven in the morning until ten at night with an hour and a half out for lunch. These were typical hours for the six days of our journey up the Alatna. On one occasion we scared up a large black bear and made camp on the spot. This stimulated a suppertime discussion about bears in which Ernie summarized years of keen observation.

"There's no question," he said, crawling under the mosquito netting, "that a bear will sometimes attack a man, just like there are occasionally crazy humans who will do the same thing, but it happens so rarely it isn't worth thinking about. I've traveled around Alaska as much as most men and I've never yet seen a bear that did anything except run away from me."

On the fifth day it also rained steadily until late in the afternoon.

The river became swifter and progress was correspondingly slower. We stopped for lunch at a place a quarter of a mile of easy walking across a low pass to Takahula Lake. It looked like an Adirondack pond with its shores thickly overgrown by spruce, aspen, more birch than we had seen during all the trip.

That afternoon was very strenuous. We pushed and tugged against a six-mile-an-hour current, until, finally, around seven o'clock we struck a good stretch of river and Ernie let the motor hum. All at once, on rounding a sharp bend, we saw two men standing at the edge of the river, waving at us. In a few minutes we ran the boat to the shore. They were two Eskimo prospectors, Jack Sackett and "Sclawick Sam"—named after the region of his origin—trying their luck on Pingaluk River, an eastern tributary of the Alatna. They were delighted at seeing the first humans in six months, cordially welcomed us to their tent, and cooked us a great banquet of fresh mountain sheep.

"We heard your motor," said Jack "when you were way down the river, I guess before you ate lunch. Then we didn't hear it again for a long time and Sam says maybe we was hearing some dooneraks. But then we heard it again about half an hour ago and first thing you know, the way the echoes was, it sounded like we heard it upstream also. I said to Sam, 'My God! Sam, we must be going crazy now. Nobody in six months, and now we are getting a boat from both directions.' Well, it sure is good to see you boys."

From Jack and Sam I learned the meaning of the names of the rivers and creeks which pour into Alatna. Iniakuk was named after the father of Kaypuk, an Eskimo woman in her late fifties who had been one of my neighbors at Wiseman during the past winter. Kutuk was named after the sister of Big Charlie, an Eskimo hunter, trapper, and miner who with his wife and 14-year-old daughter I had known at Wiseman. These place names were indicative of the fact that this whole country was a no-man's land until quite recently, because even the Eskimos had no names for its features before the life times of the fathers and sisters of the present generation. Pegeeluk means wooden bowl, from the shape of this creek's upper basin. Unakserak is a place where one goes to get wood for snowshoes. Nahtuk means owl, from the owl-shaped dome in which it rises. Pingaluk means "a little no-good," as Sam expressed it, and refers to the fact that fishing, while not terrible, falls far short of excellence.

Jack and Sam were so happy about having visitors that they did not let us leave until after lunch the next day. Then, after four hours more of strenuous hand and leg and back labor, Ernie and I finally worked our boat to the mouth of the Kutuk River. Here we made base camp for our exploration of the source streams of the Alatna.

On our first day we probed into country not entirely unknown to white men. It had been visited once, just twenty summers before, by Philip Smith when he discovered the—until then—only true glacier ever found in the Brooks Range—a glacier forming flowing ice. It lay about ten miles west of the mouth of Kutuk. Even more exciting, he discovered there the only outcropping of granite mountains in the Brooks Range. They constituted a series of sensational needlelike peaks extending for six or eight miles in a horseshoe around the gushing creek which rose in the glacier. The Eskimos called this range Arrigetch which means "fingers of the hand extended," and admirably expresses the appearance of these mountains. Since neither Ernie nor I belonged to the human-fly category, we did not try to climb the Arrigetch peaks, but instead followed more than half a dozen minor peaks on the less rugged ridge which paralleled this range about two miles to the north.

We returned to base camp by way of a creek which plunged toward the Alatna in innumerable waterfalls, from 20 to 50 feet in height. Near the mouth we found a tree which Eskimos had prepared to obtain pitch for caulking their sleds and starting fires. They had gouged out a one-and-a-half-inch cubical hole about four feet above the base of a seven-inch spruce. Into this hole the not very abundant spruce pitch was slowly gathering until after several years the hole would be filled. Then the pitch cake would be cut out and melted.

There were many old stumps of trees which the Eskimos had chopped by stone ax. Steel axes were not brought into this region until the gold rush days of 1898. Before the days of the steel ax the Eskimos had a unique way of felling trees. Some Eskimo would climb the tree to be dropped and attach a thong to the top. While several men would be hacking around the base with stone axes, all the rest of the men, women, and children in the camp would keep pulling at the thong until finally they hauled the tree over.

Next day we set out to follow the Kutuk River to its source in the Arctic Divide. In the winter of 1923 the Murie brothers, Olaus and Adolph, collecting mountain-sheep specimens for the U.S. Biological Survey, had traveled into the mountains at the head of this stream. So far as we knew we were the next white men to come into the Kutuk valley. However, all the way upstream we saw frequent evidence of Eskimos in willow and spruce stumps cut by stone axe. From this we suspected that the Kutuk must head against a low pass in the Arctic Divide, because we had both observed that Eskimo signs are almost never seen except in river valleys which are made accessible by such low gaps in the Arctic Divide.

We each carried packs of approximately 40 pounds as we tramped up the river, but our equipment totaled more than twice that much because each dog was loaded with a pack holding 30 to 40 pounds. We kept for ourselves things which should not get wet, such as blankets and photographic films. This was necessitated by the fact that the dogs, if they saw a mink or a ptarmigan across the river, were prone to swim the stream for luncheon. We wore our mosquito nets and gloves practically all the time. As we plodded along, the mosquitoes gathered thicker and thicker on the outside of the nets. After perhaps two hours they would become so dense that vision would be blurred. Then we would stop, build a big fire, get as close as we could stand the heat, and "burn the mosquitoes off," as the people in the Arctic say.

We passed last timber toward the close of our second day's journey and made camp that night on a well-drained flat among the willows at a fork of the Kutuk River, about 30 miles above its mouth. Next morning we set out to follow the left-hand and larger fork— the main Kutuk River—to the Arctic Divide. After three miles of splendid going over gravel bars which were as easy to walk on as a sidewalk, we came to a second large fork coming in from the right. We named it July Creek to contrast it with one across the Arctic Divide which Smith, FitzGerald, and Mertie of the Geological Survey had named April Creek after the month when they discovered it on their winter journey up the Alatna and Unakserak and across to the Arctic Ocean some seven years before.

We followed the main Kutuk to the left above July Creek and found the going equally good. The gravel was so well drained that miraculously we did not have to use our mosquito nets or gloves all day. We could now see ahead of us a low pass in the great mountains to the north, which we were sure must lead to the drainages flowing into the Arctic Ocean. About a mile below the pass the main Kutuk River made a fishhook bend to the right where it headed up against high mountains.

We ate a hasty luncheon before leaving the water and then started the climb to the divide. We had noticed several mountain sheep feeding among the rocks on the side hill, but as we climbed higher it turned out to be the biggest band of Dall sheep I had ever come across. We counted forty-four, including rams, ewes, and lambs.

Ernie told me that he had seen much bigger bands than this, the largest about two hundred sheep.

We had not tasted fresh meat since we left Jack Sackett's camp, but in common with most arctic pioneers Ernie was a true conservationist. "We could get one of them easy," he said, "but we've got to climb another high divide going into Unakserak, and we won't want to lug 60 or 70 pounds of meat across there, so most of the sheep would go to waste if we shot one. I guess we can live on grayling and corned beef for a few days longer."

The ground was so level on top, we could hardly tell when we reached Kutuk Pass. Any place within a mile might have been the dividing line between waters which flowed south via Kutuk River, the Alatna, the Koyukuk, and the Yukon into the Bering Sea and the Pacific Ocean, and the waters which ran north into April Creek, the Killik River, and the Colville into the Arctic Ocean. About two miles to the west was another similar flatland pass where the head of Unakserak looked as if it flowed into April Creek instead of into the Pacific watershed.

We were surprised, when we crossed the Arctic Divide, at the sudden change in the landscape. The peaks of the divide had patches of snow in sheltered pockets all along their north faces, while just beyond the head of Unakserak a high, jagged summit was half covered with snow. In contrast, we had not seen a speck of snow during the entire journey up the Kutuk. The vegetation of the flat across the divide was much sparser than in the south. The flat was filled with ten or twelve small lakes, the surface of most of them rippled by numerous wild ducks which swam around without even noticing us.

We took pictures and compass bearings and studied the vegetation of the arctic slope for three hours. Then we recrossed the divide and headed southward. While Ernie went straight for camp in the flat among the willows of the Kutuk Fork to prepare supper, I climbed a peak which rose a couple of thousand feet above July Creek, to map some of the neighboring drainages. Although I reached the top before seven o'clock in the evening, while the sun was still shining brightly, a cold wind had blown in from the north—so I called this peak Shivering Mountain. I must have shivered myself into a good appetite while I was mapping, or perhaps the thirty-mile walk had the same effect, for when I reached camp I ate ten of the juicy grayling which Ernie had caught and cooked since we separated.

We reserved the next day for the ascent of the gently sloping

mountain to the east of Kutuk River and just south of July Creek. It
was as easy to climb as it looked. We discovered that the top was
a great plateau, somewhat like the mesa country of Arizona or New
Mexico, only without any rimrock. Hence we named it Plateau
Mountain. It turned out to be an excellent place from which to map
a great expanse of territory because there were no high peaks close
enough to block the view.

This game of mapping was a most thrilling experience. First we
would identify the points of which we were certain and take compass bearings on them. Some of them we had already sketched onto
the base map of the area which we were using. Often the new compass bearings would make us change the location by several miles.
Then we would check out the drainages of which we were positive
and often materially change their location on the map. We would
take compass bearings at important junctions, and thus get at least
their direction located. One of the most puzzling features of this
pioneer mapping was the prevalence of low arctic passes which often
made it impossible to guess from a distance in which direction important valleys drained.

Ernie pointed to the north. "That must be Easter Creek over there,"
he said.

"No," I replied, "that can't be Easter. According to Smith's map
Easter flows northwest and this one goes more or less north. I bet
that flows into Chandler Lake."

"I guess you're right," said Ernie. "That's too far off for Easter
Creek anyway. It must be twenty-five miles."

We put this creek down as Chandler Creek, flowing northward,
and turned to the east to sketch the headwaters of Kevuk Creek, a
tributary of the John River. We admired the landmark which the
steep, rocky dome of Nahtuk made to the southeast.

Thirty miles southwest were the bizarre fingers of the Arrigetch
Range, startling in their contrast to the more moderate slopes all
around. We wondered what queer geological history was responsible for this one small range of granite pinnacles in the world of
metamorphic and sedimentary rocks. I was carefully sketching the
location of these peaks to the west when all of a sudden Ernie, who
had been gazing into the distant east with his eight-power field
glasses, exclaimed, "Well, I'll be damned! We're both crazy, Bob.
We both got it all wrong!"

I looked around and he lowered his field glasses, his eyes fairly
sparkling. It was the look a person might have in his face when he
discovered a thousand-dollar nugget in the gravel.

"What do you mean?" I asked. "What have you found?"

"Look through these," he said, handing me the field glasses. "Just look over to what we were calling Chandler River. Why, it don't flow into the Arctic at all. It flows southeast and it must be the John River."

I looked through the glasses. "It *does* flow southeast and not northwest," I agreed. "Only it can't be the John River either because, on the Geological Survey map, the John flows southwest in its upper course. Anyway, Hunt Fork lies between us and the John. That's what she is, all right. Hunt Fork!" We agreed that what we saw was Hunt Fork, a western tributary of John River.

In this way we gradually pieced together a rough sketch of the drainages and mountains of these unknown forty-five hundred square miles. Some day, when it is accurately mapped by transit or airplane, a number of our creeks and mountains no doubt will be several miles off. But no man by high-powered instruments and machines can ever get the thrill which we got with our pocket compass and our field glasses as we made the first rough map of an unknown empire.

The next day was short in mileage but hard in work. We and the dogs toted our 40-pound packs across the high divide between the Kutuk and the Unakserak. The day before, we had picked out the lowest point in the divide between the two rivers, but it was at least 2,000 feet above the Alatna valley. We sweated and steamed and puffed under our mosquito nets, while the dogs did likewise without nets. However, three hours of such work finally got us to the rifle notch in the divide. Suddenly Ernie in the lead called: "A sheep! Shoot him! It's all downhill from here!"

I dropped my pack, shot at the sheep which wasn't more than 200 feet away, and missed entirely. The sheep scampered up the mountainside above the pass.

"~~For Christ's sake,~~ sit down and rest your elbow on your knees!" yelled Ernie. "You got lots of time. He'll stop and look back again."

I sat down and rested the gun as Ernie directed, while the sheep stopped as he predicted. The sheep was now twice as far away, but this time I shot him through the left shoulder and he rolled down the hill again into the pass. He was a young ram and didn't dress more than 75 pounds. Despite the extra weight, our packs felt considerably lighter as we descended to Unakserak River than they had felt climbing up from the Kutuk.

We made camp a couple of miles above the last timber on Unakserak, and noticed half a dozen more sheep on the mountain above us. They must have been at least 2,500 feet out of the valley.

"Bob," said Ernie, "you've shot a sheep now, but you haven't got that picture. Let's climb up and get it."

Of course I was all in favor, so we swung around the base of the mountain to the opposite side of the ridge from where the sheep were. We climbed leisurely and comfortably, without packs. When we got a thousand feet above our Unakserak valley camp we left all the mosquitoes behind. It was now between six and eight in the evening, and rays of the sun were so pleasantly warm and peaceful that it was hard to believe there could be confusion and anxiety anywhere in the world. We would sit down frequently on some rock among the lush green vegetation and look over the unfolding drainage of Unakserak. It was considerably rougher than Kutuk, but not nearly as jagged as the country at the head of the North Fork. Everything seemed so good, so in place, so appropriate, in this remote terrain, that it didn't even seem wrong when we discovered that the sheep had somehow sensed our coming and were more than a quarter of a mile away, running hard, when we got to the place where we expected to find them.

Next day, after a delicious breakfast of sheep tongue and liver, we determined to return to our boat at the mouth of the Kutuk, by first following the course of Unakserak downstream. The main stream of Unakserak had been accurately mapped seven years before by the Smith expedition. Two miles below last night's camp was the last timber. Here we stopped more than two hours while we mapped this timber location, and I made borings into a dozen trees from which I extracted wood cores and measured and counted the rings. Queerly enough, the trees came in four distinct age classes. The trees in the baby class were between 20 and 45 years; the young-age class was 75 to 80 years; the middle-age class 120 to 130 years; and the old-age class 170 to 180 years. Why there should have been all those years when no trees started I could only guess. Perhaps they constituted a period when the temperature was too cold for seeds to germinate or when the germinating seedlings were killed by frost before they could get established.

Ernie was a modest man and never boasted that he was the most extraordinary outdoorsman among all the extraordinary inhabitants of the Arctic. However, he did have one great source of vanity—his dogs. He used to tell me how perfectly trained they were and how they would respond to his slightest wish. But when, this morning, his animals spotted a porcupine, they rushed after him and paid no more attention to Ernie's shouted commands than they did to the rushing of the nearby Unakserak. In fact, the only way that Ernie could keep them from filling themselves completely with quills was to stand over the porcupine and beat them off with the gun. Thereafter we spent a quarter of an hour pulling quills from the mouths and noses of the dogs with pliers which Ernie always carried for this purpose.

After this incident we stopped for a luncheon of fresh sheep. For supper we varied the meat diet with fresh fish. In between it was steady trudging for ten slow hard miles, covered by sedge tussocks. Although it was eight o'clock in the evening when we started again after supper, the atmosphere in the narrow valley seemed stifling, and the mosquitoes were worse than they had been at any time during the trip. We stopped several times to burn them off and in between stumbled over clumps of tundra along the side hills which came straight down to the edge of the Unakserak. After seven miles of such tedious travel we finally struck a well-drained gravel bench about ten feet above the river and followed it along to something Ernie was eager to find.

This was the home in which he had lived for an entire winter some fourteen years before—a log cabin about a mile above the place where the Unakserak empties into the Alatna.

From Ernie's cabin it was eight miles back to the mouth of Kutuk. We did not follow the Unakserak its last mile to the Alatna, but traveled cross country over a broad flat between the Unakserak and the Kutuk. The earliest hours of morning were so cool that mosquitoes virtually disappeared, and we tramped in the luxury of no nets and no gloves. Aside from getting tangled up in the soft ooze of one slough where we saw a moose, we had few difficulties and covered the distance in two and a half hours. It was just after three in the morning when we reached our base camp. We were delighted to find that neither bears nor wolverines had disturbed our boat which was pulled out on the bank, nor our food and equipment which we had slung from trees.

We slept next day till noon and spent the rest of the day loafing around camp and relaxing. Then, in three easy days, we followed the circuitous Alatna River downstream which it had taken us six days to ascend. The weather was fine, and I lay sprawled comfortably in the upturned bow of our shovel-nosed boat most of the time, while Ernie in the rear easily steered along.

A few miles above the Iniakuk River, beside the steepest rapids

on the stretch of river which we navigated, were the crumbling remains of four cabins. They had been built in the autumn of 1898
when an early freeze-up caught a group of tenderfoot stampeders
on this lonesome river and cut them off from the rest of humanity.
One can imagine the horror of these people, probably already discouraged in their quest for gold, wishing they had never left their
secure farms or cities where they had lived in safety and relative
comfort, thinking that in a day or two they would start down the
river in their boats safely ahead of the freeze-up, but wanting to
prospect just once more in the hope of still finding a bonanza which
would free them from a life of constant labor. Then suddenly,
waking up one early October morning, weeks before the date for
freeze-up even in the coldest regions to which they were accustomed,
they found the Alatna covered over and escape locked up until distant spring.

So they built these cabins which they ironically christened Rapid
City. After thirty-three years the roofs had fallen in as well as most
of the walls. We entered one of the cabins in best repair. It measured 12 by 12 feet. It had a door four feet high, and two small
windows. The floor was made out of unhewn logs. The furnishings
consisted of a bunk in one corner, remnants of a small table built
against the front wall under one of the windows, a couple of three-
legged stools, and five wooden pegs protruding from the wall above
the bed. It gave me a queer feeling to see this simple equipment
slowly rotting under the timelessness of nature, probably unseen
by human eyes for many years, completely disassociated from that
part of the earth and its processes which is human, and yet to realize that for one endless winter it constituted the most intimate
reality in the life of one lonesome person. It was easy to imagine
this futile prospector lying on his back in the hard bunk as he had
lain for many nights before, seeing the pegs in the wall, the chinked
logs, and the cold ceiling, wondering why in the world he had
ever left the comforts of a reasonable civilization, hating the misery
to which the quest for gold had led him, wishing for only one
thing in the world—that he might get away where life was safe and
gregarious. But it was also easy to imagine that in later years when
this same man was living the desired safe and gregarious life of
ordinary America, where the codes of society and the proprieties
of civilization had killed the spontaneity of the frontier, where days
and years were filled with the routine fight for a living, that he must
have often thought of the great adventure of his lonesome winter.

When we approached the mouth of Rockybottom Creek, we were

greeted by an unusual sight. Jack Sackett and Selawick Sam were out in their shallow boat, poling with all their might against the bottom of the river, and apparently trying to pull a small barren island. What in the world could that dark, smooth, low-lying mass be that they were dragging behind them in the middle of the river? Ernie didn't seem to be surprised at all. Suddenly a fetid whiff coming toward us made it dawn on me that they were dragging a giant moose.

A few minutes later Jack and Sam beached the carcass on the shore at a discreet distance from us. Sam had shot the moose the day after we left them, some nine days before. It was an unusually large specimen and would have dressed a thousand pounds. The meat was now too ripe for Jack, but it just suited Sam's taste. When it would be too ripe even for Sam, he would drag it into the fish camp where it could be used to keep the dogs plump for a good part of the summer. Eskimos do not like to waste meat any more than whites do in this remote country of conservationists.

Next day about noon we were back in civilization. Here was the Eskimo fish camp with the Kartuk and Napoleon families and that one-doonerak medicine man, old Peter Nictune, of whom Tobuk had told me. Just below was the bend where Tobuk's daughter Ekok had indicated on her map that the mysterious spruce tree with cottonwood bark was growing. The Eskimos were much interested in our quest, and Lucien, Rosie, and Clara Napoleon, ranging in ages from fourteen to seventeen, as well as Peter Nictune, volunteered to help in the search. None of the children knew anything about the tree, but old Peter assured us he could find it. The six of us spread out, about 50 feet apart, and wove back and forth over the point on which this tree was supposed to grow. Finally, when we must have covered at least two miles and it seemed we knew every tree growing on the entire area, the old medicine man walked up to what was nothing more than a large spruce tree and pointed to it in triumph. Rosie and Clara looked at it eagerly, pointed to the bark, and exclaimed in excited voices about its peculiarity.

But nothing was peculiar about it, and I reflected smugly how the mere prestige of being a medicine man could make other Eskimos think that black was white. However, when Ernie, Peter Nictune, and Lucien Napoleon had started back for the boat, Rosie turned to me and said casually: "Too bad we couldn't find your tree for you. Got to make the old man feel good, but he can't find anything. Can't hardly even start the fire in the morning!"

When we got back to camp, Lucien joined Ernie and me on our return to Allakaket. He was a bright, good-natured boy with a flair for mechanics, and we chatted together in the bow of the boat throughout the three hours of travel on the Alatna River to Allakaket. The trip was broken pleasantly by an hour's social call, including about a mile of piggy-back rides, at a lower Eskimo fish camp where Tobuk's family was spending the summer.

After a day in Allakaket, we headed up the Koyukuk River for Bettles. It started to rain again and the river was in one of its frequent flood stages. However, the water was deep and not high enough to make the going difficult. Every few hours we came to Indian fish camps where we stopped to chat.

In one respect these Indian camps were strikingly different from Eskimo camps. In the latter men and women alike chatted and joked cordially with us and pulled my whiskers, even though they had never seen me before. In the Indian camps the men were friendly, but the women stayed in their tents and came out only when I asked for permission to get a picture and the men told them to come out. This was consistent with what we had found on the dance floor where the Indian women would bury their heads in their dance partner's chest and would not talk to him or look at him during the dance. A Koyukuk Indian woman has about as much independence from her jealous husband as a Turkish harem lady.

Unless the husband happens to be away. In one of the half dozen camps which we visited, all men except Titus, a very old grandpa, were out hauling freight. Here the women chatted jovially with us, kidded us in language we couldn't understand, and sold us fifty cents' worth of fish for a dollar. The old man apparently had outgrown jealousy, because his one eye twinkled and he seemed to enjoy the women having their fling. His 16-year-old granddaughter, Elizabeth Titus, was an extraordinarily beautiful girl who had just married for the second time that spring.

When we pulled into Bettles the second evening we found Jack Dodds, caretaker of the roadhouse, the sole inhabitant. The others were out freighting on the river or mining at the distant creeks. It was a real privilege to spend two days talkings with generous old Jack who gave every cent he made from the roadhouse to help the Eskimos when they were in trouble. This, unfortunately, was often enough because of the ravages of faulty nutrition and tuberculosis.

THE JOHN RIVER

We started our next trip on August 2, bent on exploring the upper John River which empties into the Koyukuk at Bettles. We found the John River from the start less muddy and less winding, and its scenery more striking than the Alatna. We were among mountains at the first night's camp on a gravel point north of Timber Creek, an eastern tributary, while it had taken us three days on the Alatna to get above the monotonous flatlands.

Toward the close of the second day, at the mouth of Sixtymile Creek emptying into John River from the west, we met Jim Murphy, a 61-year-old Irishman who lived happily at this remote headquarters some sixty miles by river from Bettles; not sixty miles from his nearest neighbor, however, because only half an hour upstream at the mouth of Allen River, flowing into John River from the east, lived 81-year-old Mac McCamant. These nextdoor neighbors of the wilderness were as different temperamentally as two men could be. Jim was generous, liberal in his views, with a sparkling sense of humor and a philosophy of enjoying life as it passed along without regard to ultimate triumphs or failures. Mac was extremely reactionary in every view I heard him express, never laughed, and bemoaned the fortune he never made.

Perhaps nothing gives the contrast between the two men better than their view of the Eskimos. Old Mac said: "I ain't got no use for the damn natives. There ain't one of them but will try to get the best of you if he can. No, the less a man has to do with the natives the better off he is. They'll swipe everything they can get their hands on, and they haven't got the slightest sense of gratitude or appreciation."

Jim Murphy said: "They're fine people to get along with. The poor devils, they haven't got a thing in the world, but what they have got they'll share with you. I've lived with the natives for thirty-four years and I've found them better people to live with than whites. In all the years I've lived with them, I've only found one who ever stole anything from me and that was only a ball of twine. No, I've bunked with them from Dawson to the Siberian coast and I'd never ask to find a finer people."

We had a real banquet that night. Jim provided fresh sheep meat, while we gave Jim and Mac, who had come to join us, their first green vegetables in six months; we had brought a 100-pound flour sack full of young lettuce leaves just picked in Ernie's garden in Bettles.

Either the advancing season or the much better drained topography along the John River had practically eliminated the mosquitoes and we chatted comfortably around the fire after supper. Judging from the subjects of conversation among my three companions, at least Jim and Ernie must have done an impressive amount of good reading in their years of solitary arctic life. The topics included the geography of the John and the Amazon, the inexcusable wastefulness and cruelty of leaving set traps when you have finished your trapping, the brave attempt of Pancho Villa to make life better for the Mexican peons, criticism of a local hunter, Henry Ford, and John D. Rockefeller, and praise of Ekok, Senator George W. Norris, and Socialist leader Eugene V. Debs.

After we left Jim Murphy and Mac McCamant the good weather was over. We worked our way upstream while it rained most of the time. The water was much swifter than on the Alatna and sometimes threw us perilously close to cut banks and tangled sweepers. Had I been steering the boat we would have capsized frequently. Rocky mountain shoulders came down close to the edge of the water at many places. The cottonwoods and willows on the gravel bars were now well tinged with gold although it was early August.

The third day after leaving Jim and Mac the water was especially swift and shallow, and we were out in the river in our hip boots half the time tugging the boat along. Late in the afternoon we reached the mouth of the Hunt Fork, the highest of the major John River tributaries, which we had identified from the heights above Kutuk River in July. We decided we would take our boat no farther.

We had hardly made camp on top of a 30-foot bank just below Hunt Fork when we beheld a quadruple rainbow. The upper and outer bow showed a complete range of colors running from purple at the outside to red at the inside. The next bow below had its colors in reverse, being red above and purple below. There was considerable space between the two bows. The third bow was inside the second one. Its red and yellow were missing, but the green band was immediately contiguous to the second bow's purple band. The fourth bow similarly had its red and yellow missing. Its green band was against the third bow's purple, with its purple on the very inside of the whole quadruple series of arcs. The second reverse bow was much the brightest of all, and its base seemed to rest on the bar only fifty yards away.

If one rainbow is supposed to bring good weather, the four bows must have been in conflict because next day it poured harder than at any other time during the trip. I passed the time reading *War and Peace,* which Ernie had read the winter before while he was out for two months alone on the North Fork. Now he spent most of his time reading James H. Jeans's *The Universe Around Us.* In between I would go out into the thick spruce forest around camp and take borings in the trees which were from fifty to hundred-ten years old.

One interesting feature of the borings was the unusually broad growth ring for the summer of 1923, which was the hottest since white men moved into northern Alaska.

When the next morning gave every appearance of becoming the fifth consecutive rainy day, we decided we could not wait around camp any longer but would start our exploration of the unknown Hunt Fork. Unknown, that is, to white men. Eskimos frequently traveled this drainage because of two low passes into the Arctic at the head of the river. All up and down the river we saw signs of cutting among the willows and spruce trees.

We worked our boat about half a mile up Hunt Fork and left it floating there securely tied to large spruce trees growing well back from the river. In it we placed all equipment and supplies we were not packing on the backs of ourselves or the dogs, on the theory that the bears and wolverines would not be so likely to bother our goods in the rocking boat. As a matter of fact, Ernie with his arctic craftsmanship did not take kindly to the idea of leaving a boat floating in water, however securely tied; and not building a cache when leaving supplies. My anxiety to get going finally prevented him from spending two days here necessary to build a safe cache.

The dogs seemed even more delighted than I to be on the move. They tore ahead of us and swam the river six or eight times just for the lark. The two weeks since we had last been hiking had left us soft, and the sedge tussocks along the side hills were exceptionally high and quavering. The going did not get better until the close of the day, when it became feasible to travel the gravel bars. We camped that night where the Hunt Fork practically split in two. The left fork, called by the Eskimos Kevuk ("large intestines"), came from the south and headed toward the loftly dome of Nahtuk Mountain. The right hand fork, called Agak ("file"), headed toward the two low passes across the Arctic Divide.

It was raining again when we woke next morning. We decided, nonetheless, to follow Agak Creek valley. Just above camp this valley was covered by a great sheet of ice which was the residue from many years of unmelted snow. It spread from edge to edge of the gravel bars, and the river tunneled underneath. After four miles up the valley a large prong came in from the right—we called it Loon Creek, after some loons we observed—which was so swollen by nearly a week of rain that we could not ford it. Agak Creek, of course, was uncrossable unless we wanted to backtrack all the way to the ice bridge. We decided not to do this, because any creek was as exciting an exploration as any other. Hence we headed up Loon Creek to see what lay in that direction. We reached last timber on this creek very soon and observed once again that, as usual in this arctic country, the trees were making rapid growth. Timber line in arctic Alaska, I was more convinced than ever, was seldom due to climatic inhospitality.

However, the rapid growth on well-drained river bottoms is reversed on poorly drained and wind-swept hillsides, as we had already discovered during our Clear River trip. Here we saw that the most northerly trees had been fighting desperately with a hostile environment. On such a hillside above the last stand in the valley we found a lone spruce which was 173 years old and only nine feet high. More detailed examination indicated that it had taken 159 years to grow four and a half feet. At this height grew a jungle of broomed branches with evidence that year after year the wind had snapped the main shoot off at this point, probably the snowline. Finally a winter or two of less severe winds or some other fortunate chance of nature must have given the leader, which this tree had futilely shot up each year for more than a century, an opportunity to survive. Once through its critical first year or two, the tree developed so readily that in the past 14 years it had grown as much in height as in its first 159.

We made camp a mile beyond the last trees of Loon Creek, tied up the dogs, and decided to spend the night, or as much of it as we required, to search out the sources of this creek. It was a luxury to travel unencumbered by packs.

Three miles up the plunging creek we suddenly came upon a gorgeous lake, a mile and a half long and fresh as at creation. Great mountains rose directly from its shores and disappeared about 3,000 feet above the water into low-lying clouds. How far they jutted above the zone of visibility we could not even guess, but seeing the sweep of the mountains end in oblivion gave an impression of infinite heights beyond the experience of man. Nothing I had ever seen, Yosemite or the Grand Canyon or Mount McKinley rising from the Susitna, had given me such a sense of immensity as this virgin lake lying in a great cleft in the surface of the earth with mountain slopes and waterfalls tumbling from beyond the limits of visibility. We walked up the right shore among bare rocks intermingled with meadows of bright lichen, while large flocks of ducks bobbed peacefully and unmindful of us on the water of the lake, and four loons were singing that rich, wild music which they have added to the beautiful melodies of earth. No sight or sound or smell or feeling even remotely hinted of men or their creations. It seemed as if time had dropped away a million years and we were back in a primordial world. It was like discovering an unpeopled universe where only the laws of nature held sway.

Suddenly we noticed the law of nature holding sway most dramatically on the steep mountain above us. Three sheep were grazing just below the clouds. About a half a mile behind them, hidden from their view sometimes by the shoulder of the mountain and sometimes by one of the large rocks which were sprinkled liberally all around, a great black wolf was following them. He would make a swift dash for fifty or a hundred feet at a time and then crouch behind cover. Although the wind was blowing toward the wolf, some instinct seemed to make the sheep suspicious, for they would pause every little while in their feeding and look behind. Then they would continue munching the vegetation and slowly move eastward, and the wolf would bound ahead another fifty or hundred feet before hiding again. We must have watched this pursuit for half an hour while the wolf cut the distance between the sheep and himself in half, but no matter how many times the sheep looked around, the wolf was never once in the open at that precise moment. Finally they all disappeared from our sight.

Ernie decided that he wanted one of these sheep more than did the wolf, so he climbed up the side of the mountain to see whether he could knock one over. Meanwhile I started to climb above the lake to a pass which we could see about five miles upstream. It seemed as though I were headed for the world's most remote divide. I reached it exactly at midnight, which in cloudy weather was already beginning to be rather dusky. The waters on the other slope, to my surprise, did not flow into the Arctic, but apparently swung eastward to Ekokpuk Creek which empties into the upper John River.

When I returned to camp on Loon Creek three hours later, I found Ernie there without a sheep. He had cooked a pot of coffee and baked a few biscuits which we ate with cheese before retiring. Next morning it was raining harder, and the creek where we were camping was less fordable than ever. Ernie was worried that the flood might undercut the bank where our boat was tied. Since it was now out of the question to cross the creek and follow the Agak Creek fork to the divide, we decided to return immediately to our boat in one forced march.

It was nearly noon when we started downstream. The creek was a raging torrent from the timber on one edge to the other, so there were no exposed gravel bars to make for easy walking. We headed straight across country for a shoulder of the mountains about eight miles away where the valley bent sharply to the left. The tundra travel was unusually stiff and we probably did not make more than two miles an hour. After about nine miles of such travel, just below the point where Kevuk entered across the Hunt Fork valley, we came to what had been a mild Hunt Fork tributary which we had crossed easily on the way out. Two days of hard rain since then had expanded it into a wild river which was utterly unfordable. All we could do was to walk upstream until we reached a point where its volume was sufficiently diminished or its gradient sufficiently gentle to wade across.

The creek boiled for miles through a gravel cut from one hundred to two hundred feet deep. The bank on our side sloped so steeply to the edge of the water that the only possible way of walking was to follow along the top. After a mile we saw a place where the creek had flattened out sufficiently to lead Ernie to think we could get across. We slid down the loose gravel a hundred feet to the edge of the river, only to discover on closer inspection that it was absolutely unfordable. Climbing up was hard enough with 35-pound packs on our backs, but each of us had to grab a couple of dogs and drag them up as well, for the slope was too steep for them to climb without physical encouragement.

A mile further we made an equally abortive effort to cross, except that the cut bank was twice as high. After that we waited for two miles before attempting another crossing. Then Ernie spied a large spruce growing right at the edge of the water which he thought we could drop across and walk over. Under his axmanship the tree fell perfectly, and for a moment we saw the unfordable gap between us and our goal safely bridged. But before we had time to use it, the terrific force of the raging torrent had torn the dirt from around the butt end, which moved out into the stream, first slowly and then with great rapidity, until our route of escape had washed away.

By this time the problem of getting across had become a joke. "There's one safe rule in traveling this north country in summer," said Ernie unconcernedly. "If you can't get across them, you can always walk around them." So as we headed upstream once more, we christened this stream Walkaround Creek.

We had hardly gone a quarter of a mile when a side stream cut in from the bench, and we had to climb down a hundred feet and out again. There was the consolation, however, that passing this side stream meant just that much water less in the main channel. Since an equally sizeable creek came in from the other side at about the same place and the pitch of the valley leveled off very noticeably, we soon decided that the volume of the water and its swiftness were propitious for yet another attempt at crossing. This time we were finally correct, although we had to lean heavily against the sticks we cut to brace ourselves in crossing. The dogs had a harder time, and for a tense moment we thought we were going to lose Brownie in the flood. At nine o'clock in the evening, however, we were all united on the home side of Walkaround, where we dumped water out of the dogs' packs and wrung out our socks, while the dogs enthusiastically shook themselves and rolled in the sand.

Once again we took our bearing for the point of the mountain where the valley curved sharply to the left, and headed straight in that direction. The tundra travel was much harder than it would have been had we followed along the better-drained edge of the Hunt Fork, but we consoled ourselves with the thought that we were cutting off a couple of miles. Before long we came to a very steep creek which we had hardly noticed on the way out. Now it was raging so violently at the bottom of a 500-foot gorge that we knew any attempt to cross it would probably result in the drowning of ourselves or the dogs, so we had to follow it all the way down the river before its gradient leveled off enough to allow us to wade across.

From here on we decided to abandon shortcuts and to follow closely the bank of the Hunt Fork. Midnight passed and we were both still going strong. Around two in the morning, however, I got so sleepy that I couldn't keep my eyes open even when I was walking. I called a halt and curled up under a spruce, telling Ernie who had no inclination to slumber to wake me after fifteen minutes. I have never known fifteen minutes of sounder rest, and when Ernie called me promptly I was awake again.

It was five in the morning when we reached the boat and found it safely where we had left it. We were too sleepy to make camp or cook breakfast. We pulled out a few soda biscuits and a can of butter from under the canvas which covered the vessel, and after a short munching fell asleep for nine dreamless hours.

We woke at three in the afternoon, and after cooking a sumptuous meal which might have been breakfast, lunch, or supper, we traveled down in our boat to the junction of Hunt Fork and John River and the camp which we had left five days before. Here we spent another rainy day, reading and chatting. The next afternoon, when it gave promise of clearing, we moved two miles up the John River to a lovely camping spot where the ground was covered with sphagnum moss and twin flower and shaded by spruce and willows.

Between Hunt Fork and the John River was an isolated mountain, with a bare rock summit whose top we knew would furnish an ideal place to map the unknown myriad drainages which poured into the upper watershed of Hunt Fork and John River. The footing was good, the vegetation just beginning to take on the bright hues of the arctic autumn, the panorama around us became constantly brighter and more delightful, and so the 3,600-foot ascent to the summit was a rare pleasure. A whole swarm of little birds of some species neither of us knew, running and hopping around among the moss, were exceptionally interesting. They were plump and similar to grouse in shape, but no larger than curlews. Their wings, which we observed when they flew, were much narrower than those of grouse and reminded me of the wings of snipes.

The notion that this peak had ever been climbed before never entered our heads. Consequently we were mystified when we saw in the distance a square, rocky bump protruding in unnatural contours half a dozen feet above the summit of the mountain. When we got there, we found indeed a rocky cairn which apparently had been built thirty years before by the Schrader-Peters expedition when they went up the John River and down the Anaktuvuk to Point Barrow.

We spent five leisurely, luxurious hours on the top of this unnamed peak and called it Cairn Mountain; we enjoyed the vast panorama of the Brooks Range with its black summits and sparkling green slopes tumbled around in a wild confusion as far as we could see in every direction—endless mountains rising and falling as if the waves of some gigantic ocean had suddenly become frozen in full motion. One mountain to the east was of such striking gray contrast we could not resist giving it the trite name Gray Mountain. Boreal Mountain jutted up forty miles due east in all of its jagged impressiveness. It was our first tie to the more familiar geography of the North Fork country. We took more than forty compass bearings on mountain peaks, passes, river bends, junctions of streams, and other geographic features. I read the compass and Ernie wrote the bearing in the notebook. Afterward I took photographs while Ernie worked out some more of the geography. For long periods we just lay in the sunlight and enjoyed the peacefulness of a mountaintop which presumably had not been visited for thirty years.

Next day I walked fifteen miles up the John River to the most northern timber. It lay near the mouth of a minor western tributary, Yenituk ("white face") Creek, which is about sixteen miles from the Arctic Divide. Its name refers to the appearance of the hills in which the stream rises. The rapid growth of the trees was characteristic. There was nothing extraordinary about this day—thirty delightful miles among the golden foliage of a seldom-visited land.

The following day we started the return journey to Bettles. The going was easy, and for the most part I lay dreamily in the front of the boat, enjoying the sunlight which was now as persistent as the rain had been the previous week, and humming pleasant tunes as we sailed down the John River. Only at a few places, such as the mouth of Missouri Creek where the river had split into a dozen channels and we practically had to carry the boat over the rocks, was there any hard work. Ernie shot a sheep the first day. This made a welcome change in our diet, because the streams had been too flooded for fishing, and we had not tasted fresh meat since we left Murphy and McCamant. I examined this sheep's stomach contents, which included sedge, *Dryas, Arctostaphylos,* and the leaves and stems of willow.

We sailed into the Koyukuk at noon on the third day and a few minutes later pulled up in Bettles. We found the town crowded. Half a dozen prospectors had come in from the hills to take back their winter supplies before the freeze-up. Lew Carpenter, my companion of the summer, 1930, who was hauling freight on the river, was in town with his crew, and Jack Dodds was exceptionally busy at the roadhouse. In all, there must have been at least eighteen people gathered at one time in this second biggest town of the arctic Koyukuk, and this was phenomenal. It was fortunate for me, and for three and a half days I enjoyed illuminating chats with every one in town. Best of all was to talk with Ekok, who had just come down river after running my weather station in Wiseman all summer. I have never known anyone of any race so capable of adjusting to cruel necessities and yet so sensitive to fine values. All of us danced every evening until midnight, except the last evening when we just kept on and on, with every one getting more energetic as the dance progressed. The evening ended at four in the morning on a final dance with Ekok to the tune of *My Blue Heaven.*

It was a blue heaven all next day as we sailed steadily and easily up the Koyukuk River, the main artery of this part of the arctic world. The water was deep and the outboard motor pushed us along with almost no need for action on our part. The cottonwoods and the willows along the banks were bright gold although it was only August 22. The clear, cloudless sky behind them and the sparkling sunlight on the water and gravel bars and timbered hillsides and rocky summits made the world light and cheerful. Soon I would

be leaving this arctic "wilderness" where there was no unemployment, no starvation, no slums, no crowding, and no warfare, and
returning to "civilization" where, according to the issues of *Time*
and *Literary Digest* which had just come into Bettles, there was
greater misery, worse unemployment, more starvation than ever before in the history of the country.

Early next morning we reached Tramway Bar at the Middle Fork
and found Billie Burke and "Daisy" Wheeler finishing up their summer's mining with little gold but much zeal. They were the only
people we saw between Bettles and Wiseman, although we were
on the main travel route for the region. The river was shallower and
swifter this second day and we made much slower progress. At times
we had to line the boat along. At eight o'clock in the evening we
were still a couple of hours below Wiseman.

"We could make it all right," said Ernie. "We could get there by
ten o'clock and it would still be light enough to travel. Do you want
to go in?"

"No," I answered. "There'll be plenty of time in the years to come
when we'll each be wishing we could have just one night together
in camp like we had on those glorious explorations of 1931. We've
been out now forty-nine nights on this trip. Let's make it just one
more."

Ernie was delighted. We landed our boat on a gravel bar and
pitched camp in an open spruce stand on a bench about ten feet
above the river. It was an ideal location—level ground, just enough
trees to cut the wind, and a wonderful view down the spruce-flanked
river. For supper that night Ernie surpassed himself with a perfect
lamb stew. After the dishes were washed we sat together on a log
by the fire, for the evenings were cool now. It was dark enough also
that by eleven the stars began to come out, though the sky was still
not quite dark at midnight.

We didn't say very much sitting there. You don't when it is your
last camp with a companion who had shared the most perfect summer of a lifetime. We just sat, with a feeling warmer than the
crackling fire, exulting in the sharp-edged pattern which the mountain walls cut against the northern sky; listening to the peaceful
turmoil of the arctic river with its infinite variation in rhythm and
tone; smelling the luxuriance of untainted arctic valleys; feeling the
wholesome cleanliness of arctic breezes blowing on cheeks and hair.

6 Toward Doonerak

FOR SEVEN YEARS I HAD BEEN LONGING TO RETURN TO THE arctic Koyukuk. I had been thinking of the most glorious year of my life which I spent up there. I had been recalling thousands of square miles of wilderness scenery, large creeks and even rivers unvisited by man, deep canyons and hanging valleys glimpsed from a distance but never explored, great mountains which no human being has ever ascended. But most of all I had been thinking about Mount Doonerak.

Mount Doonerak is probably the highest peak in arctic America.[1]

[1] The most recent estimates by the U.S. Geological Survey through "topography from aerial photographs by photogrammetric methods," but not field checked, of elevations of the high peaks of the Brooks Range are in its 1956 series of quadrangles. These estimates have lowered Mount Doonerak to 7,610 feet. They show the highest peaks of the Brooks Range to be Mount Isto, 9,050 feet, Mount Chamberlin, 9,020 feet, Mount Hubley, 8,915 feet, and Mount Michelson, 8,855 feet. These peaks are some two hundred miles northeast of Doonerak and are in the Arctic Wildlife Range.

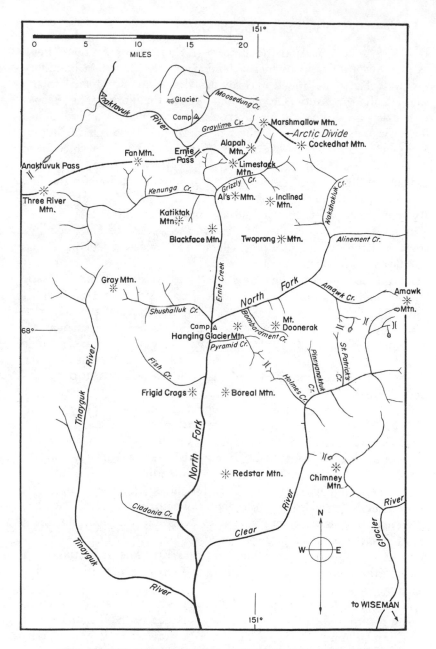

THE NORTH FORK OF THE KOYUKUK AND THE UPPER
ANAKTUVUK RIVER

It is the highest peak in the Brooks or Endicott or Arctic Range,[2] as it is variously called, which extends from the Canadian boundary nearly to Kotzebue Sound and divides the Yukon watershed to the south from the Arctic Ocean drainage on the north. The Brooks Range is one of the six major mountain systems in United States territory, but whereas the highest peaks in the Appalachian, Rocky, Sierra, Cascade, and Alaska mountain ranges have long since been climbed, no one is known to have ever been even part way up Mount Doonerak. Since I had discovered the mountain, had made the first map of it, and had named it during my trips in 1929 and 1930–31, I wanted to complete the job and also make the first ascent.

In addition, I was anxious to explore the uncharted and unknown sources of the Anaktuvuk River, which, by way of the Colville River, empties into the Arctic Ocean.

During the interval since my last trip to Alaska, my book, *Arctic Village* had been published. It stirred up a good deal of friendly interest in the Outside. However, because the study of this remarkable Koyukuk community was based primarily on my personal acquaintance with its inhabitants, it was very frank. Some people therefore questioned how it had been received on the Inside, even though all letters from there since the publication of the book had been cordial.

On my way back to Alaska in August, 1938, newspaper reporters from Ketchikan to Fairbanks had been asking me whether I was not afraid of being lynched when I returned to the people of *Arctic Village*. When the plane took off from Fairbanks and headed for the Koyukuk I felt mild qualms about my impending reception in Wiseman. These qualms may have been heightened by the company of three friends from the Outside, one of whom was Ernest Gruening, governor of Alaska. They decided to take advantage of the plane bearing me and Ernie Johnson (who had been paying a brief visit to Fairbanks) to make a fleeting trip to the Koyukuk. A hostile reception would have been bad enough, but doubly so with these friends looking on.

After an uneventful flight to the Yukon—looking as muddy as the Colorado from above—and across the sources of the Tozitna, Melozitna, and Kanuti rivers, we landed on a gravel bar at Alatna. Here

[2] Following a decision of the U.S. Geographic Board in 1925, the U.S. Geologic Survey has used "Brooks Range" to denote the entire chain across northern Alaska from the Canadian border nearly to Kotzebue Sound as described in the text. Recent U.S.G.S. maps have used "Endicott Range" to denote that part of the Brooks Range which includes the upper Koyukuk drainage to the south and the eastern part of the Colville drainage to the north.

Ernie Johnson got out to bring the boat we were going to use up the Koyukuk to Wiseman. After a couple of hours visiting with friends at Alatna, we hopped off again for the fifty-minute flight to Wiseman.

When we landed on the Wiseman field on August 4, every Eskimo and almost every white person in town was there. Oh boy, was it great to be back! I didn't realize how much I had been missing these people until I started pumping their arms and hearing their greetings, their laughter, and their good-natured banter. "Where's your oomik (whiskers)?" "What's the matter, don't they feed you Outside, you're looking poor." "You going to write 'nother book about us?" More laughter. More pumping. Piggy-back rides to children, born since I left, who knew me already as Oomik. Lots of hurried jokes and wisecracks.

Four days later Ernie arrived in Wiseman. The following morning it was raining hard so we decided to wait another day for the water on the Middle Fork to rise and make our boating easier. As a result, I spent more than five uneventful but delightful days around Wiseman.

As a matter of fact the first impression was not delightful, for I realized nostalgically that the Wiseman of 1931 had changed. There had been more of a shift from the true frontier in the past seven years, than in the previous thirty years. Only ten airplanes had arrived in Wiseman during the thirteen months I was there in 1930–31. Now there were two or three a week. Then, only one tourist visited the Koyukuk in thirteen months. In 1937, one hundred and fifty did, stopping for just a few hours, and then going back. As a result, Wiseman was no longer the isolated community, uniquely beyond the end of the world.

Another innovation which made Wiseman part of the world was the radio. In 1931 there was only the wireless station with code reception. Now there were six radios. The first automobile had come to the Koyukuk just before I left in 1931. Now it hauled men and supplies all summer to the two chief mining centers, six miles out on Nolan Creek and Hammond River. The rattling around the dirt streets of town never stopped now.

But the greatest change of all was in the people. In 1931 sixty-two of the seventy-seven whites in the entire upper Koyukuk had come to the north country by 1911. Civilization on the Koyukuk was overwhelmingly influenced by the distinctive northern mores developed in the romantic stampedes to the Klondike, Nome, and Fairbanks.

By August, 1938, twenty-eight of these seventy-seven people had left the country or died and had been replaced by forty-two newcomers to the Koyukuk of whom only five had come to the north in early days. As a result, the population of the Koyukuk, instead of having more than 80 per cent old-timers, now had half of its white people relatively recent arrivals who lacked much of the tradition of the old gold rush. Wiseman, by 1938, was no longer dominated by the pioneers of 1898.

To me it was especially saddening to find that many of those pioneers who had been among my most splendid companions seven years before, had died. When you live right along in a given environment, the deaths of friends are usually spaced enough in time to get you adjusted to them. When I returned to Wiseman, however, it was suddenly necessary to get adjusted to the deaths of sixteen white people and six Eskimos who in my mind had become an undying part of an unforgettable year.

After the first day I overcame this feeling of sadness in the throb of new life. There were eleven Eskimo children between the ages of three and seven, all born since I left, who were constantly shouting: "Give me piggy-back ride!" For all the times I obliged in the five days in Wiseman, I should have been in excellent shape for carrying 50-pound packs. There were two dances at which three little Eskimo girls aged eleven to thirteen, were among the best dancers. They apparently had a mental hangover from seven years ago, because in between dances they made me give them piggy-back rides around the hall.

One enjoyable afternoon I spent playing with the older Eskimo boys between eight and fourteen. We played a game of theirs in which you are supposed to shoot the other side by yelling "bang" and calling the name of the person you see before he does likewise to you. We had running and jumping races, and played ball with the boys' hats. They talked about school and hunting experiences. We went swimming in a frigid slough where I took colored movies of the boys who had learned to swim by the trial and error method; and then one boy grabbed the camera when I was in the water and shot pictures of me naked to the delight of the other boys.

There had been no unpleasant remarks about *Arctic Village*, in spite of the described "improprieties" in terms of Outside custom. One of the settlers, 78-year-old Verne Watts, admitted he was sore when he was quoted in his description of one girl as "so thin that a couple of macaroni sticks would make a pair of drawers for her." Another, strong-tempered Jack White, on the other hand, was delighted to find his profanity quoted and the description of his tear-ing off the roof of his house to evict a tenant. George Eaton, now seventy-seven, said seriously to me: "Of course, Bob, when I was saying how I'd slept with more women than any man in Alaska, I didn't expect you to put it in a book, but I'm a-telling you, it's true." Annie Kayak, a pretty young woman with two small children who came from the arctic tundra to Wiseman with her husband, Itachluk, in 1930, and whose rupture with him I had described in detail, invited me for an immense bowl of what she remembered was my favorite fruit, blueberries, and told me how much she liked the book and her eighteen-dollar share of the royalties. There were many pleasantries. One Eskimo girl, meeting me on the street one morning, laughingly quoted from the book: "If you meet an Eskimo girl in the morning she may look a little bit frowsy, but in the eve-ning her attire, simple though it is, will be immaculate." Such a reception to a prodigal son would only be possible with remarkably honest people who do not pretend to be what they are not and there-fore do not resent the truth about themselves.

UP THE NORTH FORK BY BOAT

In the early morning of August 10, 1938, Ernie Johnson, Jesse Allen, Kenneth Harvey, and I shoved our boat into the current of the Mid-dle Fork for the start of twenty-nine days of exploration beyond the paths of man. We were headed for Mount Doonerak and for the sources of the Anaktuvuk. (See map, page 111; also end map.)

Our rented boat was an old tub. It was too heavy for our purpose, and we soon started referring to it as "the raft," but it was the only boat available. It was 30 feet long, measured 63 inches across at the gunwale, and weighed 1,200 pounds. We had a load of 1,280 pounds dead weight, 700 pounds of us, and two large dogs.

Our journey—downstream in the Middle Fork until we reached the North Fork—was aided most of the way by a motor, although we drifted for many miles where the water was too shallow. The river was not a wilderness. Power boats had been running up and down it since 1914.

We reached the mouth of the North Fork at four in the afternoon. Here the real trip began. For six and a half days with an average of eleven and a half hours of travel per day we fought our way hundred-eighty miles up the winding North Fork. We never could see more than a couple of miles ahead at a time, and usually not more than half a mile before the next bend. On the lower, relatively much traveled, river we used the motor half the time, on the upper quarter of the route not at all. By "much traveled" I mean that, in days gone by, several hundred people had been up as far as Jack Delay Pass (about halfway to the place we were going by boat); this year, it seemed, not a human being had been on the North Fork.

We traveled until after ten the first evening to make about ten miles. We were passing through a great flat, but the clouds were so low that we couldn't see much besides mud banks with spruce, cottonwood, and willow growing. It took us only a few minutes to set our 6 by 7 foot tent and have a fire going; we cooked a hasty supper and retired in the twilight of midnight.

When we awoke six hours later, the river had risen fifteen inches and had become a boiling soup of mud. Large masses of froth and sticks of wild-looking driftwood bobbed along from the sources of the North Fork. As we continued up the river we could only see occasional low mountains through the rain and fog. We watched with interest the water birds—ducks, geese, and two loons. With even greater interest we watched a piece of "driftwood" floating down the river, which suddenly turned into a yearling black bear. Harvey jumped out of the boat and waited until his feet touched bottom. Then he blazed away with his Springfield while I did likewise with my movie camera. Then we hauled the bear ashore, dressed it, and saved the skin. It provided us and the dogs with fresh meat for four days.

On the third morning, going became hard for the first time. Just below the mouth of Glacier River we battled Squaw Rapids; named after an Indian woman who drowned in its fury more than fifty years ago, before the first white men penetrated to the Koyukuk. We hauled the boat by brute force for about three miles against the pressure of the tumbling river. For at least half the way from here up we had to "line" the boat in this way. Ernie and Harvey would grab hold of the boat, one on either end, and practically lift it over the rocks where the river was very shallow. Where it was too deep to stand against the fierce current Ernie and Harvey got in the boat and pushed with poles, while Jesse and I unwound a 150-foot rope in front of the boat and then tugged with all the power we had, walking along the edge of the river or sometimes wading with the water almost to the top of our hip boots. The greatest difficulty was keeping this tow line from getting tangled with brush and snags along the shore and with trees lying in the river where they had been carried by the flood. At places the current was so powerful that for a minute or more we could not gain an inch. We would finally get the boat over the blockade and it would go a little easier for a short distance until the river halted us again. Then it would be another tug of war between two equally balanced sides. Sometimes Ernie and Harvey gave the boat a little twist and it slipped between two rocks. Sometimes the boat got crosswise with the current and had to be straightened out. Sometimes there was no solution but pull, pull, pull, and lift, lift, lift, to the limit of endurance.

Once beyond the rapids, we were at the mouth of Glacier River, first of the four main tributaries of the North Fork. Beyond here we had smooth cruising—after having spent seven hours to cover six and a half miles to Glacier River, we covered the next thirteen miles in a mere four hours.

We made camp shortly after nine at the mouth of Ipnek Creek on the west side of the river. This had been an important focal point in the Wild River stampede of 1913–1915. It was the point where the men coming over Jack Delay Pass from Wiseman crossed the North Fork and headed over a low pass into the Wild River drainage. Many decaying cabins and tent frames remained from that rush of a quarter of a century before.

On the next day smooth traveling continued. We made twenty-five miles, our biggest day of the up-river journey. Late in the afternoon we passed the mouth of Tinayguk River, the second of the main North Fork tributaries. A mile beyond, over some still riffles, was Ernie's cabin which had been his headquarters for hunting, trapping, and prospecting during most of the period between 1919 and 1931 when he was living on this lonely river. When I was there in the deep snows during the winter of 1931 the cabin was five hundred feet back from the river and out of sight, but since then a wide strip of spruce and cottonwoods had been torn out by the floods and the cabin was within plain view. We camped here and took a look at the cabin. Apparently no human being had been here since Ernie and I hitched up our dogs and drove away on March 19, 1931, but grizzlies had smashed the cabin door and torn the inside to pieces. There were old dishes scattered hither and yon and one torn 1930 copy each of the *Literary Digest* and the *Nation*. Thumbing in them I read about the growing depression.

The next morning we passed the mouth of Clear River, third of the major North Fork tributaries. It did not rain hard, but the sky was overcast most of the day. The morning was easy going, the afternoon a constant battle against the furious current and the shallow bars on either side of Cladonia Creek. Aside from this struggle, the outstanding impression of the day was the sight of a seven-mile stretch along the west side of the river, which had been burned over the previous summer, probably as the result of lightning. The destruction of the spruce and birch timber was almost complete, but even more disastrous was the destruction of moss and lichen which had already resulted in the thawing out of the ground and the opening of deep erosion gullies in the loose gravel soil.

It did not rain on the next day, but the high peaks were covered with fog until late in the afternoon. We saw four moose along the river—first a cow and a calf, then a young bull, finally a lone calf so tame he started to follow Harvey who was pulling the boat. Harvey's dog wandered off after one of the moose, and it took us nearly an hour to find him again. The river was spread out over a wide gravel flat and at places split into a dozen different channels. We had to reconnoiter ahead to keep from going up a channel from which we could not emerge. We pulled, tugged, and lifted the boat, stumbling in the rushing water all day long. All of us went in over the tops of our hip boots and got soaked. It took us nearly twelve hours to cover twelve miles upstream.

During most of the day the Gates of the Arctic towered directly to the north, as we approached that monumental entrance to the land of Mount Doonerak, our goal. When we passed through between the jagged crest of Frigid Crags towering 4,000 feet up from the valley floor to the west and Boreal Mountain rising precipitously for 6,000 feet to the east, with the two mountains only two miles apart, it seemed as if we were leaving the world of man behind and were pioneering in a trackless wilderness. This was not far from being true. We calculated that probably no more than twelve white men had penetrated the six hundred square miles of the magnificent Koyukuk country north of the Gates of the Arctic.

Next morning the wind had shifted, and it began to rain again. We pulled and tugged our way for eight and a half more hours to cover seven miles to a place where the river swung in against a low spruce bank, two miles below Ernie Creek, the fourth major North Fork tributary. It was not ideally what we wanted, because it was not high enough above the water, but it was the best patch of timber accessible from the river which we had seen all day, and the river was getting too steep and shallow to pull a ton any farther. So here, on a peninsula between the North Fork and a slough (that extended far back from the river and seemed to lose itself in a morass), hundred-eighty miles by the turns of the river above its mouth and eighty-two miles overland from the closest neighbors on Nolan

Creek, we decided to make our base camp for half a month of exploration.

THE SOURCES OF THE ANAKTUVUK

The first task after reaching base camp was to build a cache where our extra food, bedding, and photographic equipment would be safe from the wild animals while we were away from camp for periods of a day to a week. Ernie was the architect, and he and Harvey supplied the skilled labor. Jesse did the semiskilled work while I contributed the unskilled labor. We worked on the cache for two full days, but in a pleasant, leisurely manner.

The cache consisted of a miniature spruce log cabin, built nine feet up in the air where it rested on four substantial posts. It was 5½ by 6½ feet on the outside and 3½ feet high at the front end, with a six-inch pitch to the roof. This consisted of split logs hewn into troughs to carry off the water; the cracks between them were capped with other logs having their trough on the under side. Everything which went to make the cache, except for two pounds of nails, was taken directly from the forest surrounding us.

The cache was put up on poles to keep the grizzly bear, which cannot climb, from reaching it and to exclude likewise other non-arboreal animals. The logs were fitted tightly and varied in size from six to ten inches at the small end which prevented the black bear and wolverine and the less powerful lynx, marten, weasel, squirrel, porcupine, mouse, raven, and camp robber from getting in, even if they did climb up. Without the protection of this cache much important equipment would almost certainly have been destroyed during our operation from this base.

The day after the cache was finished the weather gave promise of clearing. We crossed the North Fork in our boat and then walked to Shushalluk Creek, coming from the west two miles above, for fish and exploration. On the way we climbed an open hill, colored with the green of moss, sedge, and Labrador tea, the bright cream color of the reindeer moss, the purple leaves of the blueberries, the scarlet leaves of the Angowuk, and the brilliant red cranberries. The cranberries and blueberries were so profuse it took us a long time to reach the top of the hill.

Once there we waited while the clouds lifted off the mountains until at last we saw the goal of our expedition, the summit of Mount Doonerak. What a summit it was! It jutted so pointedly into the air that it seemed quite impossible to ascend. The northwest face, which to our vague recollection from eight years before was the one to try first, now appeared absolutely impossible. Impossible, too, was the west side, while the north face seemed to have a 2,000-foot·sheer drop. We knew that the east side, which we couldn't see, was hopeless. The only chances seemed to be (1) a ridge leading up from the northwest which we could only partly see, but which we thought we remembered might be possible; and (2) the south side rising from Pyramid Creek, which apparently had never been visited. An exploration of this creek and a reconnaissance of the mountain from this side seemed the obvious activity for the morrow.

We descended from the hill to Shushalluk Creek where we split forces. Jesse and Ernie went to fish its racing waters, swollen by the days of rain. Harvey and I set out for the upper creek to map and explore it. The lower part of the stream was bounded by crumbling slate mountains, 3,000 feet high, which were gradually sliding their way into the creek. The upper part was confined by peaks of black igneous rock and already covered with early snow. The sky, to our great disappointment, had meanwhile become overcast again.

Harvey and I returned to camp at nine o'clock and Ernie and Jesse came along a short time later. The high water had practically ruined the fishing, and it had taken them four hours to catch twenty-two grayling—an almost unheard-of low in this virtually unfished country; but the fish dinner which followed was nonetheless delicious.

It was still overcast next morning, but we thought we might as well see what we could see. Harvey decided to hunt for sheep, Ernie, Jesse, and I to explore Pyramid Creek. Before leaving I examined some spruce trees about a mile beyond camp, where I found the largest tree I had yet seen north of the Arctic Circle, a spruce twenty-one inches in diameter at breast height.

The three of us stumbled along for four miles among the soft moss and clumps of sedges, until we reached Pyramid Creek. After lunch, Jesse left us to fish in the stream while Ernie and I started up the unvisited north branch.

Almost immediately we were in a deep chasm where the bottom of the valley had narrowed into a slot only six feet wide at places between the gray rock walls. There was so much water shooting through this constricted space that we had to find toeholds on the face of the cliffs. After a mile of this going the chasm widened into a valley beyond the timber zone, with rock-faced mountains on either side disappearing into the clouds, 4,000 feet above us. The few mountains whose tops we could see were black and jagged. Every mile or less, side streams came down over the rocks in great white leaps, some of the higher waterfalls seemingly pouring down from the clouds.

About four miles above the falls we were in the broad upper valley of Pyramid Creek. The top of Doonerak, directly to the north, was hidden in the clouds, but from what we could see of its lower two-thirds and from what we had seen the day before of its very crest, this seemed the most likely side on which to make our first attempt. But it had to clear!

Instead it began to rain again about the time we reached camp. This was the tenth day of rain out of eleven on this trip, and it began to be almost depressing even though Harvey had returned with a sheep and Jesse with a fine catch of grayling to brighten our dehydrated diet. It rained steadily all night and looked worse than ever when we arose late the next morning. We ate sheep meat, chatted, and read all day, and went to bed early.

Next morning at four we were awakened by Ernie who had stepped out of the tent and was saying: "———, boys, we've got to roll out! The river's coming into camp."

The rains of the past days had raised the river three feet during the night and a side slough from it was pouring into the fireplace. We moved everything to the two-foot higher ground near the cache. It was the highest ground anywhere around. The move proved unnecessary, however, because the river soon started to drop.

We cooked an early breakfast of sheep steak and coffee and then spent a long day in camp, alternately hoping it would clear when the sky became half blue, and fearing it would never stop raining when it became all covered with black, gloomy clouds.

When it was completely overcast again the next morning we decided we had better forget Doonerak for a while if we did not want to spend our whole trip just waiting. So we packed up bedding, dishes, extra socks, photographic equipment, and food for five days and decided to attend to the second objective of our expedition— the exploration of the never-visited sources of the Anaktuvuk River.

The Anaktuvuk is one of the largest Alaskan rivers flowing into the Arctic Ocean. It does not flow directly into the ocean, however, but joins the Colville River first. The independent drainage basin of the Anaktuvuk embraces several thousand square miles and there was no record of anyone ever having been all the way to its head.

Ernie and I had probably come closer to doing so than anyone else. He had been over Ernie Pass (at the head of Ernie Creek) three different times and had descended on the Anaktuvuk side, where he had passed the main fork of the Anaktuvuk heading eastward. I had looked down into it from both Limestack Mountain and Al's Mountain—the former to the north and the latter to the south of Grizzly Creek—and had seen its headwaters disappearing eastward into limestone mountains. Now we were going to find where it really headed.

Two weeks of almost continuous rain had swollen the rivers so much that we were sure we could not ford Ernie Creek, which we had to cross two and a half miles above camp. Therefore we dragged the boat up the river and got across with its aid after two hours of hard tugging. We then tied the boat securely in a back eddy, changed from water to land travel, shouldered 30- to 40-pound packs apiece, packed 20 to 30 pounds on each of the dogs, and started stumbling our way northward through Ernie Creek valley over sedge tussocks, soggy, ankle-deep moss, and bog holes. We were all soft at back packing, so even with such light loads the going was hard. A steady drizzle all day didn't make it more pleasant. A stop for lunch at last timber was the only break in six and a half hours. We camped for the night among willows under the great black Gibraltar-like precipice at the south entrance to the Valley of Precipices which had so impressed Al Retzlaf and me on our trips up the North Fork in 1929 and 1930. Ernie had told me that in the winter following the second of these journeys, he had been calling this peak Blackface Mountain. Therefore, I used this name on my 1932 map.

While we pitched camp, we looked up at the great black rock face directly above us, but we could not see the top, because the mountain disappeared in the fog some 2,000 feet above the valley. It rained nearly all night, but our tent shed the water perfectly.

Next morning, unexpectedly, it was clearing. We could see the top of Blackface jutting almost straight into the air for 3,000 feet. On its side were many narrow ledges green with arctic vegetation, and on several of these, overhanging appalling plunges, we saw small bands of sheep moving along the cliffs.

This morning traveling was easy along the gravel of Ernie Creek up the five-mile stretch of the Valley of Precipices. I had been through this glacial gorge four times before, but its dark immensity was as awe-inspiring as ever. Underneath these great bounding walls you dwarfed into nothing.

At the upper end of this great valley Ernie Creek forks into three branches. The right-hand branch is Grizzly Creek, which Al Retzlaf and I first followed to its barren source a dozen miles to the east in September, 1930; the left-hand branch is Kenunga Creek which I first explored during the same week; and the center and smallest one is Ernie Creek itself which heads from a low pass that crosses the Arctic Divide.

Our plan was to follow the center branch, but before that I had a little piece of business up Grizzly Creek. Here was the location of my 1930 experiment of sowing spruce seeds on two adjacent plots, twelve miles north of the last timber.

Well, the seeds had not developed. My experiment was a complete, dismal failure on both plots. There was not even the sign of a dead seedling—just two patches of bare ground, marked with willow stakes set in rock. Whether the failure was due to unfertility of the seeds or faulty sowing technique or an unusually rainy autumn after sowing, which rotted them, or just unfavorable climate according to the usual theory I could not tell.

But I could not feel disappointed long, as the clouds gradually disappeared from the mountains and the great peaks of the Arctic Divide jutted all around us into the sunlight. Limestack really was a great stack of brightly shining gray lime. Alapah (Eskimo for "it is cold") certainly did look cold with its whole table-top summit covered with fresh snow. As we climbed higher toward the head of Ernie Creek, the Valley of Precipices, now behind us, became a deeper slit in the tumbled crust of the earth. When we finally reached the height of land between the Pacific and Arctic watersheds we could see the summit of the king of all arctic mountains, old Doonerak himself. He looked more unscalable than ever from the north, with several hundred feet of precipitous summit covered with snow.

It was a superlative sight, but our greatest interest for the moment lay to the north and east where the Anaktuvuk headed. Here was a world of gray limestone precipices, among the unknown recesses of which many stream valleys vanished through deep canyons. We were not sure which of them contained our goal.

We pushed northward across the broad, low gap in the Arctic Divide which is Ernie Pass and dropped into the first valley which we had thought from the top might be the main Anaktuvuk River. It was a large side creek, emerging from a canyon world exclusively made of gray limestone, with a thousand-foot sheer precipice of gray lime rising across it—so we called it Graylime Creek. It was enticing, but we pushed on across a high ridge to the place where all of us except Jesse Allen thought the main Anaktuvuk lay, in the next valley. He was right—the creek proved to be nothing but a false alarm—so we called it Fake Creek, and climbed over another ridge.

We dropped down the easy slope on its north side to what later proved to be the real Anaktuvuk. Our immediate problem was to find enough willows for camp. We followed down the river for nearly a mile to a side creek joining from the north before we found a clump of willow brush. The biggest stems were only five feet tall and two inches through at the base. Farther down the river toward the coast the willows got much bigger, but this was the highest upstream that willows grew large enough to camp in. The nearest spruce and cottonwood were across the divide, twenty-five miles to the south.

By picking up every dry stick we could find for a quarter of a mile around, and burning some green willow when the fire was going, we managed to find enough fuel for six meals. Tent poles were harder to provide. At first we thought we would not bother about setting the tent, but then the weather began to look threatening again just before bedtime. So we slung the back end from a four-foot limestone wall, and Ernie ingeniously rigged up a fairly solid five-foot pole for the front end by overlapping and lashing together the tops of three willows. For mattresses we rolled up large mats of arctic moss.

It was lucky we took this precaution, because when we rose next morning a cold fog lay low on all mountains and light rain was falling. It was not an auspicious day to set out to find the source from where the mighty Anaktuvuk started its journey to the ocean. However, fuel was so scarce that we could not afford to hang over a day, and besides the most futile of all things seemed to be to wait for a change in the weather.

Immediately upstream from camp was a broad main valley in the center of which the Anaktuvuk flowed in a little chasm, a few feet wide and 30 to 40 feet high, where the stream was cutting through the limestone bedrock. Sometimes the water foamed over rapids, sometimes it tumbled over 20-foot ledges, and sometimes it lay in clear, deep pools where we could see a few arctic trout. After a mile this chasm ended, and the main valley turned sharply to the left.

Then we suddenly found ourselves entering a glacial valley canyon. The fog lifted just enough to show us great limestone precipices on either side of us and perhaps half or three-quarters of a mile apart. We couldn't tell how high they were, because they were still rising sheer where they disappeared in the fog, but following in our imagination the thousand or two thousand feet of straight gray limestone which we did see, they seemed to rise infinitely into a world beyond the world. Ahead of us, on the floor of the valley on this twenty-fifth day of August, was a great, unmelted field of last winter's snow. We walked six hundred yards across it, and estimated that it was nine feet deep at its deepest point.

Above the snowfield the valley bent to the left again. It was still entirely bounded by limestone cliffs rising endlessly into the clouds. Sometimes these cliffs were broken by deep gorges where small side streams also tumbled out of the mist. One such stream coming in from the left, poured down at least 1,200 feet in one waterfall after another, each of them fifty to hundred feet high.

Just above these cascades, the main river forked. One-third of the water came churning out of a V-shaped trough which bent nearly ninety degrees to the right. The other two-thirds came from a stream bending almost as sharply to the left, where it raced down a half-mile straightaway. Above this straightaway it stood on end.

This is literally true. It tumbled over a waterfall, 220 feet high by barometer reading. Above the waterfall we could not even guess what might lie. From where we stood, below, we did not see a sign of river or valley—just a few rocks and fog.

We climbed up by the side of the fall and found above it a series of igneous terraces, black and pock-marked. The creek was hidden among them. We did not try to follow it, but climbed from one bench to another until we found ourselves at the foot of a broad, hanging basin. The bottom was flat enough for agriculture, but it seemed like anything but agricultural land when it began to snow steadily as we started across. It snowed for more than an hour, though the sun shone dimly most of the time. With snow and faint sunlight, this lofty barren valley with its huge rocks which had tumbled from the surrounding mountains and with its great limestone precipices still rising infinitely into the clouds, seemed an unreal world, unvisited by human beings since the dawn of time.

Not unvisited by animals, however. We saw the tracks of sheep, caribou, grizzlies, and wolves, and several old, rotten horns of caribou and sheep. But the only living things we actually saw were one ground squirrel and one water ouzel.

At the head of this basin a large creek, with almost as much water as the main river, dropped in from the right. Like the main river lower down, it also seemed to be standing on end, so we called it Standonend Creek. Above a thousand feet of cascades there seemed to be a high, hanging valley, just below the clouds.

Our main valley again turned sharply to the left. We were now going in exactly the opposite direction from that which we took when we left camp. The upper river was making a complete circle. Beyond this next bend was a third basin, paved by deep and coarse glacial rock, with hardly any vegetation. Around us on every side towered great limestone mountain walls, their tops yet hidden in the fog. Suddenly, at the head of the valley, we realized that what we had thought was a cloud against the mountain was in reality a high glacier.

We followed up the broad basin and at the head turned some more to the left into a narrow valley bounded by rockslides dropping from the limestone walls. Half a mile up the valley ended in a wall of loose rock, 200 feet high, which had been dropped by the receding glacier. We climbed around it and found ourselves at the edge of the ice sheet. Above us was a wall of stratified ice, dirty with gravel and rough-edged rock, 50 feet high and overhanging. It was indeed the edge of the glacier, a remnant of the ice age. The river had circled around so much that the ice sheet was facing northward down the valley. Behind it and to either side, on south, east, and west, the sun was shaded out for most of the year by the lofty, closely surrounding mountains. This was the second true glacier I had seen in the Brooks Range—the other had been the one discovered by Philip Smith near the Arrigetch peaks west of the Alatna, in 1911.

We climbed on top of the glacier and stopped for an hour at the center where a pile of rock had fallen from the mountain above. It seemed to be the end of the earth or the heart of another earth as we perched on top of this remnant of a long-vanished age. Everything we looked upon was unknown to human gaze. The nearest humans were a hundred and twenty-five miles away, and the civilization of which they constituted the very fringe—a civilization remote from nature, artificial, dominated by the exploitation of man by man—seemed unreal, unbelievable. Our present situation seemed also unreal, but that was the unreality of a freshness beyond experience. It was the unreality of a remoteness which made it seem as if we had landed miraculously on another planet which throughout all passage of time had been without life. There was also the unreality of countless needle pinnacles, jutting around us through the fog, alternately appearing and disappearing as the atmosphere thinned and thickened.

It was after three when we left the glacier and started back down the valley. The ceiling had raised and we could now see the summits of most of the countless snow-covered limestone mountains surrounding us. The lower we dropped, the more enormously they towered above us. Their immense precipice faces were pitted with small limestone caves and pillars. Their gray and black strata were sometimes horizontal, sometimes tilted, occasionally standing on end—usually in straight lines but at several places bent into rainbow curves. Every one of the mountains had innumerable precipices, a thousand, two thousand, even three thousand feet high. It did not really matter—there were no measures in this world—and after seeing the superlative so long, space began to lose its significance.

We descended to the valley below the fall and then followed the right-hand fork which had looked interesting on the way up. It did not flow in a broad valley, but in a narrow slit in the overtowering limestone crags through which the creek dropped in wild leaps. About a mile and a half up, it plunged over a hard, igneous wall, falling two hundred feet in a couple of jumps. Above this wall, tucked in among the mountains, was one of those startling high mountain valleys, so peaceful in contour that it seemed like a New England valley until one glanced up at the mountains above.

But even more startling was a find we made on the return journey. Just below the fall, Ernie who was in the lead called out: "If anyone had told me this, I'd say he was a damn liar!" The cause of his surprise was no spouting geyser or sensational natural bridge, but some lowly moose dung. However, not only was it in country along the backbone of the Arctic Divide where none of us had ever seen moose signs before, but in a gorge so rocky we would not have dreamed that moose could penetrate it.

The five miles from the forks back to camp between the immensity of the surrounding mountains were glorious. We were fresh and going four miles an hour at the end of thirty trailless miles when we got back to our tent at eight. Jesse, who had walked only to the forks in the morning, had a supper of pea soup, lamb stew, boiled dried applies, and coffee when we returned, and it made a delicious ending to a perfect day. Another fine touch was a band of seven sheep grazing on the hillside above camp, unaware that human beings, whom they were undoubtedly seeing for the first time, could be a source of danger.

We went to bed soon after supper, but I couldn't go to sleep for a while. I lay on my back and looked through the door of the tent at the foothills across the valley. I tried to reflect on remoteness and adventure beyond the frontiers, but I could not for long, because it seemed more secure and peaceful here, with three competent and devoted companions, than it did back home in the heart of Washington.

After breakfast the next morning Ernie and I walked far enough downstream to tie in on our maps the upper Anaktuvuk with the main river which Peters and Schrader had mapped in 1901 when they came over Anaktuvuk Pass from the head of the John River. The Anaktuvuk was broader and much tamer here, but a couple of side streams coming in on the right limit poured forth from wild limestone gorges. It would have been a delight to explore them, but food and firewood were both short, and we didn't want to take time either to hunt or move down river to willows for fear of being too long away from Doonerak. So we broke camp after lunch and hiked back to our camp at Pyramid Creek in an uneventful day-and-a-half journey. We walked into the teeth of a fierce rainstorm as we crossed back over the Arctic Divide. Thereafter we could see only the bases of the mountains around us and the valley floor.

We camped again in the willows under Blackface Mountain and slept snugly in our tight tent although it poured all night. When we reached our boat early the next afternoon we found it safe. It took us no more than an hour to fill a bucket with enough cranberries to last us four days, and then we loaded our stuff in the boat, shoved her off, and piled in. Under the power of the eight-mile-an-hour current and the skillful steering of Ernie, who stood in the back and guided the boat with an occasional deft push with his pole, we floated in nineteen minutes the two and a half miles to base camp at the North Fork below Ernie Creek, which it had taken us two hours to ascend.

AN UPSETTING EXPERIENCE

The day after we got back it rained without let-up from midnight to midnight. I wrote up my notes and sketched maps from the compass bearings I had taken on the Anaktuvuk jaunt. When we went to bed we knew we might have to move before breakfast, but we preferred to wait and let nature take its course.

Sure enough, it took it. Jesse roused us at five when the rising water was reaching the edge of the tent. We moved everything to the highest ground, at the cache, where apparently no flood waters had been. Here we thought we were safe for the remainder of our stay. We passed this day marooned between the main river to the west and a roaring slough to the east, which kept us from getting anywhere in the high water. It was another day of reading, writing, talking, and loafing—a day whose peacefulness I enjoyed despite the enforced idleness.

The following morning it stopped raining, and when the water was down enough we crossed the slough with difficulty. Jesse and Harvey decided to spend the day in camp, but Ernie and I set out to explore the south fork of Pyramid Creek.

The trip was a repetition of the one taken ten days before to the forks of the creek, but now the autumn colors had deepened. Above the forks was virgin ground. It began to rain again, and the mountaintops were covered with clouds, but we could see the lower end of splendid precipices on either side. Three miles above the main forks was a second fork. The right-hand one led into a jagged canyon among the cloud-capped crags of Boreal Mountain. However, our objective this day was to explore what from the hillside above Shushalluk Creek had appeared to be a low pass into Clear River. We were especially anxious to find one, because none had ever been discovered through that rugged range which for fifty miles separates North Fork and Clear River.

We followed up the smaller left fork, which seemed to head in our direction. After a mile of dark canyon we climbed into a broad bright green basin, with gushing water on every side. It was drizzling persistently as we rose toward the skyline ahead and we were wondering whether we could see anything on the other side. We doped it out that we should connect with a prong of Holmes Creek, which we had named in March, 1931.

When we finally reached the pass, the drizzle abated and we got a fine view down into a deep creek cutting its way among the high mountains on the other side. Because of the several bends we could not quite see as far as the point where we thought it should join Clear River. But we were able to estimate the compass bearing of the lowest straightaway of the creek and to our delight found that it checked to the nearest five degrees with the bearing I had shot from the lower end of Holmes Creek in 1931. My sketching of the main forks of Holmes Creek at that time on the basis of what I saw from the mouth was consistent with what we saw from above now, so we were sure it was Holmes Creek. Sure also we were that this was a feasible pass across one of the most difficult sections of the Brooks Range. My barometer showed the notch where we were standing to be only 3,650 feet high and the going along both Pyramid and Holmes creeks was possible for either summer foot travel or dog sledding.

We descended the 1,900 feet to camp in nine miles of glowing color. I don't know any colors so varied and brilliant as those of the arctic autumn. As a background were the greens—dark green of spruce, and lighter shades of sedge, Labrador tea, *Kalmia*, and *Dryas*. This green was interrupted everywhere over the hillsides, by the rich cream color of the various species of reindeer moss. The tops of the hills were primarily a bright red from the dwarf birch. Lower down a lurid scarlet appeared in many blotches marking rocky places where the roughened leaves of the Angowuk dominated the vegetation. At other spots purple blueberry leaves gave the tint to the coloration. The valley bottoms displayed brightest gold of cottonwood and willow.

The water in Pyramid Creek had risen so much during the day that we had a hard time returning across it. Once on the camp side, we stopped among dense cranberry clumps to pick our fruit supply for the next three days. When we got to the slough next to camp the water was too high to be forded. I had visions for a moment of repeating Ed Marsan's experience many years ago on Nahtuk Creek. He had returned to camp from a hunt to find the water so high that he could not get across. So for three days his partners had to feed him by slinging hot cakes across the creek. Fortunately we were saved from this when Harvey dropped a spruce across the slough and we walked safely and dry back to camp.

Jesse shortly served us a sumptuous supper of pea soup, sheep pot roast, hotcakes, boiled apples, and coffee. We were ready for retiring comfortably to our sleeping bags, but the water in the river to the west and the slough to the east kept rising. Soon it began to trickle into our fireplace, so we moved the fire to higher ground, 30 feet away. We dug drainage ditches with a wooden shovel we had made to dig holes for the cache posts, but the water continued to rise. It was now too dark to move camp without great inconvenience. The tents, on the very highest ground between the river and slough, were still on dry land, so we decided to sleep in shifts. Ernie and I retired at eleven with our boots on. Harvey and Jesse went to bed at one in the morning. Soon water began to trickle under the tent where they were sleeping, but we did not wake them, because they were well off the ground on boughs and it wasn't light enough yet to move camp.

Shortly after three, however, it was light enough and we rolled them out. We dropped downstream about two hundred yards to a place where the ground was a little lower but where the surrounding river and slough dropped even more, so we had two feet to spare, which we felt was ample for any additional flood with the water already so high. We spent most of the remainder of the day catching up on the sleep we had missed the night before, and walking out to the edge of the river to watch the flood.

Next morning the water in the river was higher than ever. It was still raining steadily. We walked up to the point where the slough divided from the river and marveled at the colossal power of a river in flood. It was a wildly heaving, swaying, booming mass of brown, tumbling water which carried everything before it. Cottonwood trees, full of golden leaves, came churning down; clumps of willow with large sods still adhering to their roots were turned over and over by the flood and came by us as somersaulting islands; whole spruce trees, 60 feet long, went crunching by. Just above us was a point with spruce trees which I had bored a few days before and had found to be two hundred years old. We watched the power of the river beating full blast against the point where they stood, while tree after tree slowly settled from the vertical to the horizontal as the dirt was torn from around their roots until they tumbled into the water with a splash louder than the roaring torrent.

"What would a man do if he fell into a current like that?" I asked Ernie.

"He couldn't survive thirty seconds in that ice water," my companion replied.

"But if you actually found yourself in it you'd want to fight like hell to the very end. What could you do that would be most helpful?"

"Keep your head above water, float with the current, and save your strength to work yourself out on whichever side you can."

When we were not watching the flood we read from our itinerant library. Toward noon I suggested to Harvey that he walk up again with me to the point where river and slough met, to see what the main river was doing. We found that it had broken through a barrier of driftwood and was cutting a new channel headed straight for camp. Jesse whom we met on the way back told us the water had almost reached the fire and we had better hurry if we wanted any lunch.

After a hasty meal we decided to pack up, desert the country around our cache completely and move to some bluffs half a mile to the south and forty feet above the river. We could not cross either the river or slough on foot so we pulled our boat right through the spruce forest to our cache. It had been five feet above the river when we built it, but now the water was two feet high on the poles. Our first camp was more than knee deep in water. We loaded from the cache everything we wanted to take along and then floated the boat among the spruce trees to our latest camp where we loaded the rest of the equipment. Then we let the boat down the slough, Jesse and I knee-deep in water on the bank playing out hundred feet of mountaineering rope at a time, then retying the boat by a shorter rope to bushes until we could get ready for another hundred-foot descent on the main rope. Meanwhile Ernie and Harvey were in the boat, checking its descent by poles.

When after crossing the slough we finally reached the bluffs and pitched camp on top we knew we were safe against any flood short of the one in Eskimo mythical times when the world was covered with water and the Eskimos had to take to their boats until land was finally brought back through the intervention of Toolawak the crow. Apparently some modern crow got busy during the night, because the water had dropped at least a foot by morning. The weather was still impossible for mountain climbing—the clouds hung cold and gray, less than 2,000 feet above the valley floor. We had set this as the last possible day we could wait for the weather to clear for the ascent of Doonerak. If it were still cloudy this morning we had planned to take the boat down the river. However, the water was still so high and turbulent that this was impossible. Consequently, we decided to spend the day looking for a glacier which Ernie told us he had seen ten years before while hunting in one of the numerous deep canyons emerging from the north side of Doonerak. He described the glacier as larger than the one we had explored at the head of the Anaktuvuk.

But we did not find it. There was a glacier higher up on the side of Doonerak and perhaps half a mile across, but Ernie insisted that was not the one. However, the canyons were glorious—deep limestone gorges surrounded by high limestone precipices, full of pinnacles, with tumbling water everywhere. The last one we explored had a fall which took one straight leap of three hundred feet. On the way I bored a windswept black spruce, growing on a swampy hillside, which was 6½ feet high, 3 inches in diameter, and 346 years old. Less than two air-line miles away, was a well-drained white-spruce flat which I had studied eight years before and found to contain a stand 160 years old, with sixty trees between 10 and 15 inches in diameter to the acre!

Just before we reached the last gorge, a furious blizzard struck us from the north, although it was only September 2. The driving snow hurt as it stung against our cheeks and necks. But it only lasted half an hour and was followed to our delight by the most cloudless blue sky of the trip! All mountains stood out in sharpest relief. We saw the crest of Doonerak for the third time in more than two weeks. Even though it was past our zero hour for the ascent, we decided to set out next day up Pyramid Creek to the campsite among the willows which Ernie and I had selected two weeks before as a starting point for the climb. Yet we knew that the weather, perfect as it seemed, might play us false.

It did. Next morning the blue sky was gone and the wind had shifted to the south where another storm was brewing. It had snowed on the mountains during the night and the snowline was within five hundred feet of the valley floor. Doonerak was hopeless for this year. It was time to get out.

We decided to make an easy day of it and just descend four miles down the North Fork to the mouth of Fish Creek. Here we planned to spend a day exploring the north branch of that creek which rose in never-visited igneous mountains. We knew the river was still too high for boating, but the channel which ran among gravel bars, we thought safe as far as Fish Creek.

It was snowing hard when we loaded the boat. With Ernie steering in the stern, we started down at six times the painful speed at which we had dragged the boat upstream two and a half weeks before. Several times we had to jump out and drag the boat over riffles, but otherwise the journey was peaceful. Just above Fish Creek we found that the channel had shifted 2,000 feet from the western to the eastern edge of the valley during the flood. Ernie remarked that we might as well land and make camp at the first good timber.

Then it happened.

All at once we saw that what had appeared to be an innocuous gravel bank, about 40 feet high and no different from hundreds of others along the side of the river, was not along the side of the river at all but overhanging it. The tremendous floods which had changed the course of the river by 2,000 feet pounded with full, gigantic power against the gravel bank. The force of this terrific impact had washed away the gravel from the floodline. The drop in water since the flood crest, had left a gravel bank about one foot above the river and overhanging it. The main current shot straight under this over-hang, and then turned and tore right *through* the gravel bank, tunneling underneath in a 30-foot-wide passage whose end we could not see.

All of this we observed just seconds before we hit, as we streaked along on a torrent racing at fifteen miles an hour. At that stage no human power could have thrown us out of the main current. Ernie did his best, but he was helpless. Two seconds before the crash I wondered what would happen when we hit. Then I found out.

There was a frightful crunching of shattered wood as the boat passed under the overhanging bank. All at once I was deep under icy water where no light penetrated. Immediately I felt the overwhelming certainty of death. There was no reasoning in it and there was no fear, but there was no doubt either. "A man couldn't survive thirty seconds in that ice water," Ernie had said. A tunnel in the heart of the earth with perhaps no large enough exit, a chance of having your head battered against some low point in the ceiling, a fifteen-mile-an-hour current sweeping you helplessly on, rubber boots filled with many pounds of water, icy darkness . . . I didn't "think" these things, but they must have conditioned my sense of imminent death.

But other things were coursing through my mind simultaneously. They weren't thoughts that followed each other or could be listed in order. They were there all at once.

In a very practical way I was hearing again Ernie's words of two days before: "Keep your head above the water, float with the current, and save your strength to work yourself out on whichever side you can."

In a most objective way I was feeling: "What an awfully easy way to die. Hold my breath for forty, fifty, maybe sixty seconds, trapped in this tunnel, hold it till I am ready to burst, then have to let it out, and it's all over."

There was one other thought I had very strongly, but I am almost ashamed to mention it, because it sounds so full of sweetness and light. I was also saying to myself: "I wish I had time to think over all the fine experiences of my thirty-seven years before dying—to have the satisfaction of recalling them just once more before I kick off."

Suddenly through my closed eyelids the encompassing blackness changed to bright light. I opened my eyes and saw instantly that I was out of the tunnel, on the left edge of the main current. I let it carry me along and saved my strength to push toward its outer edge. I worked my way to an uprooted spruce tree caught on the bottom. Beyond it the water was slack and I waded easily to shore. The tunnel, I now realized, had short-circuited a bend in the river.

I was safe, but I feared my three companions were drowned. I looked around. Ernie Johnson was just floating by, clinging to the upturned boat. A moment later he climbed on top of it. Directly opposite me, toward the other side of the river, Jesse Allen and Kenneth Harvey were being battered by the fierce current. Harvey would occasionally touch bottom with his feet, but the current would turn him over in a backward somersault. Jesse was being rolled over and over horizontally, like a barrel. Each time they would almost get control of their feet, only to be knocked down again. It was awful just to stand and look helplessly on. Finally, the current threw them both on a pile of driftwood where they managed to check themselves and gain their feet. They stood there, surrounded by water, almost exhausted, and shivering. I was afraid they might be too tired or numb to make land, but in a short time Jesse managed to stagger across to the opposite shore and to help Harvey over.

I looked down the river toward Ernie and saw the boat had grounded a hundred yards below me on a gravel bar on my side of the river. Ernie was pulling it up as far as he could to prevent it from floating away. I started to run down to help him, but my boots were so full of water, it was like lifting a ton at each step. By the time I had taken them off and emptied them, Ernie was coming up the bar. He yelled something across the river to Jesse, which I could not understand.

"How will they get across?" I asked.

"We'll forget that for the present," he said. "We've got to get a fire going as quick as possible. Jesse is going to do the same. We've got to hurry."

Then I noticed for the first time that it was still snowing, that the thermometer was around freezing, and that I was shivering furiously. We ran up on the side hill above the river till we came to a dead birch—a lucky break because birch makes particularly good kindling. Quickly Ernie ripped off a piece of bark and struck a dry match from his waterproof match case. But his hands were shaking and he couldn't get the match and the bark near each other, and the match went out. He struck another and I grabbed the bark and held it against the tiny flame. In a moment it was ablaze and then it was simple to heap on dead spruce twigs and later dead spruce limbs. Soon the fire was safely burning, not to go out until we could leave this spot nearly twenty-four hours later. Jesse and Harvey got their fire going at about the same time. It was not until the next day, when we were rehashing the experience, that I realized what Ernie and Jesse knew, that if we had not started the fires promptly we might have perished from exposure in this freezing weather.

But here we were, safe and sound, the four of us peeling off and wringing out our soaking clothes by two good fires on opposite sides of an unfordable river. We were seventy-five miles from the nearest neighbors or assistance, with a shattered boat and, so far as we knew, not another possession in the world—food, bedding, tents all gone.

"If only an ax and a gun might have gotten stuck in the boat, we could live in luxury off the country," Ernie said. "I've got a fishline in my pocket and Jesse probably has, and we can walk back to Wiseman in three days and not suffer, even if we haven't any food, but an ax and a gun would be nice."

After about an hour we were fairly well dried out and warmed up, so Ernie and I started down to the boat to see if anything could be salvaged. I have never been a dog enthusiast, but it gave me a warm feeling, to see our dogs sitting on top of the shipwreck, waiting patiently for their friends to return. We always kept them chained to the side of the boat when we were traveling on the river, and when the boat tipped the dogs had been dragged underneath it until it had run aground. An air pocket between the water and the boat must have kept them from drowning. After making the boat fast, Ernie had unchained the dogs and they had climbed on top of the boat and waited.

We reached under the boat and found that some of our possessions had neither sunk when it tipped nor floated away when it drifted down the river. The difficulty about salvaging them was that the stern of the boat was yet in two feet of very swift water, and if we tried to turn it right side up everything underneath would float away before we could grab it. Consequently, Ernie lifted the boat just enough for a few things to float out while I, standing downstream, would make a dive for a butter can or a sack of beans or the small tent or a box with shoepacs as it came floating along. By this procedure we managed to save almost everything we needed from what was imprisoned under the boat.

The prospect for the return journey now looked brighter. We found ourselves supplied with about five pounds of once-dried peas, three pounds of beans, five pounds of rice, ten pounds of flour, two pounds of saturated sugar, three pounds of salt, four pounds of butter, two pounds of coffee, two cans of dried eggs, and what had been fifteen but was now probably fifty pounds of rolled oats. This may not have been a balanced diet, but it was more than ample to get home. We cooked the oats for the dogs before leaving.

Aside from food, we saved only Jesse's and Harvey's shoepacs, everybody's extra socks and shirts, except my own, a couple of sewing kits, all films and movie magazines, which were seriously soaked,

Harvey's still camera and my movie camera (which was in my large shirt pocket at the time of the upset), all three six-shooters and the ammunition for them, two fishlines, our small open tent, a piece of canvas, my field notes, Jesse's and Harvey's packboards, four waterproof bags, and, most important, fifty-five dry matches among our four match cases.

Among the more important things we had lost were all our bedding, the larger tent, all axes, Harvey's rifle and Ernie's .22 Special, Ernie's and my still cameras, all cooking utensils and dishes, my two packsacks, and the dog packs. Also all books and a barometer.

To a Nansen living two years on the ice, a Stefansson subsisting in luxury off the Arctic with almost nothing but a rifle and his own skill, to an Ellsworth wandering for months across Antarctica with almost nothing saved from a plane wreck, it would mean nothing to be left with all of this equipment in a fish- and game-filled country, only seventy-five miles from people. To me, spoiled as I was by civilization, it seemed adventuresome.

We shouted across the river to Jesse and Harvey. They wanted to wait until morning before trying to cross to our side, which was the one from which to start for Wiseman. Ernie thought he could patch up the boat enough to ferry them over. A reconnaissance confirmed that the river was unfordable at this stage of water. Jesse and Harvey had half a bar of chocolate which Jesse had in his pocket. Ernie and I, of course, had lots of food. We spent the six hours of darkness in comfort by roaring fires on opposite sides of the river.

Shortly after daylight Ernie and I started to work on the boat. It had a crack ten feet long and one-fourth of an inch wide on the side where the boat had struck the bank, and the bow was all stove in. However, with caulking cotton and some boards and nails from a box which we had saved, Ernie the carpenter deftly fixed the boat soon to leak only slowly. Then he cut an eight-foot pole from a spruce tree by pocket knife and shoved off. In less than five minutes we were all reunited on the east side of the river.

We spent most of this day finishing the process of drying out equipment, making new packsacks and dog packs out of the waterproof bags and the canvas, fashioning two pots and a griddle out of various cans, and sorting out the soaked films to see which looked like being worth backpacking on the slim chance of development.

We decided that the shortest and easiest route back to Wiseman would be over the new pass between Pyramid and Holmes creeks which Ernie and I had discovered a few days before, then down the unknown stretch of Holmes Creek, across the low pass beneath

Chimney Mountain from Clear River into Glacier River, which Ernie
and I found in 1931, then down Glacier River, and finally across
the hills to Nolan. We moved camp that afternoon four miles back
up the North Fork to Pyramid Creek. Here we found lots of dry
spruce trees which we uprooted and carried whole to the fire without benefit of an ax. Harvey and I walked out to the cache to get
some more sugar, a little tea, and a few dried peaches. The water
had dropped five feet, but our old campgrounds were covered with
up to eighteen inches of silt from this one flood. We made the
seventy-five miles from Pyramid Creek to Wiseman easily in three
days. We traveled every day from about seven in the morning until
six in the evening, with two generous hours out for lunch. Generally,
the going was good, although not as easy as on a trail. There were
four hard miles of uphill work across soft moss and through brush-
filled gullies to the first forks of Pyramid Creek; a climb of 2,000
feet to Holmes Pass; sedge tussocks from the mouth of Holmes Creek
to Chimney Pass and for a couple of miles just before we left Glacier
River; and plenty of highly adhesive mud deposited by the recent
flood all the way down Glacier River. These, however, were small
matters.

Our packs of course were light, ranging from 10 to 25 pounds. For
Ernie and me the only real trouble was our footgear, for we had lost
our shoes and had nothing but heavy rubber boots which reached
to the hips. For myself, an advocate of light footwear, this was a
nuisance. However, when fording the high creeks Ernie and I had
a big advantage and we would carry Jesse and Harvey across on
our shoulders to keep their feet dry.

Each night we set up our small tent with the open side toward the
fire, four or five feet away. After the fire had been started with spruce
twigs and willows, we got our fuel by pulling dead spruce trees up
by the roots. The roots gave out the most heat. The first two nights
we let the fire burn down until someone felt cold enough to put on
more wood. As a result we all felt cold half the night. The last night
we divided into one-hour watches during which one of us would
sit up and keep the fire burning all the time. By this method we
were comfortable all night, except when I got overambitious toward
the close of one of my watches and nearly drove everyone out of
the tent by excessive heat.

Under Jesse's skillful handling of peas, beans, rice, and the impro-
vised hotcake griddle, our meals were delicious. We ate out of coffee
and butter cans with our fingers and with spoons which we whittled

from alder. Harvey shot three ptarmigan, but aside from that we did not take time to live off the country.

Our trip down Holmes Creek was a real elation. From the pass to which Ernie and I had first climbed the week before, to the mouth at Clear River by which Ernie and I had mushed seven and a half years earlier, no white man had probably traveled.

Holmes Creek emptied into the lower end of the upper Clear River valley. When Ernie and I spent four days there in the winter of 1931 I thought this Yosemite-like valley with its sensational ten side canyons the most beautiful place I had ever seen. Seeing the valley now in autumn, I had the feeling of meeting the son of an old friend whom I had not seen for years. There was a strong resemblance, and yet it was a different person. Whether I preferred the valley in winter or autumn I could not fairly say, because the weather was not clear enough now, and there was no time for exploration.

The jaunt down Glacier River, almost from its source, was made enjoyable by the fresh autumn colors—the bright cream of reindeer moss, the reds and scarlets of dwarf birch and Angowuk all over the hillsides, and the glowing gold of cottonwood leaves. The willows, however, had lost their leaves, though it was only early September.

The last day we saw more and more signs of civilization—cut stumps and old camping spots littered with tin cans. We ate lunch on Yankee Creek, in a log cabin which, we discovered, old George Eaton had left just the day before. There, for the first time in many days, we prepared a meal on a stove. Ernie and Harvey, who had used up their last tobacco that morning, kept assuring me that they could go indefinitely without tobacco, all the while they were hopefully rummaging through old cans, under George's bed, and among dark corners, for some he might have left. When we saw him in town he told us he had come back only because he had run out of tobacco.

A 700-foot climb took us over our last divide at Snowshoe Pass. Thereafter we walked four miles downhill along wood roads to Nolan Creek. When we stepped up to Jack White's boiler house on the creek and were greeted by Verne Watts who was running the hoist, it was just four weeks since we had seen our last human being.

We hung around Nolan Creek until after supper, chatting with friends. We heard the news of the four weeks since we had left the world—Albert Ness having both legs broken; all of Europe mobilizing; the worst rain and floods since white men had come to live permanently in the upper Koyukuk in 1899. About Albert we were sorry; about Europe we still felt remote; about the rain and floods, we were quite satisfied. If our ascent of Doonerak was blocked and our boat wrecked, we comforted ourselves, it was only by the worst weather and the worst high water in the memory of the oldest inhabitants.

The six miles to Wiseman we walked after dark. We found that two landslides had blotted out the road for a couple of hundred feet each. In town we learned that innocuous little Wiseman Creek had broken over its banks and washed out half the gardens in town. The bridge was gone and the creek unfordable, so Wiseman was two separate cities for the night.

When, an hour later, we lay down on soft beds inside dry and well-heated cabins, the trip was indeed over. We had failed in our major objective—climbing the Arctic's highest peak. We had had twenty-seven days of rain in twenty-nine. We had lost our boat, much of our equipment, and—as turned out later—part of our pictures; fortunately not all were ruined. Nevertheless, we had explored the upper reaches of the Anaktuvuk; and, for purely a good time, it would be hard to beat our four weeks' adventure in unexplored wilderness.

7 North Doonerak, Amawk, Alhamblar, and Apoon

IN JUNE, 1939, NINE MONTHS AFTER OUR UNSUCCESSFUL ATtempt to climb Mount Doonerak, I was fortunate enough to be able to return, for the fourth time, to Alaska. I could not resist the lure of unconquered Doonerak.

As the plane circled the Wiseman landing field it was exciting to recognize each cabin, to observe which of the women had their laundry on the line, to pick out the individual Eskimo children running to the field. We landed at one o'clock in the afternoon on what should have been the longest day of the year, except that for all practical purposes every day for three months was equally long, with twenty-four hours of daylight.

As soon as the welcomes were over and my baggage carried the quarter mile to the roadhouse, Jesse Allen and I retired to his cabin to discuss plans for our next trip. (See map, page 143.) Our foremost objective would be Mount Doonerak. We decided on five days hard back packing overland for another attempt at a first ascent. Afterward we would explore the unknown Arctic Divide at the heads of the North Fork of the Koyukuk and the Hammond River. We would be out for twenty-four days.

We had planned the autumn before, when the previous expedition was not yet completed, that Jesse Allen, Kenneth Harvey, and I would be partners in another attempt at Doonerak. Ernie Johnson was busy with mining and could not come. In his place, Nutirwik, a Kobuk Eskimo, who had the reputation of being the best hunter in the Koyukuk, joined us. Unlike most other Eskimos in the region, he lived alone. This small man—he was scarcely more than five feet tall—with his thin face, high cheekbones, and little gnarled hands more than held his own with his sturdier-looking companions. His prominent eyebrows were in sharp contrast with his thin eyes. He had a strong, sensitive face and remarkably few wrinkles for a man close to sixty who had lived out of doors all his life. His name literally means blizzard. When he came to live among the whites about 1903 he changed it to Harry Snowden, but we continued to use his Eskimo name on these wilderness adventures. He brought with him his dogs, Coffee and White-eye, while Harvey brought his dog, Moose; they aided materially in dispersing the load.

This load consisted of 285 pounds, of which approximately one-third was photographic and scientific equipment, which would not get lighter; one-third tent, bedding, dishes, packsacks, rifle, ammunition, ax, extra socks and shoes, first aid material, and the like, which likewise would not diminish; and only one-third food, which would gradually decrease until we obtained fresh meat. A few weeks before my arrival, Jesse had packed out staples to a cache on upper Hammond River.

Most of Wiseman was at the roadhouse when we hoisted our packs to our shoulders on the evening of June 23. Harvey, Nutirwik, and I each carried about 55 pounds; one-armed Jesse, who was sixty years old, took 40 pounds; and the three dogs who were soft from months of inaction, 25–30 pounds each. But if dogs get soft from just sitting around and getting fed, so does a bureaucrat, and it was pleasant that for our first day's journey we were taking only the six-mile climb on the road to Nolan Creek. Pleasant also was the chatter of Verne Watts who accompanied us from town with a pack of his own. Pointing to Harvey's advancing baldness, he said: "You'll have to tie a string around your head pretty soon to tell how high to wash your face in the morning." But most pleasant of all was a cold rain

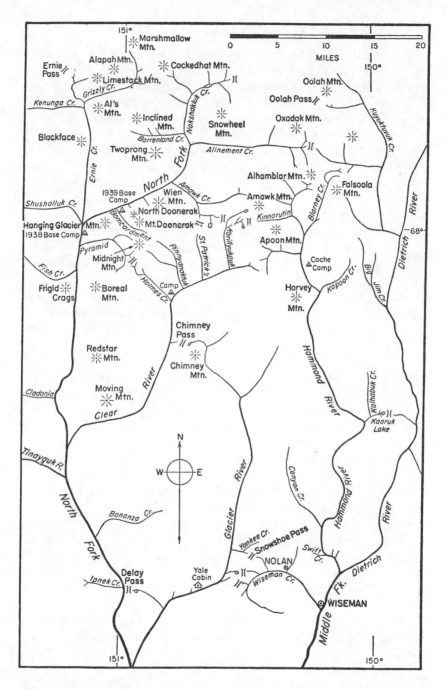

THE NORTH FORK OF THE KOYUKUK AND THE HAMMOND RIVER

which struck us fiercely for a few minutes when we were halfway to Nolan; it put an end to the heat of the evening and to the mosquitoes which had been swarming in great masses around us.

At Nolan Creek we scattered to the cabins of different genial hosts who had invited us to spend the night. I went for nine hours of luxurious sleep to the cabin of George Eaton, now seventy-eight, with whom I had stopped in 1929, 1930, and 1931. Then, although about 70, he had still been a powerful man, boasting that he could outshovel any man in the Koyukuk, and apparently expecting to be active until he was a hundred years old. Now he was old and unhappy in the realization that active life was over, but still unbroken. He said: "It's terrible to me, Bob, to think my legs is so bad I can't go on a trip like you fellows is going on, but it doesn't bother me a bit that I'm going to die some day soon. I've got to go, and I don't know when, and I'm glad I don't."

We spent the sunny next day on Nolan Creek while I went up and down the valley, chatting with old friends. Almost every one on the creek dropped in afterward to say good-bye as we headed out at eight in the evening.

We planned to travel during the night hours in these days of twenty-four hour daylight, because the temperature was cooler then and the mosquitoes a little less thick. But on the steep ascent to Snowshoe Pass perspiration and mosquitoes were both profuse until the low sun was temporarily hidden behind the mountainside we were climbing. When we crossed the height of land at ten in the evening we stepped back into the sunlight. Just to the right of the sun, forty miles to the north, black and massive and immense, was old Mount Doonerak, looking utterly unscalable from this angle. But we were not discouraged, knowing a mountain has many angles.

Besides, a person could not be discouraged with bright evening sunshine making flowers and moss fairly glow all around. There was the yellow green of sphagnum, the creamy yellow of reindeer moss, the pure gold of Arctic cinquefoil and poppy, the rich purple of lupine, and the white, cottony tassels of millions of sedge plants waving everywhere.

But these white tassels, for all their beauty, were flags of warning to tell us they waved over sedge tussocks. We avoided them wherever we possibly could as we lugged our packs over the side hills of Glacier River. We made travel as easy as possible by resting at fifty-minute intervals for ten minutes and by stopping for over an hour in the middle of the journey to eat a midnight supper of canned ham and tea. At four o'clock in the morning we made camp near the remains of an old igloo built many years before by arctic Eskimos, over here for a hunt.

Camp consisted of a 10 by 11 foot rectangular canvas, sloping back-ward from a horizontal front ridgepole, held taut by other poles and ropes, and covering a patch of level ground where we laid spruce boughs. On the boughs we spread our sleeping bags. There was also ample space under the fly to place supplies we wanted to keep dry. Directly in front of the fly we built a fire of dry spruce and cottonwood. After a supper of macaroni and cheese, canned ham, bread and butter, and green tea, we retired for the "night" at the odd hour of seven in the morning and did not stir until four in the afternoon.

With this upside-down schedule the evening meal became breakfast, hence we had oatmeal, bacon, and coffee. It was shortly before eight when we started again. We followed the right bank of Glacier River for mile after mile of slow, plodding travel. It is hard to describe how slow and plodding it really seems when you are out of practice and there is no trail and you have a 55-pound pack tugging on your head-strap and shoulders. You have hardly gone five minutes when the muscles in your neck are so sore that you know every step for the next six or seven hours will be pain. You throw off the headstrap to rest the neck and the pack pulls so violently on your shoulders you imagine it is turning them inside out. You go back to the headstrap again, push-ing against it for all you are worth, perspiring freely in spite of the hour of evening, swatting at fifty mosquitoes which have lighted on your forehead and your cheeks and your neck, letting down your black mosquito net which instantly makes the whole world dark, pulling it up again when you almost stifle in the sultry evening, noticing sud-denly that your ankle is sore where the boot has rubbed off the skin, stumbling over sedge tussocks, forcing your way through thick willow brush, sliding along on uncertain side hills ankle deep with sphagnum moss, neck aching, shoulders aching, ankle aching, on, on, on.

But surprising things happen in the midst of such travel. Unex-pectedly you notice a clump of lovely *Pyrola* you almost stepped on, with round, shiny leaves and with stalks topped by almost bell-shaped five-petaled white flowers. Now, under a clump of spruce, you discover those gayest of white flowers, the *Dryas*, fairly sparkling with their eight bright petals set off against the light green of the sphagnum moss. Now your attention is drawn to fresh sheep or moose or bear tracks on the mud of the river bar or, on occasion, to tracks of wolves travel-ing together.

Then, as you get into the swing of it, the pack seems to bother less the farther you go. You no longer look at your watch every ten minutes to see how soon the end of the fifty-minute shift will come. You enjoy more and more the freshness and the freedom from trails and human signs in this remote country, and you realize that one incentive for setting out to climb Mount Doonerak is the satisfaction in conquering the seventy-five miles of back packing across untamed country, which is necessary to reach its base.

Around eleven at theoretical night it started to rain steadily, though not hard. This did not deter us from thirty-eight hearty back slaps at midnight as Harvey moved into his thirty-eighth birthday. A short time later, as we were starting up after midnight supper, something in Moose's swagger seemed to irritate White-eye, who was still virtually a stranger to him, and amid frightful snarls we had the one and only dog fight of our expedition.

We pitched camp at three in the morning directly under the great limestone tower of Chimney Mountain. It rose sheer on three sides for three to four-hundred feet, but on the fourth it sloped at an angle that could be climbed. The chimney was perched on top of a 1,500-foot mountain, and it was a stirring feeling to be camped directly underneath it. Weird and amazing, too, when I woke after hours of unbroken slumber, expecting to see the familiar alley back of an old stable converted into a garage which had greeted my eyes upon awaking all of a Washington winter, to find this wild chimney overhanging me. It took a while to connect with reality and convince myself that I was not dreaming.

The next night we traveled across the low pass between Glacier and Clear rivers with no adventures, but with the pleasing sight of a moose feeding along the marshy edge of a small lake in the middle of the pass. We made what proved to be an exceptionally comfortable three-day camp in the willows at the junction of Holmes Creek and Clear River.

Next evening it was overcast, but the clouds were high, so Harvey and I decided to seek out the never-visited source of Pinnyanaktuk Creek, one of ten large creeks flowing into that super-Yosemite of the North, the eight-mile glacial valley of upper Clear River. On the winter trip of March, 1931, I had named this creek with the Eskimo word meaning "superlatively rugged." Looking up into it was like looking into a great basin which instead of being hollow, was filled with sharply pointed peaks packed together closely.

We pushed our way across two and a half miles of sedge tussocks and soft moss and Labrador tea in full white blossom, to the point where Pinnyanaktuk flows into Clear River at the foot of the mountains. Within the first three miles of its boulder-filled course, two large forks plunged in from the right, and the view up each revealed many unknown crags. Shortly after passing the second fork, Harvey spied four sheep on the hillside to the left. As we needed fresh meat badly, he decided to go after them.

Meanwhile I continued up the valley. The main Pinnyanaktuk climbed rapidly, sometimes cutting through steep dirt banks, sometimes splashing over bedrock, often tearing its way through yet unmelted snowbanks. The bluish white of the anemone profusely speckled the sphagnum. Wherever I looked was the deep purple of phlox and shooting star. The heather was thick; its delicate white bells were lovely and filled the atmosphere with a delightful scent. The creek roaring in the rocky gorge below made stirring music, and every sense seemed satisfied except the sense of touch, which to my unpleasant surprise was just as much abused by mosquitoes above 3,000 feet, with the ground all excellently drained, as it had been in the boggy lowlands.

When I reached a bench along the uppermost forks of Pinnyanaktuk I could see the final divide between Clear River and North Fork less than two miles away. Shortly before, I had heard a shot echoing in the steep valley and felt confident that Harvey had got his sheep. Although it was midnight, I snapped several pictures. In the middle of this occupation I was startled by small rocks bounding down the hillside above me. I looked up in time to see four sheep beating a retreat across the slide rock.

When I rejoined Harvey he had a fine 90-pound ram. We cut him up and divided the load among ourselves and Moose. At the mouth of Pinnyanaktuk we left the meat on a gravel bar, and hiked briskly along the river bottom five miles up to the source branches of Clear River valley. The clouds had all vanished during the night and the air was crisp and clear. We enjoyed exciting views up St. Patrick's Creek (which runs parallel to Pinnyanaktuk) on our side of the Clear River and up a couple of deep, nameless creeks on the other. On the return journey the sun over the mountains kept lighting more and more of the valley and the great precipice walls which bounded it.

Back at the mouth of Pinnyanaktuk we picked up the sheep and strode into camp among the willows of the Holmes Creek–Clear River junction at four in the morning. Jesse and Nutirwik had caught a nice mess of grayling, so we were now plentifully supplied. That morning we enjoyed the first sheep meal, which as usual consisted of those choice morsels, heart, tongue, and liver.

When I awoke at two in the afternoon the sun was still shining so brightly that I rushed up on the hill back of camp to photograph everything in sight. The whole gay valley seemed to be white and green with millions of flowers and plants. Not the white and green of lifeless paintings, but living, vivid colors sparkling from miles of hillside in the crystal-clear atmosphere. So they had sparkled for many millenniums since the last ice sheet receded, without any purpose of being looked upon by man, but as just a part of great objective nature.

The fresh sheep plus my journey to upper Pinnyanaktuk Creek somewhat changed our plans. I got the notion that instead of reconnoitering Mount Doonerak from the mountains of upper Pyramid Creek, as we had originally planned, we could climb the wall at the head of Pinnyanaktuk Creek and see the south side of Mount Doonerak just as well from there. At the same time we could eat another day's worth of meat and thereby save packing that much extra load over Holmes Pass.

So Harvey and I set out again for Pinnyanaktuk Creek. The first miles to the upper forks were a repetition of the previous night's gay blossoms and jagged pinnacles. Above the upper forks we climbed over slide rock and snowbanks to the very source of Pinnyanaktuk, and then by easy grade to the 5,000-foot divide.

There, just ahead of us, was the great black bulk of Mount Doonerak, rising gigantically into the sky, directly in front of the sun. To our left was one of the steep mountains at the head of Pinnyanaktuk, and this peak we decided to climb in order to get a better picture of the lay of the land. The best possible picture was certainly needed, because the land, as seen from the top, did not look as we expected. We at first had thought that the deep creek behind which Mount Doonerak rose was Pyramid Creek; then, after checking the known topography, we realized this could not be right. Suddenly I discovered that Bombardment Creek, which we always supposed had its source only a few miles south of the North Fork (on the north side of Doonerak and Hanging Glacier Mountain), actually cut a deep gorge between the two peaks. Pyramid came nowhere near Mount Doonerak, and the fog-covered mountain at its head which Ernie and I had assumed was Mount Doonerak the previous summer, in reality was part of Hanging Glacier Mountain. Worst of all, while that mountain could be climbed from the south side, just as we reported, Mount Doonerak's south side was almost sheer for 6,000 feet and appeared utterly unscalable. The only possibility in the half of its circumference which we could see was a very steep ridge running toward lower Bombardment Creek. Even this possibility seemed highly remote, but at least we knew that Bombardment Creek and not Pyramid Creek, as we had thought, was the best site for our first base camp.

We spent more than an hour, equally distributed around midnight, on the summit, and called our peak Midnight Mountain. As if to celebrate the christening, at exactly midnight the sun suddenly illuminated the finger of Chimney Mountain, jutting into the sky a dozen miles southward. Twenty minutes after midnight the sun shot out from behind Mount Doonerak. Even the sun, however, did not make us warm and we had to pound each other frequently to stop shivering. Yet we savored the intimate view of hundreds of nearby, never-scaled pinnacles, blackly puncturing the midnight arctic sky.

Next evening we broke our comfortable three-day camp at the Holmes Creek junction and started the long uphill drag toward Holmes Pass, eight and a half miles to the northwest and 1,300 feet above us. First we stumbled over sedge tussock- and moss-covered hillsides for a couple of hours, scrambling through the dense brush of the dwarf birch, pushing for all we were worth against headstraps as we gained steep grades. A heavy rainstorm broke shortly after we started and soon had us soaked to the skin. We stopped for a lunch of tea and cold mutton chops at the last dry willows big enough to make a fire. Then we splashed along up Holmes Creek, sometimes on gravel bars, sometimes through willow brush, often right through the water. At one place the creek narrowed into a canyon not more than ten feet wide and half barricaded by a huge wall of yet unmelted ice. In order to get around this we had to climb a steep bank for several hundred feet and then descend again into the creek.

We reached the broad pass just before midnight. It was completely barren of woody growth, but profusely covered by many-colored flowers and the lovely greens and yellows of mosses and lichens. To the west, was the familiar North Fork.

The steep descent into Pyramid Creek was almost as hard as the ascent to Holmes Pass had been. We had to be constantly on edge to keep from falling in as we stepped over the water-splashed boulders. Lower down, the creek became too deep to be forded comfortably, so we took to the side-hill moss. This was slippery, but not hard going except at half a dozen steep, brushy gulches. At one place the brush tore into the breeching on the pack of White-eye, and we had to repair it on the hillside.

It was nearly four in the morning when we made camp in ankle-deep sphagnum moss under a thrifty young spruce stand near the mouth of Pyramid Creek. The scene of last autumn's shipwreck was only four miles to the south, but none of us had any inclination to visit it. We had, however, a great desire to sleep, and after a huge supper of pea soup, sheep steak, and boiled dried apples, we retired at seven-thirty in the morning for ten hours of slumber.

Another night's hard scrambling through thick brush and along soft, slippery, moss-covered hillsides, with 65-pound packs tearing at our neck and shoulder muscles, brought us the nine and a half miles to our destination at the junction of Bombardment Creek and the upper North Fork. Here we set up base camp for our assault on Mount Doonerak.

It was a lovely location on a spruce flat between the two streams. The sphagnum moss covered the ground in great, dry mats, fifteen inches thick, which beat a feather bed for softness. The early morning sun, rising upriver, gave a sparkling brightness to a 200-foot waterfall tumbling off the side of Hanging Glacier Mountain which loomed high over our camp.

When we awoke next evening, the bright sunlight had given way to an ominous sky. Just as we finished our oatmeal and mutton it started to rain hard. Nevertheless, we decided to spend an active night. Jesse and Nutirwik walked back eight miles to our cache of last year where we had left 44 pounds of food, and picked up some sugar, rice, butter, and dried apples. Harvey and I set out to explore the intriguing recesses of Bombardment Creek.

This little eight-mile creek had cut out a fabulous gorge between Hanging Glacier rising 4,000 feet above it to the west and Doonerak rising 6,000 feet directly to the east. Higher and higher, as we ascended the valley, the great rock crags of these two towering mountain masses rose. Loftier and loftier grew the sheer rock faces. At places waterfalls dropped over them, a hundred, two hundred, even three hundred feet high.

With mosquitoes swarming about us all the time, we picked a route just below the base of the precipices, on unstable slide-rock slopes, lying at too steep an angle for repose. Every now and then we would start small avalanches. After three and a half miles we came to a sharp turn in the valley beyond which, we decided, it was not safe to go, with the rain making the rock so slippery and with frequent slides starting from the mountainside above. Even while we were discussing the return a small rock from far up the mountainside went bounding over Harvey's head.

The downhill route over the sliderock was much easier than the ascent. We reached Bombardment Creek just below its plunge over a 125-foot wall. We followed up the narrow gorge, crawled under a massive icebank which overhung for ten feet, and stood in the spray at the base of the fall, which dropped through a narrow chute, rock on one side and ice pillar on the other. At one place the chute was not more than eighteen inches wide. The fall set up a strong breeze, which, together with the cold of the surrounding ice chased away the mosquitoes which had followed us all evening.

The two following nights were also stormy. Jesse and I spent the first in camp, while Harvey and Nutirwik went hunting—and came back empty-handed, because they would not shoot a ewe with a lamb. The second evening it rained only intermittently, so I decided to climb a gray foothill of Mount Doonerak about three miles west of camp, from which I would get a better view of the north side of the mountain and look directly down on what the autumn before had appeared to be a glacier. Harvey and Nutirwik went out after sheep again.

The sky cleared to the north and west, and I climbed 3,000 feet through a garden of bright flowers, keeping pace with the setting sun as shadows rose ever higher on the mountain. Growing luxuriantly were the many-blossomed white heads of bear cabbage (*Veratrum*), the gold of the arctic poppy and the buttercup, the sparkling white of *Dryas octopetala* nodding above its fernlike leaves, the deep purple clumps of phlox.

Now I could look directly over to the black pinnacle of Mount Doonerak, jutting almost straight up for 4,000 feet. It seemed utterly unscalable from this side. At the lower edge of this wall was the glacier indeed, darkened by centuries of tumbling rocks which had mingled with the ice. It was half a mile away and five hundred feet below me. There appeared to be no possible way of climbing to the glacier for measurements. I estimated it was 2,000 feet long and 800 feet wide, and the surface sloped at thirty degrees. The face must have been about 50 feet thick, and a large chunk had apparently broken off just a few days before, because it lay yet unmelted where it had tumbled into a hollow a thousand feet below.

At eleven-fifteen the sun finally dipped behind the mountains across the North Fork and I returned to Bombardment Creek camp. An hour later, Harvey, Nutirwik, and Moose trudged in under the load of a large sheep. Since we were all back in camp by one-thirty in the morning, we decided this would be a good time to change from night to day schedule, which would be better for climbing mountains.

In the later morning, after breakfast, our first job was to cut up the meat, set it on poles under willow shade, and protect it from flies by a mosquito tent. The sky was overcast, but the clouds were high and the top of Mount Doonerak clear, so we decided to make an attempt. Unfortunately we started up a ridge which ended in sheer limestone precipices only 3,000 feet above the valley. We were completely stopped for this day, but we could see that the next ridge to the south would permit us to rise higher, even though the summit now appeared impossible.

Next morning the sky was cloudlessly blue. Harvey, Nutirwik, and I set out at six-fifteen, Jesse remaining in camp as his one arm made steep rock work not feasible. We followed up the bench above Bombardment Creek for a mile and then started up a steep, green shoulder leading to the ridge we had, on the previous day, decided to follow. When we reached it we got a fine view into the upper gorge of Bombardment Creek where, to our amazement, we saw a half-mile-long lake which was still frozen on this July 5.[1] Below it, Bombardment Creek spilled over a waterfall, a hundred feet high.

As we followed the ridge on good footing we were suddenly face to face with Mount Doonerak. About half a mile away its northwesterly abutment rose straight up for 2,000 feet. Nowhere did we see a chance to scale it, and yet from a distance this had seemed the most feasible side. The only other remote possibility was some shoulder leading up from the northeast.

We continued climbing easily until we were nearly 6,000 feet high. Then we had precarious footing for a quarter of a mile over tumbling slide rocks toward the base of a rocky dome, a thousand feet high, to the north of Mount Doonerak itself, but sitting on the same massif. We called this dome North Doonerak and started to work our way up it in the hope that from there we would be able to see what the chances for a northeastern ascent of Doonerak might be. We proceeded with great caution, the rock being loose and crumbly.

We labored up almost vertical chimneys, crawled around the edges of great cliffs, took toe and finger holds and pulled ourselves up ledges. By slow degrees we worked higher until finally, five hours after leaving camp, we reached a knife-edge ridge which dropped precipitously on one side toward the North Fork and on the other toward Bombardment Creek. It was a short and easy climb on the crest of this ridge to the summit of North Doonerak. Here was a most comfortable little flat, about ten by six feet, covered with reindeer moss, *Dryas*, and heather. We sprawled out in comfort and leisure to enjoy mountains everywhere under the blue sky.

Dominating the scene, of course, was the great black face of old Doonerak, less than half a mile away and jutting straight up for nearly 2,000 feet. I did not believe that any climber, however expert, could make that face. The northeast shoulder which had been our one remaining hope, we could now see plainly. Some day, probably, people

[1] On June 30, 1952, George W. Beadle, Gunnar Bergman, and Alfred Tissieres, an American-Swedish-French team of scientists from the California Institute of Technology saw this lake from Midnight Mountain. When they returned from their trip, they recommended to the U.S. Geographic Board in Washington, D.C., that it be called Marshall Lake. The name was adopted by the board.

with years of rope-climbing experience will succeed in reaching the top by this route. We all knew that we never could.[2]

There were other superb views. Northward we looked over the black crests of Inclined Mountain and Blackface Mountain toward those lofty gray lime summits where the Anaktuvuk originates, including Marshmallow Mountain, which next to Mount Doonerak is probably the highest mountain in the Brooks Range. Directly west, across Bombardment Creek, was Hanging Glacier Mountain, a great black wall against the sun, considerably higher than our 7,250 feet. In the far west, in the hazy distance, we could see the dome of Nahtuk, shaped like an owl's head, lying sixty-five miles away between the Alatna and John rivers in country I had not looked into since 1931. In all the vast panorama we could see on this clear day there probably was not a human being outside our party.

Time on the mountaintop passed quickly. First we just sat and enjoyed the view while munching our lunch. After a while we began to discuss and identify dubious geographic features. Then Harvey and I took still and moving pictures, got compass shots on more than thirty points, and measured the vertical angle to most of them by means of a Brunton pocket transit. Meanwhile Nutirwik scanned the panorama with field glasses to pick out sheep. For three and a half hours we stayed on North Doonerak, this superb observation point of the Arctic, before we returned to camp.

AMAWK

Next morning it was raining intermittently. Having given up Mount Doonerak, this was all right with us, because we had only a short day in mind, to pack six miles to the junction of Amawk Creek and the upper North Fork. The footing was relatively good, there was little climbing, and the journey consequently was easy, although our packs, owing to the large amount of fresh meat, were the heaviest of the trip, weighing about 70 pounds. We camped in a clump of cottonwoods with a fine view up the upper North Fork toward the last spruce trees, less than a mile to the north.

From this remote junction near the sources of the Koyukuk we spent

[2] On June 30, 1952, George W. Beadle, Gunnar Bergman, and Alfred Tissieres climbed to the top of Mount Doonerak by way of the south face. For an account of their climb see "Up Doonerak—An Arctic Adventure" by G. W. Beadle in The Living Wilderness XVII (Winter, 1952–53), 7 ff. and "Up Doonerak—Climbing Bob Marshall's Mountain" by G. W. Beadle in The Land XII (Winter, 1953–54), 413 ff.

two glorious days of exploration in never-visited terrain. Aside from the first five miles of the first day, which I had covered nine years before, every bend in every valley held beyond it the glamorous mystery of unknown worlds. The two days' exploration showed clearly that the guesses I had made on my old map for this unknown country meant little.

The first day we set out to follow the upper North Fork upstream, to a point where we could see its source. Five miles up, it split almost exactly in two. The right fork came from the east and flowed along just south of that series of well-alined high mountains after which I had named it Alinement Creek when I followed it for eight miles in the autumn of 1930.

At that time, I had named the left-hand fork Nakshakluk. It appeared to emerge from an impassable canyon about a mile upstream. We climbed high on the mountainside to the west of Nakshakluk to avoid this slate canyon and in a couple of miles found an even deeper canyon in a major tributary entering from the west. We had to follow the top of the precipices two and a half miles up this tributary to find a place where we could cross it.

We stopped for lunch at the edge of foaming white water dropping from a bright green basin, entirely devoid of any sort of tree growth. While Jesse and Nutirwik were making tea, Harvey and I followed that tributary upstream a couple of miles to a point where we could see the entire head of this valley. It was fascinating in its barrenness, so we called the drainage Barrenland Creek.

After lunch I repeated the experiment which I had tried with negative results nine years before—the experiment to test my theory that lack of time, not unfavorable climatic conditions had prevented the further progress of the northern timber line. I had brought with me this time some white spruce seeds which the Lakes States Forest Experiment Station had provided.

I marked two square plots on a flat about ten feet above the creek. On the larger one, 12 by 12 feet, I sowed the seeds directly among the sphagnum moss, *Dryas octopetala,* and dwarfed willow. On the other plot, which was 8 by 8 feet, I scraped away the vegetation and sowed the seed on mineral soil.

When the plots were completed we headed diagonally across the corner of the hill toward Nakshakluk Creek. Tediously circumventing additional canyons, we finally worked ourselves to a point high up on the west side of Nakshakluk from which we could see its very head and the low pass across the Arctic Divide. There were several blue lakes on our side of the divide of which the longest must have been half a mile. Beyond the pass was the source of the Itkillik River which flows north a couple of hundred miles to join the Colville River near the Arctic Ocean. It was a sore temptation to follow it northward among the unexplored mountains stretching as far as we could see. However, that would have been a whole summer's journey, and we had only ten days left. So we classed that as a fine dream, unattainable as the end of the bright double rainbow in the canyon below us.

Reluctantly we turned south, after mapping all source streams of the Nakshakluk, and noting with pleasure that our present position tied in perfectly with Cockedhat Mountain which I had mapped from the Grizzly Creek side in 1930. On the return journey we got a splendid view of hundreds of feet of black slate precipices south of Barrenland Creek. The rock strata were folded back and forth in amazing loops, sometimes in hairpin bends.

As exciting as the rock were the sheep. We saw eighteen in four different bands. A band of nine watched us calmly as we descended toward them, and would not run until we were within fifty yards. Then they tore for the steepest rocky point where wolves could not climb and relaxed as they looked back at us from their secure perch. There were six ewes and three lambs in this band, and we imagined the small number of the latter was a result either of the wolves, of which we saw many signs, or of the eagles, of which we saw one. According to Nutirwik, eagles feed on very young lambs up to two or three weeks old.

Nutirwik told us other interesting things about the feeding habits of animals he had observed during more than half a century of intimate dependence on them. Bears, he said, are as fat when they come out of the ground in the spring as when they go in during the fall, and there is nothing in their stomachs but a little water. Wolves, Nutirwik had found, feed on mice and birds when they cannot get sheep.

"Funny animal eagle," he said. "Never eat him hind leg. Leave him hind leg all time. Fox, lamb, squirrel, siksik, siksikbok, all the same. Eagle won't eat hind leg." "Siksik" means ground squirrel—so named for the noise it makes. "Bok" means big—hence "siksikbok" means "a big ground squirrel," which is the woodchuck or arctic marmot.

Next morning heavy cumulus clouds hung in the sky. The high mountains were covered with fog. It did not seem a very auspicious day to try one of the higher peaks, but Jesse felt convinced it would clear and that today was a better gamble with weather than tomorrow. We had set as our objective a flat-topped, nonprecipitous mountain, about nine miles away, air-line, at the head of Amawk Creek. The summit was about 4,600 feet above camp.

We followed the tumbling, plunging waters of Amawk Creek over boulders ground smooth by constant action until, after three miles, we reached a major fork. The left branch flowed for several miles through a deep lime canyon and headed in high mosslands to the east. The right branch came through a schist canyon after rising in a series of lakes and springs in a large flat between the upper North Fork and Clear River drainages. A ridge covered with sphagnum, *Dryas*, and Angowuk separated the two and led toward our summit.

We climbed along it for miles. The vegetation became scarcer as the sandy soil diminished, and we found ourselves walking over disintegrated schist, slate, quartzite, and volcanic tuff. The whole mountain seemed to be crumbling away at a rapid rate, entirely unlike any other peak we had seen in this arctic territory. To pick one's way through this loose, sliding, rock rubble was like climbing in loose snow. When we occasionally reached a ledge which had not disintegrated, it was a relief to take a few steps in substantial footing before bucking the rubble again.

Of great assistance through this loose footing were the trails which sheep had walked over so much that at places they appeared almost graded. Near the top we followed them altogether. The sheep had plowed out a path even over several large snowbanks which we had to cross.

The summit of the mountain was a flat, thirty or forty acres in extent, covered entirely with fine, disintegrated rock, except for one point, a few feet higher than the rest, which was solid slate. To this very summit not only the sheep had climbed, but also their chief predatory enemy, judging by the wolf sign which was lying there. We named the peak Amawk Mountain—Amawk meaning wolf in Eskimo.

But if the crumbling rock and the fresh wolf sign gave one a feeling of wildness, this was mild compared with the feeling aroused by the panorama of jagged mountains and uncharted valleys. Dominating everything was Mount Doonerak, about twelve miles away to the west. It jutted up into the sky more forbidding than ever. It had the shape of an isosceles triangle from here, with the apex angle only a few degrees and the black sides so steep that ascent seemed as impossible as scaling the craters of the moon.

Four miles southeast of us the twin summit of Apoon rose across Kinnorutin Pass from which I had first seen Apoon in midwinter, eight years before. Then the mountain had made an overwhelming impression on me with the highest unbroken snow slope I had ever seen, rising 4,500 feet out of Kinnorutin Creek. Even now in July it had, in the gully leading downward between its two peaks, the deepest midsummer snow of our experience. We estimated its depth at one hundred feet. We were particularly impressed by a great domeshaped mountain northeast of where we stood.

Toward the Arctic, the limestone summits formed an unknown gray ocean. They were the beginning of unmapped country stretching northward to salt water. Eastward, beyond the Middle Fork, were those yellow limestone precipices which had been so impressive when we were climbing beneath them in the short November days of 1930.

We made interesting geographical discoveries. Alinement Creek cut clear around the head of Hammond River, which did not rise in the Arctic Divide as people had been supposing for thirty-five years. The low pass which Ernie had reported leading from Amawk Creek into the Arctic was in reality a very high pass into Hammond River. Three hours passed rapidly here while we sketched watersheds, took compass shots and vertical angles on mountains, took movies and still pictures, and in general enjoyed the vast, extending landscape.

When we finally left the summit at five in the afternoon it had become so chilly that we ran down the slide-rock slope to get warm. On one snowbank we coasted a couple of hundred feet. We dropped 1,600 feet in short order and soon found ourselves at the edge of a deep-blue lake just under the summit. Its elevation of 5,400 feet here probably made it the highest lake in the Brooks Range, so we called it Inyirik Lake, inyirik meaning mountain.

We then skirted the shoulder of a hill and reached a lake-filled benchland extending for miles in every direction. It seemed a trifle crazy to have this smooth, rolling flat right in the midst of these wild mountains. The sun, which had been obscured by clouds much of the afternoon, at last came out to stay and turned the mosses and leafy plants into a carpet of vivid green. Set in this carpet, everywhere as far as the eye could see, was the golden gleam of the arctic poppy and the snow-white petals of the *Dryas*. The green, the gold, the white—all were so unblemished under the bright sunlight, the rich vegetation so entirely untouched by man, and everything around so peaceful and pure that it seemed a pattern for the Eden of men's dreams.

Unfortunately we were only four lucky people among millions in the world to whom this paradise was as unattainable as Mount Doonerak was to us. Besides, if the millions wanted this sort of perfection and could attain it, the values of freshness and remoteness and adventure beyond the paths of men would automatically disappear. The "paradise" would become a green lawn in Prospect Park, covered with picnicking throngs. Actually, only a small minority of the human race will ever consider primeval nature a basic source of happiness. For this minority, tracts of wilderness paradise urgently need preservation. But mankind as a whole is too numerous for its problem of happiness to be solved by the simple expedient of paradise, whether it lies in Eden or the flower-filled Amawk divide.

Jesse's weather sense proved excellent, for next day it was raining. We spent it chiefly between the tent and the fireplace, except that Nutirwik went out with his .22 on an unsuccessful hunt for a siksikbok. Harvey and I checked our notes and made corrections on the map. Jesse took care of the cooking, and we helped ourselves generously to the last of the sheep meat. We wanted to finish it before packing across the high divide to the Hammond River.

THE SOURCES OF THE HAMMOND; ALHAMBLAR

When we set out next morning our packs were the lightest of the trip. Not only was our meat gone, but we had purposely allowed our food supply to run down in order to reduce as much as possible the work of climbing across the untraveled mountains which separated Amawk Creek and Hammond River. This we did with confidence, because we were counting on the staples which Jesse had cached, before my arrival, on upper Hammond. Of course we uneasily joked about the possibility that bears or wolverines had raided everything, but even in this eventuality we would not really have worried, because there was plenty of game, fish, and wild plants on which we could have lived almost indefinitely.

Thus, with light packs the going up Amawk Creek was good. Above the forks we climbed to a moss-covered bench in order to avoid the box canyon through which the right fork dropped its turbulent waters. In a couple of miles this stream emerged from its cage of andesite rock. From here on we followed it, among the rich green vegetation of damp bottomlands and the deepest sky-blue forget-me-nots, to the pass on the Clear River divide.

This pass had an elevation of 4,450 feet, so we had climbed about 2,000 feet. Before us the country dropped rapidly into the upper stretch of Clear River, which Ernie and I had followed to its snowbound source in March of 1931. Less than three miles away, at the very head of this river, was the pass leading into Hammond River.

By making a wide semicircle to the east we reached it with little loss of elevation and soon were standing where Ernie and I had stood, on that 30-below morning more than eight years before when we thought we were looking down into arctic waters, when actually, as Jesse,

Harvey, and I discovered a few months later, we had seen Kinnorutin Creek.

One thing Ernie and I could not observe that March morning, with the deep snow all around, was the fact that just before we reached the pass, where the uppermost prong of Clear River heads sharply to the south into high mountains, was a genuine glacier. Its front consisted of a 50-foot ice wall. This was the fourth genuine glacier ever discovered in the Brooks Range. Like the Arrigetch, Anaktuvuk, and Doonerak glaciers, it was on the north-facing side of the mountain, in a deep valley whose east, south, and west walls kept out the sunlight most of the time. Like the other three, it also appeared to be receding rapidly.

We took our way down the steep course of Kinnorutin Creek enjoying the sight of many sheep feeding among the surrounding precipices. We saw twenty-one in the five-mile stretch from Kinnorutin Pass to Hammond River. Halfway down, at five in the afternoon, we stopped for an hour at the first willows big enough for building a fire, to warm a luncheon of pea soup and tea.

Where Kinnorutin enters Hammond we stopped for another hour on a mossy flat and repeated the spruce-seed experiment of Barrenland Creek. Here also we were eight miles beyond the last stand of spruce timber. The remaining seven miles of the day, down Hammond River, were easy traveling. We were going strong when we reached the cache —eleven hours, twenty-six miles, and 3,000 feet of climbing beyond our Amawk Creek camp. The cache had not been invaded and we found all the food we needed for the six remaining days of the trip.

On the first of these, Harvey, Nutirwik, and I decided to spend a rainy day tying up the topography to the east between the Hammond and Dietrich rivers—the two major source rivers of the Middle Fork of the Koyukuk, which joined some twenty-eight miles to the south, at a point about four miles north of Wiseman. A memorable feature on that day was an encounter with two sheep which we practically climbed onto as we were skidding along some slippery slide rocks. The sheep had apparently been asleep in a sheltered nook. I have never had such an opportunity to enjoy the intimate facial expression of wild sheep.

Next morning the rain was over and we started on a rambling adventure to follow Blarney Creek, a tributary of Hammond Creek, to the Arctic Divide or wherever it might lead us. About a mile above its mouth, and at least three miles from the next most northerly spruce, we found a young and vigorously growing spruce tree. Assuming that no experiment-minded Eskimos had tried a Stone Age variation of my experiment, the only explanation for the existence of that tree seemed to be a heavy windstorm which had blown spruce seeds three miles from the nearest source, or a bird with unusual appetite which had brought a seed in its digestive tract and deposited it here.

Blarney Creek valley, after twisting around until it was well within the hills, soon turned northward and became bare, straight, and limy. After six miles it split into almost equal forks. A high ridge between the two appeared to offer firm footing to the divide which all of us, except Harvey, thought must separate Koyukuk waters from those flowing into the Arctic via the Itkillik River.

Harvey was right. When we reached the summit we found ourselves looking into a large, unknown stream which flowed eastward to the Kuyuktuvuk Creek, which in turn flowed southward into Dietrich River and hence the Middle Fork. We sat on a high rock and tried to understand the new topography spread before us. Jesse and I reasoned that this unexpected creek, originating a few miles to the northwest, must come from Oolah Pass—a pass important as the gate across the Arctic Divide which most Eskimos from the arctic coast had followed on their way to Wiseman.

Harvey was again skeptical. He thought Oolah Pass was on the main fork of the Kuyuktuvuk. I tried to overwhelm him with the logic of the situation. I pointed to the mountain just beyond the pass and said it looked exactly like an oolah (an Eskimo tool, used for scraping hides, which the mountain above the pass was supposed to resemble). Harvey said he had never seen an oolah and was not convinced. Then I pointed out that this creek entered the main Kuyuktuvuk at just the angle the Eskimos at Wiseman had told me the creek from Oolah Pass entered. Harvey did not know at what angle the creek from Oolah Pass entered, but nevertheless felt sure it must be farther north. I became indignant that Harvey could not see something so obvious, and my righteous rationalization must have sounded like a senator expounding on eternal truth in connection with an appropriation bill. Nutirwik, the Kobuk Eskimo from country far to the west, knew nothing about Oolah Pass, and maintained a discreet silence. Jesse was on my side, but less vociferous.

We proceeded westward along the high ridge dividing Blarney and Kuyuktuvuk creeks. The farther we went, the more apparent it seemed that we were approaching Oolah Pass. About fifteen miles from camp we reached the summit of a very pointed pinnacle where Jesse and Nutirwik decided to return to camp. Harvey and I wanted to be sure of our topography, so we agreed to climb the next peak along the ridge.

At the next peak it looked more like Oolah Pass than ever, but we wanted to learn about the drainages on the other side of the divide so we climbed some more until we reached a height from which we looked down into what I thought was the very head of the Itkillik River. To my surprise it was flowing westward from what certainly must be Oolah Pass, instead of northward. By this time the eternal varieties had become so obvious that Harvey had almost consented that Oolah Pass lay below us. But I was still curious to know where Alinement Creek ended, so I suggested that we climb the highest peak in the neighborhood, which lay about a mile beyond. Harvey was the perfect partner for such an expedition and agreed at once, although it was already seven o'clock in the evening and camp was seventeen miles away.

As we plowed our way up the skiddish slide rock, it was exciting to anticipate what lay on the other side of the mountain. Harvey was about thirty seconds ahead of me reaching the summit, and almost immediately let out the triumphant shout: "Alinement Creek!" I could not understand why he should be so triumphant, since we both thought the creek might head against the other side of the mountain. But when I reached the peak, I immediately saw that the stream flowed westward from "Oolah Pass" was not the Itkillik River after all, but Alinement Creek; that we were not on the Arctic Divide at all, but merely on the divide between the North Fork and Middle Fork waters; and that for all my unimpeachable logic, Harvey was right, and Oolah Pass was farther north.

But if logic was not triumphant, beauty certainly was on this July evening as the low sun crept ever closer to the tumbled horizon of the north and we looked into a world of unknown mountains and valleys. It was the finest view we had yet had of the peaks at the head of the Chandalar River to the east. A surprising number of them rose to more than 7,000 feet, but standing out conspicuously above all the rest was the great dome-shaped mountain we had observed from Amawk. As we deliberated how to name it, we recalled a conversation I had had a year ago with jolly, wrinkled old Nakuchluk discussing Koyukuk geography. Nakuchluk, who with her husband, Big Jim had been among my neighbors in Wiseman in the winter 1930–31, had traveled in the Arctic all her nearly seventy years and had crossed the Arctic Divide to the east on a number of migrations. When I asked her which was the highest peak in the Brooks Range, she drew a sketch map of some mountain at the head of the north fork of the Chandalar River. As the domed mountain which we now saw was almost exactly where the old Eskimo woman had shown her peak, we named it Nakuchluk Mountain. It was not as high as Mount Doonerak, but certainly one of the great peaks of the Brooks Range. Even more impressive, though not quite so high, was the black mountain, only five miles north of us, which I had taken to be Oolah Mountain. Actually it turned out to be a different peak, which we named Oxadak, after a venerable oldster of the arctic Eskimos.

The sun was still half an hour above the mountains to the north when we left our summit at nine o'clock. It had become quite cold on top and we were shivering. Because the waters rising on this peak flowed into the three drainages of Alinement Creek, Hammond River, and Blarney Creek, we gave it the compound name of Alhamblar Mountain.

The descent from Alhamblar to upper Hammond River led down one of those not-too-steep slopes of soft rock, moss, and *Dryas,* where it is such a luxurious pleasure to let gravity have her way. In half an hour we had plunged down 2,500 feet. We sketched the tributaries of upper Hammond, stopped to drink from the large springs which bubbled from the lower hillsides, and crawled to the edge of what was almost a natural bridge, a hundred feet high. In relatively recent times a small strip of rock in the center of the bridge had broken off, leaving a three-foot gap in the igneous arch. We commented that one could easily jump the gap, but having made this objective observation, neither of us felt inclined to do so. We reached the cache and camp at one in the morning after fifteen hours and thirty-four miles of solving mysteries of geography.

APOON

Next day was our last one for side trips. Harvey and I decided to spend it climbing Apoon Mountain which was probably higher than any peak ever climbed in arctic Alaska. Jesse and Nutirwik were going to spend the day taking life easy and doing a little fishing.

The summit of Apoon was only about five miles airline to the northwest of camp. We forded Hammond River and followed up Shinningnellichshunga ("I am Sleepy) Creek which I had named eight years before on my hike to the head of Hammond. Harvey was still jocularly rolling the name on his tongue. Jesse boycotted it and refused to say anything lengthier than Sleepy Creek. This morning, however, we were wide awake and covered four uphill miles in little more than an hour. Then we left the creek and started the real climb. It was steeply but not precipitously up, first over flowers and green vegetation, then over loose slide rock, finally on sharply rising bedrock which varied from slate to quartz to andesite. At one place a 20-foot sheer drop on a knife-edge ridge made us backtrack and detour, using fingerholds to get around a minor bump on the skyline which we had not noticed from Amawk and Alhamblar. Here it took us fifty minutes to gain 150 feet in elevation.

Mostly, however, the going was good, and less than five hours after leaving camp we stood on a wild summit in the midst of the Koyukuk's most spectacular topography. Across the Clear River country we could see an arctic thunderstorm was just breaking over Boreal, giving an exceptional impression of nature unconquerable and infinitely more powerful than man.

To the right of the storm was Doonerak, just as unconquered as the thunder. There it rose, crowned by 2,000 feet of bleak rock precipice—as unconquerable to us in 1939 as the Atlantic Ocean must have seemed five hundred years ago.

The ascent of Mount Doonerak had been the first objective of our journey. We had intensely wanted to climb the mountain. Now, obviously, our goal was unattainable for us. We had made and would make first ascents of many lesser peaks, but someone else would accomplish the superlative, not we.

Our view, to be sure, was gorgeous perfection. Not even Mount Doonerak could have surpassed it. Indeed, we tried to persuade ourselves that the greater height of Mount Doonerak would tend to flatten the appearance of lesser summits and of the jaggedness of the topography. Also, the storm had spread northward from Boreal, and Mount Doonerak's tip was just being enveloped in clouds. We speculated that if we were now on that peak, there would be no more enjoyment of scenery, but a hasty retreat from the storm. Nevertheless, Mount Doonerak alone could have brought highest fulfillment, the highest honor.

Was our happiness on Apoon diminished because we could not climb 2,000 feet of sheer rock? Is it possible to reconcile oneself to the second best and feel satisfied with the best one can attain? That was the question in everything. One in a million, perhaps, could be a Nobel Prize winner or a President of the United States. The other 999,999 might burden their lives in gnashing their teeth over unrealized ambitions for greatness, or they might adjust to limitations and fate and get the greatest possible happiness out of the North Dooneraks, the Amawks, and the Apoons which they could attain. Perhaps this philosophizing on a windswept pinnacle of rock might seem a little forced, but I could not help it, because I had talked only recently with an assistant manager, an associate professor, and a division chief whose lives for several years had been unhappy because they had not been promoted to head manager, full professor, and bureau chief.

The storm was swinging eastward. Boreal and Doonerak, emerging from the clouds, were saturated in a weird light, as if they had suddenly dissolved in air but not yet blown away. In the opposite direction, far to the east across the deep valley of Hammond River, beyond the widely branching drainage of the Middle Fork, far out among the unknown, unexplored source streams of the Chandalar, against the most distant horizon where fact and infinity merged, the sun was shining brilliantly on countless lofty peaks without name and beyond the scope of human knowledge. All around us were gorges, thousands of feet deep, great snowbanks, bright green valleys, gaily colored rocks. All was peace and strength and immensity and coördination and freedom.

Next morning we broke camp in the rain and started our fifty-three miles of back packing necessary to get back to Wiseman. We all hated the thought of the approaching end. The longer you are out on a wilderness trip, the smoother things work. Making and breaking camp, and all the little chores go more and more automatically. You become so used to your equipment and its inevitable limitations that soon the fact that you have just twenty inches between your head and the back wall of the fly for storing equipment which you want to keep dry has become entirely accepted. All the time you are getting physically hardened so that 55 pounds, which seemed like quite a load whether you had come fresh from a winter of shoveling gravel or of sitting at a Washington desk, is now an easy pack. Saddest of all was the thought of leaving these fine partners—these energetic, stimulating, considerate, kindly, intelligent men, with whom not a single harsh word had been exchanged during the entire journey.

The first day we reeled off fourteen miles along the gravel bars of the Hammond River. We traveled again in fifty-minute shifts with ten-minute rests between. It rained all day steadily but not hard. By ten in the evening we had reached the yellow reindeer moss flats at the mouth of Kalhabuk Creek.

While the fellows were setting up camp and preparing supper, I walked three and a half miles up the right branch of Kalhabuk Creek to Kaaruk Lake on the low divide between Hammond and Dietrich rivers sparkling with the freshness of arctic moss and arctic flowers at arctic midnight. At the lake a bull moose was feeding with no concern for the first man to visit his domain in many years.

Not the first visitor, however, for old ax marks along the creek indicated both Eskimo and white-man invasions in the past. Later, when we compared notes with Verne Watts after our return, we found that he and three partners had camped at the mouth of Kalhabuk Creek for one mid-winter night when they saw in the new year of 1902.

Next day we covered eighteen easy miles to Canyon Creek, a tributary of Hammond River, where we spent our last night together, just beyond the zone of man. It was one of our most comfortable camps, although I chided Nutirwik jokingly for the large-size sticks he started to incorporate in the bed.

"Nutirwik, those spruce boughs you've got there, are more like spruce logs."

"Big sticks good for you," he replied. "Get up early, no loaf in bed."

Next day at noon at a mining camp on Swift Creek we saw the first people outside of our party that we had seen in twenty-two days. We learned from them that it was Sunday, that the whole world was not yet at war as it had appeared to be when we emerged from the wilderness the year before, and that Joe Louis had knocked out Tony Galento in four rounds.

We had only half a mile of trail and seven miles of "auto road" from Swift Creek to Wiseman. The auto road was actually being used for the first time since the previous summer by the Koyukuk's one and only car, with whose owner, Joe Ulen, we chatted briefly. Half an hour later we walked up to the Wiseman roadhouse.

Now we were back among people in Wiseman. In a day I should be in Fairbanks, in two more in Juneau, in a week in Seattle and the great, thumping, modern world. I should be living once more among the accumulated accomplishments of man. The world with its present population needs these accomplishments. It cannot live on wilderness, except incidentally and sporadically. Nevertheless, to four human beings, just back from the source streams of the Koyukuk, no comfort, no security, no invention, no brilliant thought which the modern world had to offer could provide half the elation of the days spent in the little-explored, uninhabited world of the arctic wilderness.

EDITOR'S POSTSCRIPT TO THE FIRST EDITION

A quarter of a century, more or less, has passed since Robert Marshall wrote the accounts which make up this book. When I had finished editing his journals, I wondered what had become of his friends and major companions of his trips and where I might reach them, if they were still alive, to send them a copy of this book.

Through responses to inquiries from Alaska, I heard that Ernie Johnson continues to hold claims up the Alatna River and spends some time there each year. Al Retzlaf, still fascinated by gold, runs a dredge near Fairbanks. Kenneth Harvey works as a mechanic for an Alaska airline. Only Jesse Allen has left Alaska and now lives in Red Bluff, California.

Nutirwik died ten years ago. At about the same time Ekok, the friendly and intelligent Eskimo woman who ran Bob's scientific station, was burned to death with her husband and several children in a fire which destroyed their cabin. Martin Slisco, the Wiseman roadhouse proprietor, was murdered by a man who picked a quarrel with him and then pumped him full of lead with a rifle; the murderer was quickly convicted and sent to prison.

I have been told also that not so many in northern Alaska now care for the pioneer life as in Bob's time. Wiseman itself has changed with fewer people in camp, and very few left of those whom Bob knew. More planes penetrate the north country, and DC-3's land in Bettles on scheduled flights. However, despite increasing threats to the continuing primitive wildness of northern Alaska, much of the vast country north of the Yukon and across the Arctic Divide remains a wilderness.

G. M.

1956

EDITOR'S POSTSCRIPT TO THE SECOND EDITION

It is forty-one years since Robert Marshall made his first exploration of the Upper Koyukuk region and thirty years since his last trip and the year of his death. Changes had occurred between then and the publication of the First Edition of Arctic Wilderness *in 1956 as we have noted. Additional changes have occurred during the thirteen years since then, and three of his closest friends and companions of his journeys died.*

Jesse Allen, except for two trips to see relatives in Ohio and West Virginia, spent his last years at Red Bluff, California, where he died in November, 1956. Some of his friends believed that life in California was too mild and tame for a man who had spent most of his years in the rigors of the Arctic. His family, who had not seen him for many years, had a warm feeling toward him and were enthusiastic about Arctic Village *and* Arctic Wilderness, *copies of which made the rounds of his brother's family and some twenty cousins. These books were placed in The Hardy County Public Library in Moorefield, West Virginia, Jesse's home town, as a memorial to him.*

His sister-in-law wrote: "It didn't seem strange for Jesse to go pioneering, but for Robert Marshall, born and brought up in a great city, it did. And yet, Robert Marshall's forebears were real pioneers and pathfinders. I wonder if when he stood on the top of North Doonerak, his thoughts went back to that day so long ago when another stood on a mountaintop gazing on the land he was not privileged to enter."

Ernie Johnson, who moved to Fairbanks with his brother Rudolph, never liked the city and longed for the hills. Each year he visited his claim on the Alatna, but probably did little prospecting and no mining. Although he had the prospector's eternal optimism, he was at heart a hunter and trapper and loved the remote river and mountain country, and welcomed any reason to go there. He wrote to me in 1957:

"Last summer in the hills prospecting. Don't know how it will turn out but I don't build high hopes. Been at it too many years for that. Am going on seventy-five years now. I intend to stay in the Hills until the end." The end came for him in 1961 with a heart attack.

Four years later Kenneth Harvey also died of a heart attack. After 1956, he continued to work for an airline as troubleshooter, travelling over much of Alaska to repair downed planes. Later he was in charge of the airline's instrument shop in Fairbanks. He went to Wiseman quite often during the summer to do a little prospecting with his old partner, Bob Jones.

Commenting on this book, Harvey wrote:

"I received a copy of Arctic Wilderness *which was very good. It brought back memories of the good times we had running around the mountains. I like Bob's books as he printed the truth in them."*

G. M.

January, 1970

Index

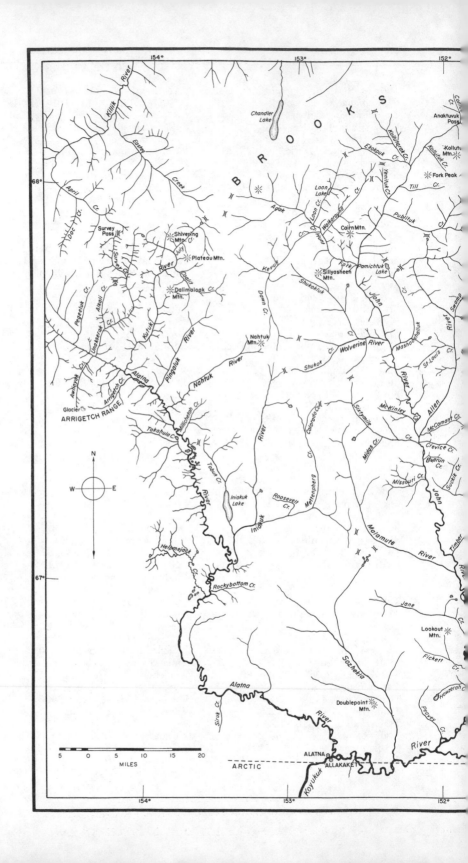

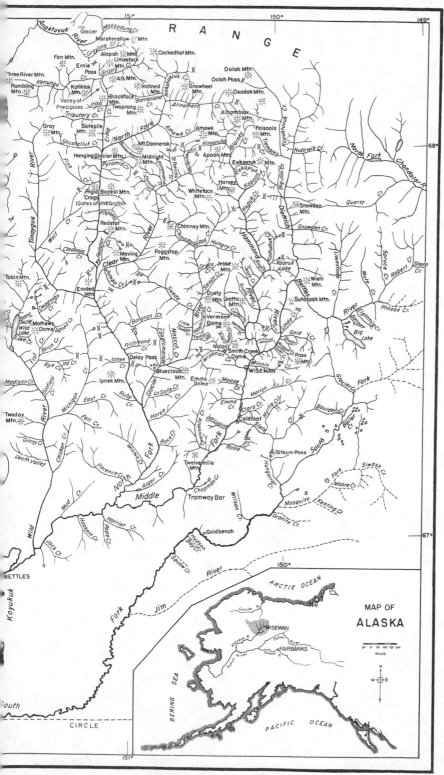

Source: Based on maps by Robert Marshall NORTHERN KOYUKUK DRAINAGE